QUICK & LIGHT

Over 200 Great Taste - Low Fat Recipes
Ready in 30 Minutes or Less

TIME® LIFE BOOKS

ALEXANDRIA, VIRGINIA

First printing. Printed in U.S.A.

3 5 7 9 10 8 6 4 2

TIME-LIFE is a trademark of Time Warner Inc. U.S.A.

ISBN 0-7370-1146-7

CIP data available upon application.
Librarian, Time-Life Books
2000 Duke Street
Alexandria, VA 22314

TABLE OF CONTENTS

Steak au Poivre with Peppers and Potatoes

~

page 119

Italian Pork Parmesan Salad

~

page 289

INTRODUCTION

This cookbook is designed to take the work and worry out of everyday low-fat cooking; to use quick, streamlined methods and available ingredients; to provide delicious, fresh, and filling recipes for family and friends; and, within every recipe, to keep the percentage of calories from fat under 30 percent.

Quick recipes have become a necessity of modern life. Although some people can happily spend hours creating a sumptuous meal—traveling far and wide for obscure ingredients and starting at dawn to produce a spectacular dinner—it's more often the case that family members (including the one who does the cooking) dash in, ravenous, just in time for supper. We're particularly proud of this special Great Taste-Low Fat volume, which enables you to come up with a delightful variety of dinners on even your busiest days. We've streamlined the recipes to bring you satisfying dishes guaranteed to take no longer than 30 minutes to prepare.

BEATING THE CLOCK

You can find hundreds of so-called "short-cut" recipes in magazines and newspapers. You'll notice, however, that these recipes tend to rely heavily on highly touted "instant" ingredients like processed cheese spreads and powdered sauce mixes. These products save time, but sacrifice taste and texture in the process; and they're often loaded with preservatives, artificial flavors, and other undesirable additives. And from looking at the recipes, you might get the idea that streamlined techniques and good nutrition simply can't co-exist: For instance, the creators of short-cut

dishes often resort to a topping of potato chips or fried onion rings (to disguise the boring flavor of the dish) or call for high-fat ingredients like mayonnaise or frankfurters.

So how did we manage to come up with over 200 fresh tasting and original recipes, all low in fat and ready in less than half an hour? The solution was obvious: We asked someone with real-life experience to create the recipes. Sandy Gluck is a wife and mother with a full-time career, and is accustomed to creating family-pleasing meals on a tight schedule. "I refuse to live on pizza, Chinese take-out, and fast food, although those are the easy options," says Sandy, "and eating the same thing every day can be dreary. I've always believed in using fresh ingredients, and if you're well organized, it doesn't take a lot of time to cook from scratch."

Pasta is a natural for fast meals, and our intriguing array of sauces—salsa, chili, basil, curry, sesame, and more—will banish boredom. Quick-cooking boneless chicken breasts are the starting point for many of Sandy's recipes, but chicken thighs, turkey breast, and turkey sausage add variety to the poultry selections. Beef, pork, and lamb can be main ingredients if sliced thin, cubed, or ground; stir-frying, grilling, and broiling are the fastest ways to cook these meats, but Sandy has also created some stews and salads. Fish & shellfish cook in minutes, so they're well represented in this cookbook; and there's a tempting array of vegetable main courses, that make use of satisfying staples such as rice, potatoes, and beans.

The "Secrets of Quick Cooking" section of this book suggests some efficient meal preparation techniques; there's also a guide to the timesaving ingredients we use. These are predominantly basic, healthy foods in more convenient forms, such as quick-cooking couscous, evaporated low-fat and skimmed milk, and frozen broccoli florets. We steer clear of inferior convenience products such as garlic salt. If you have some spare time on weekends, you can employ one of Sandy Gluck's favorite time-saving tricks and lay in your own supply of healthful ready-to-use staples, including cooked rice and beans; we've supplied storage directions and times as well as reheating directions.

When you expect a week to be especially busy, choose your recipes and do your shopping in advance; then relax, confident that you'll be putting delicious, low-fat meals on the table—despite work pressures, traffic jams, and the dizzyingly active schedule of the average energetic family.

CONTRIBUTING EDITORS

Sandra Rose Gluck, *a New York City chef, has years of experience creating delicious low-fat recipes that are quick to prepare. Her secret for satisfying results is to always aim for great taste and variety. By combining readily available, fresh ingredients with simple cooking techniques, Sandra has created the perfect recipes for today's busy lifestyles.*

Grace Young *has been the director of a major test kitchen specializing in low-fat and health-related cookbooks for over 12 years. Grace oversees the development, taste testing, and nutritional analysis of every recipe in this book. Her goal is simple: take the work and worry out of low-fat cooking so that you can enjoy delicious, healthy meals every day.*

Kate Slate *has been a food editor for almost 20 years, and has published thousands of recipes in cookbooks and magazines. As the Editorial Director of this book, Kate combined simple, easy-to-follow directions with practical cooking tips. The result is guaranteed to make your low-fat cooking as rewarding and fun as it is foolproof.*

NUTRITION

Every recipe in this book provides per-serving values for the nutrients listed in the chart at right. The daily intakes listed in the chart are based on those recommended by the USDA and presume a nonsedentary lifestyle. The nutritional emphasis in this book is not only on controlling calories, but on reducing total fat grams. Research has shown that dietary fat metabolizes more easily into body fat than do carbohydrates and protein. In order to control the amount of fat in a given recipe and in your diet in general, no more than 30 percent of the calories should come from fat.

Nutrient	Women	Men
Fat	<65 g	<80 g
Calories	2000	2500
Saturated fat	<20 g	<25 g
Carbohydrate	300 g	375 g
Protein	50 g	65 g
Cholesterol	<300 mg	<300 mg
Sodium	<2400 mg	<2400 mg

These recommended daily intakes are averages used by the Food and Drug Administration and are consistent with the labeling on all food products. Although the values for cholesterol and sodium are the same for all adults, the other intake values vary depending on gender, ideal weight, and activity level. Check with a physician or nutritionist for your own daily intake values.

SECRETS OF QUICK LOW-FAT COOKING

QUICK COOKING

No matter how busy you are, there are still seven days in every week, each day requiring an evening meal. Calling for a pizza, picking up some take-out, or microwaving a frozen meal are some not-so-healthy answers to the question, "Quick—what's for dinner?" This book offers a superior solution: recipes for delicious, low-fat meals that can be made in half an hour or less.

GETTING ORGANIZED

Many factors contribute to cutting down on the time you spend preparing meals. For starters, base your shopping on a week's worth of recipes, and organize the list according to the layout of your market. Determine which of your kitchen gadgets and appliances really speed up the work, and which are just in the way (clear out the latter). Efficient habits make for streamlined cooking: You can cook two foods in one pan (we cook pasta and vegetables together in some of our recipes), and you can often prepare ingredients during the "down time" in a recipe (mincing herbs while the chili simmers, for instance). Cleaning up as you go ensures that you won't be left with a sinkful of dishes after dinner. Don't forget to enlist other family members in the kitchen brigade: Even young children can help with simple tasks.

QUICK-COOKING TECHNIQUES

The two principal techniques for quick cooking are broiling (or grilling) and sautéing (or stir-frying). Both methods use high heat to speed up the cooking process. Broiling is by far the simplest of the approaches: Food is either marinated or rubbed with seasonings and then quickly cooked under high heat (and generally quite close to the heat source). Grilling, though similar, presents a special problem in low-fat cooking, though one that is easily solved by properly preparing the grill (see "Quick on the Grill," below).

QUICK ON THE GRILL

It's hard to beat the outdoor grill for quick cooking. But low-fat recipes present a special problem: Since their fat content is naturally low, the food is more likely to stick to the grill rack or grill topper. To solve the problem but maintain the low fat content of the dishes, our chefs use nonstick cooking spray (rather than oil) to prevent sticking. However these sprays, whether aerosol or pump, can cause flare-ups, so follow these steps for safety: Preheat the grill as directed; just before grilling, put on oven mitts, remove the rack or grill topper, and spray it with nonstick cooking spray. Carefully return the rack or topper to the grill.

But when all is said and done, the most important techniques to master for quick cooking are the sauté and the stir-fry. Few cooking techniques allow for as much variety as stir-frying and sautéing. And even in recipes that don't identify themselves as sautés/stir-fries, this important technique is used. For example, to make a quick pasta sauce, the ingredients are first stir-fried. All soups and stews start with a stir-fry. And many dishes that are traditionally slow-cooked in deep saucepans, here are quickly cooked in a skillet.

THE FINER POINTS

In a mixed stir-fry or sauté—one in which, for example, several different vegetables plus meat, poultry, or seafood are cooked together—each ingredient must be timed so it's perfectly cooked and not overcooked: Dense vegetables like turnips and parsnips take longer to become crisp-tender than delicate sugar snap peas, zucchini, and the like. We accommodate these variations in two ways: First, you can cook the various ingredients one at a time, removing each one from the pan as it's done. We often use this method for meat, poultry, and fish, which are stir-fried or sautéed until cooked through, then set aside, to be returned to the pan after the other ingredients are cooked.

You can also add the ingredients to the pan cumulatively in a logical order, beginning with those that require the longest cooking and gradually adding the quicker-cooking foods; flavoring vegetables, such as onions and garlic, often go in first. For example, in our Chicken Stir-Fry with Broccoli, Garlic, and Basil (page 143), the scallions, garlic, and ginger are cooked until fragrant, then the broccoli is added. In this recipe,

wet vegetables such as cucumber and fresh tomatoes are added early on so they can break down and contribute to the sauce. Delicate fresh basil is added at the very end to preserve its flavor.

Cutting ingredients into small or thin pieces (see page 9) exposes more surface area to the heat for faster cooking. It also helps the food to become more thoroughly coated with seasonings, and allows for more all-over browning (which enhances

flavor, especially in meat, poultry, and fish).

To brown properly and not create excess steam, foods to be sautéed or stir-fried must be dry. Meat, poultry, and fish are often dredged with flour or cornstarch to create a dry surface: Sometimes herbs and spices are added to the dredging mixture for extra flavor.

Stir-frying is traditionally done over very high heat, but our recipes, with their minimal amounts of oil, should be stir-fried over medium heat. Still, the food should sizzle as it hits the pan. When our recipes say to add ingredients to the pan and stir-fry, keep the pan over the heat, tossing the ingredients with a spatula or spoon and shaking the pan occasionally.

CHOOSE YOUR TOOLS

Most recipes in this book are prepared in a large nonstick skillet—large, because if the pieces of food are crowded together, steam will be trapped and the food will turn out soggy rather than delicately crisp. Your nonstick skillet should be 10 to 12 inches across, of heavy-gauge steel or aluminum with a flat bottom. A handle that doesn't conduct heat is a plus—otherwise, you'll have to hold the pan with a potholder as you cook.

Nonstick finishes have been greatly improved since they were first invented, and today's non-stick pans are extremely durable. If your old skillet is badly scratched (or if it tends to scratch easily), you may want to replace it with one of the newer models. Just to be safe, always use smooth nylon, plastic, or wooden spatulas and spoons on nonstick pans; they're gentler on the finish than metal utensils.

For stir-fries, you also have the option of using a nonstick wok, the Chinese pot developed for this cooking technique: Its wide, bowl-like shape is ideal for stir-frying. Whichever you choose, a good quality utensil makes cooking more efficient. A wok should be big enough (at least 12 inches across) to allow for vigorous tossing and stirring, and must conduct heat evenly without

---

COOKING IN FOIL

One of the most efficient ways to cook all of the components of a meal at the same time is to assemble them in foil packets. This saves time not only in the preparation of the meal, but also at clean-up time. To make a packet, cut off a large rectangle of foil and place the food in the middle. To seal the packets, draw the short ends of the foil together; then roll the edges together, making a series of ½-inch folds, leaving some breathing room for the steam. Leave the final fold up to act as a handle. Last, fold in or crimp the sides of the packet. You can also use this method to cook food on a grill, but be sure to use a double layer of heavy-duty foil to prevent tearing.

---

hot spots. A round-bottomed wok works best on a gas range: Its bowl-like base will rest in the burner, letting the flame rise along the sides. If you have an electric stove, a flat-bottomed wok will stand steady on the flat burner and heat evenly.

THE QUICK COOK'S LOW-FAT PANTRY

In keeping with today's guidelines for healthy meals, our recipes call for lots of vegetables, grains, legumes, and pasta. Fortunately, these foods come in convenient forms that don't require complicated or lengthy preparation.

• **Prepared vegetables:** New at the supermarket are ready-to-use fresh vegetables—washed, cut, and all set to go into stir-fries or salads. Slaw mix, mini carrots, and spinach are some of the options. Salad bars are a wonderful source for small quantities of prepared vegetables such as salad greens, shredded carrots, and sliced mushrooms.

• **Frozen vegetables:** Frozen vegetables are better than ever. Standbys like frozen broccoli are great because of their uniformly high quality; they boast fine flavor and retain most of their nutrients (without added salt or preservatives). Frozen vegetables also save hours of kitchen labor: Think of the time it would take to prepare fresh artichoke hearts or pearl onions in quantity.

continued on page 10

TECHNIQUES FOR QUICK AND EVEN COOKING

For sautéing and stir-frying, foods that are to be cooked together should be of a uniform size. For speedy cooking, the pieces should be either small or thin—or both.

For sautéing, this means that meat and poultry are sliced thin, and sometimes pounded to flatten the meat into a thin cutlet or scallop. (Fish steaks and fillets, and shrimp and scallops, are already just right for pan-cooking.) Vegetables for a sauté may be sliced, diced, or julienne-cut.

For stir-frying, the ingredients are usually cut quite small: Meat, poultry, and thick cuts of fish may be cut into cubes or strips. Thin vegetables such as bell peppers are cut into strips or squares, while solid vegetables like sweet potatoes or carrots may be sliced or julienned. Cutting vegetables crosswise on a diagonal exposes more surface area for quicker cooking.

Our recipes call for lean cuts of meat that are cut very thin and cooked quickly. The quick-cooking keeps the meat juicy, and cutting it into small pieces tenderizes it by shortening the meat fibers. Chilling the meat before cutting it firms up the texture, making it easier to slice: Fifteen minutes in the freezer will do the trick.

Pounding

A boneless chicken breast half is naturally thicker at one side. To even it out a bit, place the chicken breast between two sheets of plastic wrap or waxed paper. Pound the thicker side lightly with a meat pounder or the flat side of small skillet.

To make quick-cooking cutlets from boneless pork chops, place the chops between two sheets of plastic wrap or waxed paper and with a meat pounder or the flat side of a small skillet, pound the chops to a ¼- to ⅛-inch thickness.

Cutting Chicken Strips

This is how to cut the chicken when the recipe calls for "chicken breasts cut crosswise into ½-inch-wide strips" (crosswise means across the grain). For easier cutting, chill the chicken breasts in the freezer for about 15 minutes first.

Cutting Beef Strips

To cut the very thin strips of meat called for in our stir-fry recipes, first chill the steak in the freezer for about 15 minutes to make it firmer. Then with a long, sharp knife, cut the steak in half horizontally, using a careful sawing motion.

Separate the two pieces of meat and return them briefly to the freezer, if necessary, to refirm them. Then cut each piece crosswise (across the grain) into thin strips; our recipes call for strips that are either ⅛ or ¼ inch thick.

Diagonal Slicing

Cutting long, slender vegetables—especially hard vegetables that require longer cooking times—such as carrots and parsnips, on the diagonal exposes more surface area to the heat for quicker cooking; it also gives the slices an appealing oval shape.

continued from page 8

• **Processed foods:** Although you wouldn't want to make a meal solely from packaged foods, a health-conscious cook can do wonders with the contents of carefully selected jars and cans. When buying canned goods, pay close attention to the ingredient and nutrition labels, and look for "no-salt-added," "reduced-sodium," or "low-sodium" products. Canned beans are notable timesavers; to freshen their flavor and reduce their sodium content, always rinse and drain the beans. Among vegetables, canned beets are a great pantry standby; and most good cooks appreciate canned tomato products for their convenience and rich, consistent flavor. Other canned goods to keep on hand include: water-packed tuna, reduced-sodium chicken and beef broths, evaporated skimmed milk, and juice-packed pineapple and other fruits.

• **Quick-cooking grains:** Whole grains take quite a while to cook, but they also come in short-cut forms: Quick barley is done in 15 minutes (hulled barley takes 40 to 45) and bulghur—presteamed cracked wheat—is ready in 15 minutes (whole wheat berries must cook for more than an hour). Lentils cook in about 20 minutes with no pre-soaking. A pantry full of pasta is basic to a repertoire of speedy suppers. Stock up on all shapes and sizes, from tiny couscous and pastina to chunky rigatoni and radiatore; keep some "yolkless" egg noodles and spinach pasta on hand, too.

A WELL-STOCKED FREEZER

Store-bought frozen foods are great timesavers for busy cooks, but choices are limited. Set aside some time on a weekend and fill your freezer with healthy staples tailored to your family's tastes. When freezing foods, make sure they are wrapped well and be sure to label and date each package. Here are some suggestions and storage guidelines:

• **Beans.** Many people prefer dried beans to canned: Home-cooked beans are lower in sodium and have a firmer texture than canned. It's easy to cook a big batch of beans and freeze them in amounts suited to the recipes you'll be using. Soak the beans in water overnight, or, to save time, quick-soak them: Place the beans in a large pot with cold water to cover by 2 inches. Bring to a boil and simmer for 2 minutes, then cover and let stand for 1 hour. Drain, add fresh water, and cook the beans according to the directions on the bag. Drain and cool the cooked beans, then store them

in freezer bags or plastic containers for up to 6 months. To reheat frozen beans, place them in a pan with ¼ cup water per 1 cup beans. Cover, bring to a simmer over low heat, and cook until heated through.

• **Rice.** Brown rice takes 45 minutes to cook, but it can be made ahead and frozen. To reheat rice, steam the rice in a double boiler or steamer or microwave it on high power for 3 to 5 minutes. Frozen rice will keep for at least 6 months.

• **Onions.** You can buy pre-chopped onions, but it's simple (and less expensive) to lay in your own supply of this frequently used ingredient. Peel the onions, chop them by hand or in a food processor, and seal in large or small bags. Cut-up leeks and scallions can be frozen the same way. Frozen raw onions will keep for 6 months or longer, but the flavor will fade with time. Onions that have been frozen should be used only for cooking.

• **Bell peppers.** Diced bell peppers also freeze well. Wash, stem, and seed the peppers, then dice them or cut them into squares, as your recipes require. Package, seal, and freeze for up to 6 months. Peppers that have been frozen should be used only for cooking.

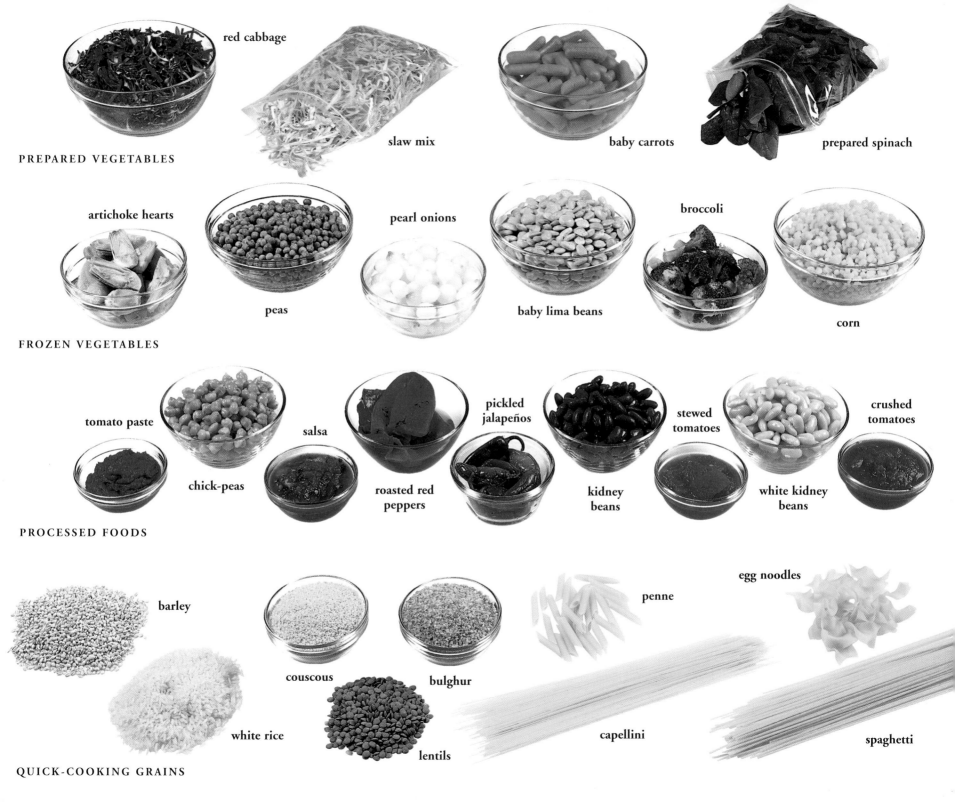

PREPARED VEGETABLES

red cabbage

slaw mix

baby carrots

prepared spinach

FROZEN VEGETABLES

artichoke hearts

peas

pearl onions

baby lima beans

broccoli

corn

PROCESSED FOODS

tomato paste

chick-peas

salsa

roasted red peppers

pickled jalapeños

kidney beans

stewed tomatoes

white kidney beans

crushed tomatoes

QUICK-COOKING GRAINS

barley

white rice

couscous

lentils

bulghur

penne

egg noodles

capellini

spaghetti

SOUPS & STEWS

Left, Hearty Chicken and Corn Chowder
Above, Sicilian-Style Ragout of Beef

CHICKEN GOULASH WITH EGG NOODLES

SERVES: 4
WORKING TIME: 20 MINUTES
TOTAL TIME: 30 MINUTES

12-ounce jar roasted red peppers or pimientos, rinsed and drained

2 tablespoons no-salt-added tomato paste

1 tablespoon mild paprika

1½ teaspoons olive oil

2 medium onions, chopped

4 cloves garlic, minced

2 green bell peppers, diced

3 tablespoons chopped fresh dill, or ¾ teaspoon dried

1¼ cups reduced-sodium chicken broth, defatted

½ teaspoon salt

1 pound skinless, boneless chicken breasts, cut into 2-inch chunks

8 ounces wide egg noodles

⅓ cup plain nonfat yogurt

2 tablespoons flour

3 tablespoons light sour cream

1. In a blender or food processor, combine the roasted peppers, tomato paste, and paprika and purée until smooth. Set aside.

2. In a large nonstick skillet, heat the oil until hot but not smoking over medium heat. Add the onions and garlic and cook, stirring frequently, until the onions are lightly golden, about 4 minutes. Add the peppers and dill and cook for 3 minutes. Stir in the pepper purée, broth, and salt and cook for 1 minute. Add the chicken, bring to a boil, reduce to a simmer, cover, and cook until the chicken is cooked through, about 5 minutes.

3. Meanwhile, in a large pot of boiling water, cook the noodles until just tender. Drain well.

4. In a small bowl, combine the yogurt and flour, stir into the chicken mixture, and cook, uncovered, until the sauce is just thickened, about 3 minutes longer. Place the noodles on 4 plates, spoon the chicken goulash on top, and serve with a dollop of the sour cream.

Suggested accompaniments: Crusty peasant bread, followed by a warm cherry crisp topped with toasted oats for dessert.

FAT: 8G/15%
CALORIES: 485
SATURATED FAT: 2G
CARBOHYDRATE: 63G
PROTEIN: 40G
CHOLESTEROL: 124MG
SODIUM: 595MG

We've flavored this version of the Hungarian specialty with a piquant blend of paprika, tomato paste, and roasted red peppers. Nonfat yogurt adds a creamy texture to the stew. We've mixed it with flour to both thicken the sauce and to stabilize the yogurt so it won't separate during cooking. Light sour cream tops it off.

SPICY BLACK BEAN CHILI

SERVES: 4
WORKING TIME: 15 MINUTES
TOTAL TIME: 30 MINUTES

The flip side of "chili, no beans," vegetarian chili has been around for some time. Along with the usual chili powder and jalapeños, this version is seasoned with tomato-vegetable juice, which contains extracts of celery, beets, watercress, and other vegetables. White rice is the perfect foil for this mildly spicy chili, and the combination of beans and rice is an excellent source of low-fat protein.

1 cup long-grain rice
¾ teaspoon salt
2 teaspoons olive oil
4 scallions, thinly sliced
3 cloves garlic, minced
1 pickled jalapeño pepper, finely chopped
1 red bell pepper, diced
1 zucchini, quartered lengthwise and cut into ½-inch pieces
14½-ounce can no-salt-added stewed tomatoes
Two 19-ounce cans black beans, rinsed and drained
5½-ounce can reduced-sodium tomato-vegetable juice
⅓ cup chopped fresh cilantro (optional)
2 tablespoons fresh lime juice
1 teaspoon chili powder

1. In a medium saucepan, bring 2¼ cups of water to a boil. Add the rice and ¼ teaspoon of the salt, reduce to a simmer, cover, and cook until the rice is tender, about 17 minutes.

2. Meanwhile, in a large saucepan, heat the oil until hot but not smoking over medium-low heat. Add the scallions, garlic, and jalapeño and cook, stirring occasionally, until the scallions are softened, about 4 minutes. Add the bell pepper and zucchini and cook until crisp-tender, about 5 minutes.

3. Stir in the stewed tomatoes, beans, tomato-vegetable juice, cilantro, lime juice, chili powder, and the remaining ½ teaspoon salt and cook, stirring occasionally, until the chili is slightly thickened and the flavors are blended, about 7 minutes. Divide the rice among 4 bowls, spoon the chili alongside, and serve.

FAT: 4G/9%
CALORIES: 398
SATURATED FAT: 0.5G
CARBOHYDRATE: 76G
PROTEIN: 16G
CHOLESTEROL: 0MG
SODIUM: 988MG

Vegetable-Bean Soup

Serves: 4
Working time: 25 minutes
Total time: 30 minutes

1 tablespoon olive oil

4 cloves garlic, minced

1 tablespoon finely chopped fresh ginger

1 red bell pepper, cut into 1-inch squares

1 green bell pepper, cut into 1-inch squares

1 Granny Smith apple, cored, peeled, and cut into ½-inch cubes

2 teaspoons paprika

½ teaspoon salt

2 tomatoes, coarsely chopped, or 2 cups canned no-salt-added tomatoes, chopped with their juices

¾ pound green beans, cut into 1-inch lengths

16-ounce can red kidney beans, rinsed and drained

2 tablespoons balsamic vinegar

1. In a large saucepan, heat the oil until hot but not smoking over medium heat. Add the garlic and ginger and cook, stirring frequently, until the garlic is softened, about 1 minute. Add the bell peppers and cook, stirring frequently, until the peppers are crisp-tender, about 5 minutes. Add the apple, paprika, and salt and cook, stirring frequently, until the apple is crisp-tender, about 4 minutes.

2. Add 4 cups of water, the tomatoes, green beans, and kidney beans to the pan and bring to a boil. Reduce to a simmer, cover, and cook until the green beans are crisp-tender, about 5 minutes. Stir in the vinegar and serve.

Helpful hint: Green and red bell peppers differ not just in color, but in flavor: Red peppers have been left on the vine longer than green, and are therefore sweeter.

Fat: 5g/23%
Calories: 196
Saturated Fat: 0.6g
Carbohydrate: 33g
Protein: 9g
Cholesterol: 0mg
Sodium: 429mg

Adding beans to just about any meatless soup makes a more satisfying meal. Here, the kidney beans contribute starchy sturdiness and protein, while green beans, bell peppers, and apple cubes bring a fresh, crisp quality to the soup. The lively finishing touch is a splash of vinegar; mellow balsamic works particularly well, but red wine vinegar could be used instead.

OLD-FASHIONED VEGETABLE-BEEF SOUP

SERVES: 4
WORKING TIME: 15 MINUTES
TOTAL TIME: 30 MINUTES

*2 cups reduced-sodium beef
broth*

1 tomato, coarsely chopped

3 cloves garlic, minced

½ teaspoon dried thyme

½ teaspoon dried rosemary

½ teaspoon Worcestershire sauce

¼ teaspoon salt

4 ounces elbow macaroni

1 cup frozen baby lima beans

*¾ pound well-trimmed top
round of beef, cut into ½-inch
dice*

1 cup frozen corn kernels

3 tablespoons ketchup

1. In a Dutch oven or large saucepan, combine the broth, tomato, garlic, thyme, rosemary, Worcestershire sauce, salt, and 3 cups of water. Bring to a boil over medium heat, cover, and cook for 5 minutes to blend the flavors.

2. Stir in the macaroni and lima beans, cover, and cook for 5 minutes. Stir in the beef, corn, and ketchup, cover, and cook until the meat is cooked through and the macaroni is tender, about 5 minutes.

Helpful hint: Worcestershire sauce "beefs up" soups and stews with a complex blend of ingredients that includes anchovies, soy sauce, molasses, garlic, onions, and vinegar.

FAT: 4G/11%
CALORIES: 337
SATURATED FAT: 1.1G
CARBOHYDRATE: 46G
PROTEIN: 30G
CHOLESTEROL: 49MG
SODIUM: 657MG

You'll find row upon row of soup cans labeled "old-fashioned" on your supermarket's shelves, but we think you'll be much happier with this recipe, which uses fresh beef, tomato, and garlic for maximum flavor, and frozen corn and lima beans for convenience. You might want to double the recipe so your family can enjoy the soup as a take-along lunch later in the week.

ASIAN-STYLE MUSHROOM STEW

SERVES: 4
WORKING TIME: 15 MINUTES
TOTAL TIME: 25 MINUTES

1 cup long-grain rice

3 tablespoons flaked coconut

¾ teaspoon salt

1 teaspoon olive oil

4 scallions, thinly sliced

2 tablespoons finely chopped fresh ginger

¾ pound mushrooms, thickly sliced

14½-ounce can no-salt-added stewed tomatoes

1 tablespoon rice vinegar or cider vinegar

1 teaspoon sugar

15-ounce can baby corn, rinsed and drained

8-ounce can sliced water chestnuts, drained

½ cup chopped fresh mint

8 ounces firm tofu, cut into 1-inch cubes

1. In a medium saucepan, bring 2¼ cups of water to a boil. Add the rice, coconut, and ¼ teaspoon of the salt. Reduce to a simmer, cover, and cook until the rice is tender, about 17 minutes.

2. Meanwhile, in a large nonstick skillet, heat the oil until hot but not smoking over medium heat. Add the scallions and ginger and cook, stirring frequently, until the scallions are softened, about 2 minutes. Add the mushrooms and cook, stirring occasionally, until the mushrooms are almost tender, about 4 minutes.

3. Stir in the stewed tomatoes, vinegar, sugar, and the remaining ½ teaspoon salt and bring to a boil. Add the corn, water chestnuts, and mint and simmer gently for 3 minutes to blend the flavors. Stir in the tofu and simmer just until the tofu is warmed through, about 3 minutes. Divide the rice among 4 bowls, spoon the stew alongside, and serve.

Helpful hint: It's best to buy tofu in sealed packages; when it's displayed in an open tub of water at room temperature, the tofu may be contaminated with bacteria (thorough cooking, however, will destroy the bacteria).

FAT: 9G/21%
CALORIES: 378
SATURATED FAT: 2G
CARBOHYDRATE: 62G
PROTEIN: 17G
CHOLESTEROL: 0MG
SODIUM: 474MG

Coconut-flavored rice is a lovely surprise with this unusual stew, which is dotted with cubes of tofu (bean curd) instead of chunks of beef or pork. The tofu absorbs the tangy sauce faster than meat or poultry would, and that's the key to tofu's versatility: It readily takes on the flavors of the foods you cook with it. Be sure to buy firm tofu; soft tofu will disintegrate in the stew.

In Portugal, cooks often sauté slices of linguiça—a garlicky pork sausage—to get soups and stews off to a savory start. (We've substituted Spanish chorizo, which is very similar to linguiça but more widely available in the United States.) Golden cubes of butternut squash make a lovely change from potatoes in this stew.

Portuguese Fish Stew

SERVES: 4
WORKING TIME: 25 MINUTES
TOTAL TIME: 40 MINUTES

3 ounces chorizo sausage (see tip), thinly sliced, or 3 ounces Canadian bacon, cut into julienne strips

1 onion, diced

3 cloves garlic, minced

1½ cups reduced-sodium chicken broth, defatted

½ cup dry white wine

2 cups peeled, cut butternut squash (1-inch cubes)

1 cup no-salt-added canned tomatoes, drained and chopped

1½ teaspoons paprika

1 teaspoon hot pepper sauce

¼ teaspoon salt

1 cup frozen corn kernels

1½ pounds sea bass, halibut, or flounder fillets, cut into 2-inch pieces

1. In a Dutch oven or flameproof casserole, combine the chorizo, onion, garlic, and ½ cup of the broth over medium heat. Cook, stirring frequently, until the onion is softened, about 7 minutes. Add the wine, increase the heat to high, and cook until almost evaporated, about 3 minutes.

2. Add the squash, stirring to coat. Add the remaining 1 cup broth, the tomatoes, paprika, hot pepper sauce, and salt. Reduce to a simmer, cover, and cook until the squash is tender, about 7 minutes. Stir in the corn, place the fish on top, cover, and cook until the fish is just opaque, about 4 minutes. Divide the stew among 4 bowls and serve.

Helpful hint: There is also a Mexican sausage called chorizo, but it differs from the Spanish type in that it is made from raw, rather than smoked, pork. If you can't find firm Spanish-style chorizo, use Canadian bacon instead.

TIP

Spanish-style chorizo is made from coarsely ground smoked pork, garlic, and spices. It is formed into links that are about ¾-inch in diameter and 8 inches long.

FAT: 12G/29%
CALORIES: 374
SATURATED FAT: 4G
CARBOHYDRATE: 26G
PROTEIN: 41G
CHOLESTEROL: 87MG
SODIUM: 695MG

Mexican Tomato and Tortilla Soup

Serves: 4
Working time: 15 minutes
Total time: 25 minutes

exican cooks sometimes use crisped tortilla strips in place of soup noodles, adding both heartiness and a textural contrast. Each bowl of this well-spiced soup brims with Mexican flavors— jalapeño, lime juice, cumin, cayenne, sweet corn, and tangy jack cheese.

2 teaspoons olive oil
Four 6-inch corn tortillas, cut into ½-inch-wide strips
4 scallions, thinly sliced
3 cloves garlic, minced
1 jalapeño pepper, seeded and minced
2 large tomatoes, coarsely chopped
8-ounce can no-salt-added tomato sauce
2 cups reduced-sodium chicken broth, defatted
1 teaspoon ground cumin
¼ teaspoon salt
⅛ teaspoon cayenne pepper
1 pound skinless, boneless chicken breasts, cut crosswise into ¼-inch-wide strips
1 cup frozen corn kernels
1 tablespoon fresh lime juice
3 tablespoons shredded Monterey jack cheese

1. In a nonstick Dutch oven or flameproof casserole, heat the oil until hot but not smoking over medium heat. Add the tortilla strips and cook until lightly crisped, about 1 minute. With a slotted spoon, transfer the strips to paper towels to drain.

2. Add the scallions, garlic, and jalapeño to the pan and cook until the scallions are softened, about 1 minute. Stir in the tomatoes, tomato sauce, broth, cumin, salt, and cayenne and bring to a boil. Reduce to a simmer, cover, and cook until the flavors are blended, about 5 minutes.

3. Add the chicken and corn, cover, and cook until the chicken is just cooked through, about 3 minutes. Stir in the tortilla strips and lime juice. Ladle into 4 soup bowls, sprinkle with the cheese, and serve.

Helpful hint: There's no need to cut each tortilla individually: You'll save time if you stack them and cut them all at once with a heavy knife.

Fat: 7g/20%
Calories: 313
Saturated Fat: 1.8g
Carbohydrate: 31g
Protein: 34g
Cholesterol: 72mg
Sodium: 624mg

SPICED SHRIMP STEW

SERVES: 4
WORKING TIME: 15 MINUTES
TOTAL TIME: 30 MINUTES

You might call this a chowder, but that word brings to mind a creamy, gentle dish. Cumin, ginger, and paprika, the alluring spices used here, are suggestive of exotic Middle Eastern cuisines; the sweet potatoes are a nice change from the white potatoes used in chowders. Like a curry, this stew has a yogurt sauce, and is served with rice.

1 cup long-grain rice
½ teaspoon salt
2 cups reduced-sodium chicken broth, defatted
3 cloves garlic, slivered
1 teaspoon ground ginger
1 teaspoon paprika
¾ teaspoon ground cumin
1 large sweet potato, peeled and cut into ½-inch cubes
1 red bell pepper, diced
1 pound large shrimp, shelled and deveined
½ cup plain nonfat yogurt
2 tablespoons flour
⅔ cup frozen peas

1. In a medium saucepan, bring 2¼ cups of water to a boil. Add the rice and ¼ teaspoon of the salt, reduce to a simmer, cover, and cook until the rice is tender, about 17 minutes.

2. Meanwhile, in a large skillet, combine the broth, 1 cup of water, the garlic, ginger, paprika, and cumin. Bring to a boil over medium heat, add the sweet potato, and cook until almost tender, about 7 minutes. Add the bell pepper, shrimp, and remaining ¼ teaspoon salt, cover, and simmer until the shrimp are opaque on the outside but still a bit translucent in the center, about 3 minutes.

3. In a small bowl, combine the yogurt and flour. Stir the yogurt mixture and peas into the skillet and cook, stirring, until slightly thickened, about 2 minutes. Serve with the rice.

Helpful hint: Normally you would want to remove the pan from the heat before adding the yogurt; but stirring flour into yogurt stabilizes it so it will not "break," or curdle, when heated.

FAT: 3G/7%
CALORIES: 403
SATURATED FAT: 0.5G
CARBOHYDRATE: 65G
PROTEIN: 29G
CHOLESTEROL: 140MG
SODIUM: 793MG

SPEEDY BEEF STROGANOFF

SERVES: 4
WORKING TIME: 25 MINUTES
TOTAL TIME: 25 MINUTES

Chefs in Imperial Russia probably didn't have to worry about whipping up quick meals or cutting calories. But our adaptation of this 19th-century Russian classic is a fast-cooking marvel, and it's a luxurious but lean dish when you use top round, reduced-fat sour cream, and yolkless egg noodles. Add a simple accompaniment such as steamed summer squash.

8 ounces "yolkless" egg noodles
2 tablespoons flour
2 teaspoons paprika
¾ teaspoon salt
¼ teaspoon freshly ground black pepper
¾ pound well-trimmed top round of beef, cut into ¼-inch-thick slices
1 tablespoon olive oil
4 cups sliced mushrooms
¾ cup reduced-sodium beef broth
4 scallions, cut into julienne strips
¼ cup reduced-fat sour cream
1 teaspoon Worcestershire sauce

1. In a large pot of boiling water, cook the noodles until tender. Drain well.

2. Meanwhile, in a sturdy plastic bag, combine the flour, paprika, salt, and pepper. Add the beef to the bag, tossing to coat.

3. In large nonstick skillet, heat the oil until hot but not smoking over medium heat. Add the beef and mushrooms and cook until the mushrooms are tender, about 5 minutes. Add the broth and scallions, bring to a simmer, and cook until the sauce is slightly thickened, about 3 minutes.

4. Remove the skillet from the heat and stir in the sour cream and Worcestershire sauce. Divide the noodles among 4 plates, spoon the beef mixture alongside, and serve.

Helpful hint: Removing the pan from the heat before stirring in the sour cream prevents the sauce from curdling.

FAT: 10G/22%
CALORIES: 406
SATURATED FAT: 2.7G
CARBOHYDRATE: 49G
PROTEIN: 32G
CHOLESTEROL: 54MG
SODIUM: 509 MG

Tex-Mex Beef Stew

SERVES: 4
WORKING TIME: 20 MINUTES
TOTAL TIME: 30 MINUTES

1 cup long-grain rice

¾ teaspoon salt

2 tablespoons flour

½ teaspoon freshly ground black pepper

10 ounces well-trimmed beef sirloin, cut into ½-inch chunks

2 teaspoons olive oil

6 scallions, cut into 1-inch lengths

3 cloves garlic, minced

2 cups no-salt-added canned tomatoes, chopped with their juices

4½-ounce can chopped mild green chilies, drained

2 tablespoons fresh lime juice

1½ cups frozen corn kernels

½ cup chopped fresh cilantro or basil

1. In a medium saucepan, bring 2¼ cups of water to a boil. Add the rice and ¼ teaspoon of the salt, reduce to a simmer, cover, and cook until the rice is tender, about 17 minutes.

2. Meanwhile, on a sheet of waxed paper, combine the flour, ¼ teaspoon of the salt, and the pepper. Dredge the beef in the flour mixture, shaking off the excess.

3. In a large nonstick skillet or Dutch oven, heat the oil until hot but not smoking over medium heat. Add the beef and cook, stirring frequently, until browned, about 4 minutes. Stir in the scallions and garlic and cook until the scallions are softened, about 3 minutes. Add the tomatoes, chilies, lime juice, the remaining ¼ teaspoon salt, and ¼ cup of water. Bring to a boil, reduce to a simmer, cover, and cook until the beef is just cooked through and the sauce is slightly thickened, about 10 minutes.

4. Stir the corn and cilantro into the pan and cook just until the corn is heated through, about 2 minutes. Divide the rice evenly among 4 plates, spoon the stew alongside, and serve.

Helpful hint: For an extra touch of flavor and color, sprinkle the rice with 1 teaspoon chopped fresh herbs—cilantro, basil, or parsley.

FAT: 7G/16%
CALORIES: 395
SATURATED FAT: 1.6G
CARBOHYDRATE: 63G
PROTEIN: 23G
CHOLESTEROL: 43MG
SODIUM: 672MG

Many of the dishes Texas is famous for begin with beef—the pride of the state—and the Mexican flavorings that Texans have come to love. This beef stew makes the most of both: Sirloin chunks, corn kernels, and scallions get the Tex-Mex treatment with tomatoes, garlic, green chilies, lime juice, and the herby kick of fresh cilantro. Fresh biscuits or rolls are a fine accompaniment.

GOLDEN BUTTERNUT-APPLE SOUP

MAKES: 6 CUPS
WORKING TIME: 25 MINUTES
TOTAL TIME: 30 MINUTES

3 cups peeled, seeded, and cut butternut squash (2-inch chunks)

2 Granny Smith apples, peeled, cored, and cut into 1-inch chunks

1 medium onion, coarsely chopped

2 cups reduced-sodium chicken broth, defatted

2 tablespoons firmly packed dark brown sugar

½ teaspoon ground ginger

¼ teaspoon cinnamon

½ cup low-fat (1%) milk

2 tablespoons dark rum

¼ cup reduced-fat sour cream

2 scallions, thinly sliced on the diagonal

1. In a Dutch oven, combine the squash, apples, onion, broth, brown sugar, ginger, and cinnamon. Cover and cook over medium-high heat, stirring occasionally, until the squash is very tender, about 10 minutes.

2. With a slotted spoon, transfer the solids to a blender or food processor and purée until smooth. Return the purée to the pan, add the milk and rum, and stir well to combine. Cook over low heat, uncovered, until the soup is just heated through, about 3 minutes.

3. Ladle the soup into bowls and spoon 2 or 3 small dollops of the sour cream on top of each. With a skewer or knife, cut through the sour cream to form a decorative pattern. Sprinkle the scallions on top and serve.

Helpful hints: Prepare the squash purée up to 2 days ahead, refrigerate, and then stir in the milk and rum just before serving and gently heat. If desired, cook the squash mixture in the microwave: Combine the ingredients in step 1 in a microwave-safe bowl, and microwave on high power for 10 to 15 minutes, stirring halfway through.

VALUES ARE PER 1 CUP
FAT: 2G/13%
CALORIES: 128
SATURATED FAT: 0.8G
CARBOHYDRATE: 24G
PROTEIN: 4G
CHOLESTEROL: 4MG
SODIUM: 231MG

Set your holiday table with candlelight, and present this colorful soup as a festive first course. It's guaranteed to spark appetites— tart apples and a hint of rum delicately sweeten the squash, while ginger and cinnamon lend an invitingly spicy scent. Ladle into pottery soup bowls, or into heavy mugs for a more casual gathering around the fire.

S*tews
usually require long,
slow cooking to render
meat or poultry
perfectly tender. But
meatless stews can cook
considerably quicker.
Tofu and cannellini
(white kidney beans),
the protein components
of this stew, just need
to be heated through;
the vegetables, in true
Asian style, are briefly
cooked until crisp-
tender.*

ASIAN-STYLE VEGETABLE STEW WITH TOFU

SERVES: 4
WORKING TIME: 20 MINUTES
TOTAL TIME: 25 MINUTES

1 cup long-grain rice

¼ teaspoon salt

2 teaspoons vegetable oil

4 scallions, thinly sliced

2 cloves garlic, minced

1 red bell pepper, cut into ½-inch pieces

⅓ cup orange juice

¼ cup chili sauce

2 tablespoons plum jam

2 tablespoons reduced-sodium soy sauce

¾ teaspoon ground ginger

½ pound snow peas, fresh or frozen, halved crosswise (see tip)

½ cup canned sliced water chestnuts, drained

19-ounce can white kidney beans (cannellini), rinsed and drained

8 ounces firm tofu, cut into ½-inch cubes

1. In a medium saucepan, bring 2¼ cups of water to a boil. Add the rice and salt, reduce to a simmer, cover, and cook until the rice is tender, about 17 minutes.

2. Meanwhile, in a large skillet, heat the oil until hot but not smoking over medium heat. Add the scallions and garlic and cook, stirring frequently, until the scallions are tender, about 2 minutes. Add the bell pepper and cook until crisp-tender, about 2 minutes.

3. In a small bowl, combine the orange juice, chili sauce, plum jam, soy sauce, and ginger. Add the orange juice mixture to the skillet, stirring to combine. Add the snow peas and water chestnuts and bring to a boil. Stir in the white kidney beans and cook just until heated through, about 2 minutes. Add the tofu and cook, stirring gently, until heated through, about 3 minutes. Divide the stew among 4 plates, spoon the rice alongside, and serve.

Helpful hint: For this recipe you'll want to buy firm tofu, which looks like little pillows, rather than soft tofu, which comes in straight-edged blocks; soft tofu would crumble apart in the stew.

TIP

To prepare fresh snow peas for cooking, trim the stem end and pull off the string along the straight side. For the best flavor and texture, cook snow peas just until they are crisp-tender and a vibrant green.

FAT: 9G/17%
CALORIES: 470
SATURATED FAT: 1.1G
CARBOHYDRATE: 78G
PROTEIN: 23G
CHOLESTEROL: 0MG
SODIUM: 853MG

PORK AND RED BEAN CHILI

SERVES: 4
WORKING TIME: 20 MINUTES
TOTAL TIME: 30 MINUTES

Chili—the Southwest's favorite "bowl of red"—is an earthy, sustaining meal that's subject to fascinating variations. This one is mostly red, with just a touch of green in the mild chilies that flavor it. It's made with sizeable chunks of pork rather than ground meat and is sure to be a stick-to-the-ribs dinner.

2 teaspoons vegetable oil
¾ pound well-trimmed pork tenderloin, cut into ¾-inch chunks
1 onion, coarsely chopped
1 clove garlic, minced
1 tablespoon chili powder
1 teaspoon fennel seeds
19-ounce can red kidney beans, rinsed and drained
15-ounce can no-salt-added tomatoes
7-ounce jar roasted red peppers, drained and diced
4½-ounce can chopped mild green chilies, drained
½ teaspoon salt

1. In medium nonstick saucepan, heat 1 teaspoon of the oil until hot but not smoking over medium heat. Add the pork and cook until browned, about 5 minutes. With a slotted spoon, transfer the pork to a plate.

2. Add the remaining 1 teaspoon oil to the pan along with the onion and garlic. Cook, stirring, until the onion is softened, about 4 minutes. Stir in the chili powder and fennel seeds and cook until fragrant, about 1 minute. Add the beans, tomatoes, roasted red peppers, green chilies, and salt. Bring to a boil, reduce to a simmer, and cook, breaking up the tomatoes with the back of a spoon, until slightly thickened, about 10 minutes.

3. Return the pork to the pan and cook until warmed through, about 1 minute. Transfer to a large tureen or serving bowl and serve.

Helpful hint: Veteran chili-lovers may want to substitute canned jalapeños for the mild green chilies to increase the heat in this dish. Feel free to add more chili powder as well.

FAT: 7G/22%
CALORIES: 289
SATURATED FAT: 1.4G
CARBOHYDRATE: 30G
PROTEIN: 27G
CHOLESTEROL: 55MG
SODIUM: 818MG

A

light Italian-style soup of spinach cooked in broth—"in brodo"— becomes a filling main dish with the addition of potatoes and chick-peas. Legumes, such as beans, chick-peas, and split peas, are excellent low-fat protein sources, making them both healthful and satisfying substitutes for meat and poultry.

CHICK-PEA AND SPINACH SOUP

SERVES: 4
WORKING TIME: 20 MINUTES
TOTAL TIME: 30 MINUTES

1 tablespoon olive oil

1 onion, finely chopped

6 cloves garlic, minced

2 carrots, halved lengthwise and thinly sliced

¾ pound all-purpose potatoes, peeled and cut into ½-inch cubes

2 cups reduced-sodium vegetable broth

16-ounce can chick-peas, rinsed and drained

½ teaspoon salt

½ teaspoon grated lemon zest

¼ teaspoon freshly ground black pepper

10-ounce package fresh spinach, shredded (see tip)

1. In a large nonstick saucepan, heat the oil until hot but not smoking over medium heat. Add the onion and garlic and cook, stirring frequently, until the onion is softened, about 7 minutes. Add the carrots and cook, stirring, until the carrots are crisp-tender, about 3 minutes.

2. Add the potatoes to the pan, stirring to coat. Add the broth, 1 cup of water, the chick-peas, salt, lemon zest, and pepper and bring to a boil. Reduce to a simmer, cover, and cook until the potatoes are firm-tender, about 7 minutes. Stir in the spinach and cook for 1 minute to wilt. Divide among 4 bowls and serve.

Helpful hint: There are three basic types of spinach. Savoy is the crinkly-leaf spinach usually sold pre-washed in bags. There are also semi-Savoy (less crinkly) and smooth-leaved types. Any of the three can be used in this recipe.

TIP

The easiest way to shred spinach or other broad-leaved greens is to stack the leaves and then slice them crosswise.

FAT: 6G/23%
CALORIES: 233
SATURATED FAT: 0.6G
CARBOHYDRATE: 38G
PROTEIN: 10G
CHOLESTEROL: 0MG
SODIUM: 604MG

CHUNKY NEW ENGLAND COD CHOWDER

SERVES: 4
WORKING TIME: 10 MINUTES
TOTAL TIME: 20 MINUTES

*J*ust one ounce of Canadian bacon suffuses this stew with rich, old-fashioned flavor. Serve with oyster crackers or saltines.

¾ pound small red potatoes, cut into 8 wedges each

2 teaspoons olive oil

3 tablespoons chopped Canadian bacon (1 ounce)

1 red bell pepper, cut into 1-inch squares

1 green bell pepper, cut into 1-inch squares

3 cloves garlic, minced

2 tablespoons flour

1½ cups low-fat (1%) milk

½ teaspoon salt

¼ teaspoon cayenne pepper

1 pound skinless, boneless cod steak, cut into 8 chunks

1. In a medium pot of boiling water, cook the potatoes until just tender, about 8 minutes.

2. Meanwhile, in a large nonstick skillet, heat the oil until hot but not smoking over medium heat. Add the Canadian bacon, bell peppers, and garlic and cook, stirring frequently, until the bell peppers are crisp-tender, about 5 minutes.

3. Sprinkle the flour into the skillet, stirring to coat. Gradually stir in the milk, salt, and cayenne. Bring to a boil, place the cod on top, reduce to a simmer, cover, and cook until the cod is just opaque, about 5 minutes. Divide the cod mixture among 4 bowls and serve.

Helpful hint: Red potatoes add a nice note of color, but small round white potatoes would work perfectly well. If you can only get long white boiling potatoes, halve them crosswise, then cut each half into eight wedges.

FAT: 5G/17%
CALORIES: 259
SATURATED FAT: 1.2G
CARBOHYDRATE: 26G
PROTEIN: 27G
CHOLESTEROL: 56MG
SODIUM: 488MG

Green Chili

SERVES: 4
WORKING TIME: 20 MINUTES
TOTAL TIME: 30 MINUTES

1 pound all-purpose potatoes, peeled and cut into ½-inch dice

2 teaspoons olive oil

4 scallions, thinly sliced

3 cloves garlic, minced

1 pickled jalapeño pepper, finely chopped

2 green bell peppers, diced

Two 4½-ounce cans chopped mild green chilies, drained

1 cup reduced-sodium chicken broth, defatted

16-ounce can red kidney beans, rinsed and drained

1½ cups frozen corn kernels

½ cup chopped fresh cilantro

2 tablespoons fresh lime juice

½ teaspoon dried oregano

½ teaspoon salt

¼ cup reduced-fat sour cream

1. In a large pot of boiling water, cook the potatoes until tender, about 8 minutes. Drain well.

2. Meanwhile, in a large nonstick skillet, heat the oil until hot but not smoking over medium heat. Add the scallions, garlic, and jalapeño and cook until the scallions are tender, about 1 minute. Add the bell peppers and cook, stirring occasionally, until tender, about 5 minutes.

3. Add the green chilies, broth, kidney beans, corn, cilantro, lime juice, oregano, and salt and bring to a boil. Reduce the heat to a simmer, cover, and cook until the flavors are blended, about 5 minutes. Stir in the potatoes and cook until warmed through, about 1 minute. Divide the chili among 4 bowls, top each with a dollop of sour cream, and serve.

Helpful hint: A large lime will yield about 2 tablespoons of juice; if using smaller limes, you'll need more than one. Buy limes that feel heavy in your hand—they'll be juicier.

FAT: 6G/19%
CALORIES: 289
SATURATED FAT: 1.4G
CARBOHYDRATE: 51G
PROTEIN: 13G
CHOLESTEROL: 5MG
SODIUM: 903MG

Accompany this light, sassy chili with warm corn tortillas; garnish it with lime wedges for an extra citrusy jolt.

HEARTY CHICKEN AND CORN CHOWDER

SERVES: 4
WORKING TIME: 15 MINUTES
TOTAL TIME: 25 MINUTES

Creamed corn helps thicken this soup to a satisfying chowder consistency, without the added calories and fat of cream. When roadside farm stands are stacked high with sweet corn, certainly substitute freshly cooked corn off the cob for frozen in this chowder. For a variation, replace the parsley with fresh cilantro.

1 teaspoon olive oil

1 large onion, finely chopped

1 red bell pepper, diced

1 all-purpose potato, peeled and diced

1 ounce Canadian bacon, diced

1 cup reduced-sodium chicken broth, defatted

1 cup evaporated skimmed milk

1 cup canned creamed corn

¾ pound skinless, boneless chicken breasts, diced

½ teaspoon salt

¼ teaspoon freshly ground black pepper

¾ cup frozen corn kernels

2 tablespoons chopped fresh parsley

1. In a medium saucepan, heat the oil until hot but not smoking over medium heat. Add the onion, bell pepper, potato, and bacon. Cover and cook, stirring occasionally, until the vegetables begin to soften, about 5 minutes. Stir in the broth, evaporated milk, and creamed corn. Bring to a boil and reduce to a simmer. Cook, uncovered, stirring occasionally, for 10 minutes.

2. Stir in the diced chicken, salt, and black pepper and cook until the chicken is cooked through, about 5 minutes. Stir in the corn kernels and cook until the corn is just heated through, about 2 minutes longer. Ladle the chowder into 4 bowls, sprinkle with the parsley, and serve.

Suggested accompaniments: Green salad with a balsamic vinaigrette. For dessert, broiled peach halves topped with a little brown sugar.

FAT: 4G/12%
CALORIES: 296
SATURATED FAT: .8G
CARBOHYDRATE: 37G
PROTEIN: 31G
CHOLESTEROL: 57MG
SODIUM: 896MG

A

favorite Tuscan way of flavoring cannellini (white kidney beans) is by stirring puréed tomatoes into the freshly cooked beans; garlic and sage are the other dominant flavors in the dish. For this robust stew, potatoes, carrots, and leeks join the beans; fragrant rosemary takes the place of the sage, and ground ginger adds a lively note.

TUSCAN VEGETABLE STEW

SERVES: 4
WORKING TIME: 15 MINUTES
TOTAL TIME: 25 MINUTES

1 pound small red potatoes, cut into ½-inch cubes

2 cups peeled baby carrots

1 tablespoon olive oil

2 leeks (white and light green parts only), diced, or 8 scallions, thickly sliced

3 cloves garlic, slivered

Two 19-ounce cans white kidney beans (cannellini), rinsed and drained

8-ounce can no-salt-added tomato sauce

¾ cup reduced-sodium chicken broth, defatted

1 teaspoon ground ginger

½ teaspoon dried rosemary

½ teaspoon salt

1. In a medium pot of boiling water, cook the potatoes for 5 minutes. Add the baby carrots and cook until the potatoes are just tender, about 3 minutes. Drain well.

2. Meanwhile, in a large nonstick skillet, heat the oil until hot but not smoking over medium heat. Add the leeks and garlic and cook, stirring occasionally, until the leeks are tender, about 4 minutes. Stir in the potatoes and carrots and cook, stirring occasionally, until the vegetables are tender, about 4 minutes.

3. Add the beans, tomato sauce, broth, ginger, rosemary, and salt and bring to a boil. Reduce the heat to a simmer, cover, and cook until the stew is slightly thickened and the flavors are blended, about 5 minutes.

Helpful hint: You can make the stew up to 8 hours in advance and keep it covered in the refrigerator. Reheat it, covered, on the stove over low to medium heat.

FAT: 6G/14%
CALORIES: 398
SATURATED FAT: 0.6G
CARBOHYDRATE: 70G
PROTEIN: 19G
CHOLESTEROL: 0MG
SODIUM: 781MG

TIP

When a recipe calls for leeks to be sliced or diced, first trim the root end and the dark green leaves, then cut the leeks as directed. Place the cut leeks in a bowl of tepid water, let them sit for 1 to 2 minutes, then lift the leeks out of the water, leaving any dirt and grit behind in the bowl. This is easier and faster than splitting and washing whole leeks before slicing them.

Tex-Mex Turkey Sausage Stew

Serves: 4
Working time: 10 minutes
Total time: 25 minutes

1 cup long-grain rice

½ teaspoon salt

½ pound hot Italian-style turkey sausage, cut into 1-inch pieces

⅓ cup reduced-sodium chicken broth, defatted

1 green bell pepper, cut into 1-inch squares

14½-ounce can no-salt-added stewed tomatoes

4½-ounce can chopped mild green chilies

½ teaspoon ground cumin

½ teaspoon dried oregano

1 cup frozen corn kernels

1. In a medium saucepan, bring 2¼ cups of water to a boil. Add the rice and ¼ teaspoon of the salt, reduce to a simmer, cover, and cook until the rice is tender, about 17 minutes.

2. Meanwhile, spray a large nonstick skillet with nonstick cooking spray. Add the turkey sausage and cook over medium heat just until lightly browned, about 3 minutes. Add the broth and bell pepper and simmer until the pepper is tender, about 4 minutes.

3. Stir the tomatoes, chilies, cumin, oregano, and remaining ¼ teaspoon salt into the skillet. Bring to a boil, reduce to a simmer, and cook until the sausage is cooked through and the sauce is slightly thickened, about 5 minutes. Stir in the corn and cook just until warmed through. Divide the rice among 4 plates, spoon the stew alongside, and serve.

Helpful hint: If your family doesn't go for spicy food, use sweet sausage instead of hot. If, on the other hand, you like things extra hot, add a pinch of cayenne or a few shakes of hot pepper sauce to the stew before serving.

Fat: 7g/18%
Calories: 344
Saturated Fat: 1.8g
Carbohydrate: 57g
Protein: 16g
Cholesterol: 30mg
Sodium: 915mg

Mexican cooks would make this stew with the spicy pork sausage called chorizo, which is not very widely available here. In its place, we've used Italian-style turkey sausage, which contributes its own wonderful seasonings to the chilies, cumin, and oregano in the dish. Of course, turkey is also lower in fat than pork. Accompany the stew with a lightly dressed salad to refresh the palate.

FISH STEW GIARDINIERA

SERVES: 4
WORKING TIME: 20 MINUTES
TOTAL TIME: 30 MINUTES

Here's how a gardener in Italy (una giardiniera) would cook up a fish stew—with an abundance of vegetables. The "meat" of the matter is sizeable chunks of cod, a neutral-flavored firm-textured fish that works well in savory tomato-based dishes. Be sure to offer some crusty Italian bread to soak up every last drop of the broth.

2 teaspoons olive oil

4 scallions, thinly sliced

3 cloves garlic, minced

1 red bell pepper, diced

2 carrots, thinly sliced

14½-ounce can no-salt-added stewed tomatoes

½ cup bottled clam juice

8¾-ounce can red kidney beans, rinsed and drained

½ teaspoon dried oregano

¼ teaspoon salt

1 pound skinless, boneless cod steak, cut into 12 chunks

1½ teaspoons cornstarch mixed with 1 tablespoon water

1. In a large nonstick skillet, heat the oil until hot but not smoking over medium heat. Add the scallions and garlic and cook until the scallions are wilted, about 1 minute. Add the bell pepper and carrots and cook, stirring occasionally, until the vegetables have softened, about 4 minutes.

2. Stir in the tomatoes, breaking them up with the back of a spoon. Add the clam juice and bring to a boil. Stir in the beans, oregano, and salt and cook, stirring occasionally, until slightly thickened, about 5 minutes. Place the cod on top, cover, and cook until the cod is just opaque, about 5 minutes.

3. With a slotted spoon, transfer the cod to 4 bowls. Add the cornstarch mixture to the skillet, and cook, stirring, until slightly thickened, about 1 minute. Spoon the vegetable mixture over the cod and serve.

Helpful hint: Clam juice brings a nice seaside fragrance to the stew, but you can substitute chicken broth if you like.

FAT: 4G/17%
CALORIES: 217
SATURATED FAT: 0.5G
CARBOHYDRATE: 21G
PROTEIN: 25G
CHOLESTEROL: 49MG
SODIUM: 372MG

SICILIAN-STYLE RAGOUT OF BEEF

SERVES: 4
WORKING TIME: 20 MINUTES
TOTAL TIME: 30 MINUTES

Sicilian cuisine upholds an ancient tradition of accenting savory dishes with sweet ingredients: Raisins, oranges, honey, and sweet Marsala wine go into many Sicilian meat, fish, or poultry dishes. This delicious beef ragout, served over golden ribbons of fettuccine, is simmered in a broth flavored with orange juice, raisins, ginger, and fennel seeds.

¼ cup golden raisins

½ cup hot water

2 tablespoons flour

½ teaspoon salt

¼ teaspoon freshly ground black pepper

¾ pound well-trimmed top round of beef, cut into ½-inch cubes

1 tablespoon olive oil

1 large onion, coarsely chopped

4 cloves garlic, minced

6 ounces fettuccine

2 large tomatoes, coarsely chopped

⅓ cup orange juice

½ cup reduced-sodium chicken broth, defatted

½ teaspoon fennel seeds

¼ teaspoon ground ginger

1. Start heating a large pot of water to boiling for the pasta. In a small bowl, combine the raisins and hot water and set aside to soften. On a sheet of waxed paper, combine the flour, ¼ teaspoon of the salt, and the pepper. Dredge the beef in the flour mixture, shaking off the excess.

2. In a Dutch oven or flameproof casserole, heat 2 teaspoons of the oil until hot but not smoking over medium heat. Add the beef and cook until lightly browned, about 4 minutes. With a slotted spoon, transfer the beef to a plate and set aside. Add the remaining 1 teaspoon oil to the pan along with the onion and garlic and cook, stirring frequently, until the onion is lightly golden, about 5 minutes.

3. Cook the fettuccine in the boiling water until just tender. Drain well.

4. Meanwhile, stir the tomatoes, orange juice, and the raisins and their soaking liquid into the stew and bring to a boil. Stir in the broth, fennel seeds, ginger, and the remaining ¼ teaspoon salt and return to a boil. Reduce to a simmer, cover, and cook until the flavors are blended, about 7 minutes. Uncover, return the beef to the pan, and cook until the beef is just cooked through, about 2 minutes. Divide the fettuccine among 4 plates, spoon the beef mixture alongside, and serve.

FAT: 8G/18%
CALORIES: 396
SATURATED FAT: 1.8G
CARBOHYDRATE: 52G
PROTEIN: 28G
CHOLESTEROL: 89MG
SODIUM: 418MG

CURRIED PORK AND CHICK-PEA STEW

SERVES: 4
WORKING TIME: 20 MINUTES
TOTAL TIME: 30 MINUTES

*J*ust about any food will cook quickly if cut into small pieces; that's why timesaving recipes often call for meat to be cut into strips or dice. The small cubes of pork tenderloin used here will cook in about five minutes. The apple juice-based curry sauce will strike a familiar chord in anyone who likes applesauce with roast pork.

1 cup basmati or long-grain rice

¾ teaspoon salt

1 tablespoon olive oil

1 red onion, cut into ½-inch cubes

1 green bell pepper, cut into ½-inch squares

1 teaspoon curry powder

1 teaspoon ground cumin

2 tablespoons flour

1 tablespoon no-salt-added tomato paste

2 tablespoons honey

1 cup apple juice

¾ pound well-trimmed pork tenderloin, cut into ½-inch cubes

19-ounce can chick-peas, rinsed and drained

2 teaspoons chopped fresh parsley

1. In a medium saucepan, bring 2¼ cups of water to a boil. Add the rice and ¼ teaspoon of the salt, reduce to a simmer, cover, and cook until the rice is tender, about 17 minutes.

2. Meanwhile, in a nonstick Dutch oven, heat the oil until hot but not smoking over medium heat. Add the onion and bell pepper and cook, stirring occasionally, until the onion is softened, about 5 minutes.

3. Add the curry powder and cumin and cook until fragrant, about 1 minute. Sprinkle on the flour, stirring to combine. Add the tomato paste, honey, and apple juice and bring to a boil. Reduce the heat to a simmer, add the pork, chick-peas, and the remaining ½ teaspoon salt, cover, and cook, stirring occasionally, until the pork is cooked through, about 5 minutes. Divide the mixture among 4 plates, spoon the rice alongside, sprinkle the parsley over the rice, and serve.

Helpful hint: If you chill the pork in the freezer for a scant 15 minutes, it will be much easier to cut into cubes.

FAT: 10G/18%
CALORIES: 504
SATURATED FAT: 1.6G
CARBOHYDRATE: 75G
PROTEIN: 29G
CHOLESTEROL: 55MG
SODIUM: 635MG

PEPPERY FISH AND CORN CHOWDER

SERVES: 4
WORKING TIME: 20 MINUTES
TOTAL TIME: 30 MINUTES

W*e've used Canadian bacon here for old-fashioned flavor, and lots of vegetables. Red snapper or halibut could easily replace the cod.*

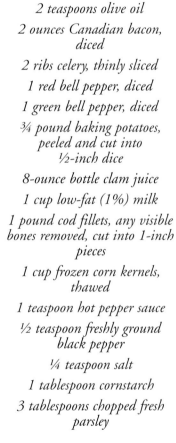

2 teaspoons olive oil

2 ounces Canadian bacon, diced

2 ribs celery, thinly sliced

1 red bell pepper, diced

1 green bell pepper, diced

¾ pound baking potatoes, peeled and cut into ½-inch dice

8-ounce bottle clam juice

1 cup low-fat (1%) milk

1 pound cod fillets, any visible bones removed, cut into 1-inch pieces

1 cup frozen corn kernels, thawed

1 teaspoon hot pepper sauce

½ teaspoon freshly ground black pepper

¼ teaspoon salt

1 tablespoon cornstarch

3 tablespoons chopped fresh parsley

1. In a Dutch oven, heat the oil until hot but not smoking over medium heat. Add the bacon and cook until lightly crisped, about 1 minute. Stir in the celery and bell peppers and cook, stirring frequently, until the vegetables are just tender, about 5 minutes.

2. Add the potatoes, stirring to coat. Add the clam juice, milk, and 1 cup of water. Bring to a boil, reduce to a simmer, cover, and cook until the potatoes are almost tender, about 7 minutes.

3. Stir in the cod, corn, hot pepper sauce, black pepper, and salt, cover again, and simmer until the cod is just opaque, about 4 minutes.

4. In a cup, combine the cornstarch and 1 tablespoon of water and stir to blend. Return the cod mixture to a boil over medium heat, stir in the cornstarch mixture, and cook, stirring constantly, until the chowder is slightly thickened, about 1 minute longer. Stir in the parsley and serve.

Suggested accompaniments: Oyster crackers, and a tossed green salad with buttermilk dressing. For the finale, blueberries garnished with lemon zest and a dollop of vanilla nonfat yogurt.

FAT: 5G/17%
CALORIES: 271
SATURATED FAT: 1.2G
CARBOHYDRATE: 28G
PROTEIN: 28G
CHOLESTEROL: 58MG
SODIUM: 606MG

GREEK-STYLE COD AND LEMON SOUP

SERVES: 4
WORKING TIME: 20 MINUTES
TOTAL TIME: 30 MINUTES

2 cups reduced-sodium chicken
broth, defatted

½ teaspoon grated lemon zest

¼ cup fresh lemon juice

½ cup chopped fresh mint

4 scallions, finely chopped

2 cloves garlic, minced

½ teaspoon dried oregano

½ teaspoon salt

½ cup orzo or other small
pasta shape

1 yellow summer squash,
halved lengthwise and thinly
sliced

1½ pounds skinless cod fillets,
cut into large pieces

1 teaspoon cornstarch mixed
with 1 tablespoon water

1. In a large nonaluminum saucepan, combine 4 cups of water, the broth, lemon zest, lemon juice, mint, scallions, garlic, oregano, and salt. Bring to a boil over medium heat and cook for 5 minutes to blend the flavors.

2. Add the orzo and yellow squash to the pan and cook for 5 minutes. Reduce to a simmer, add the fish, and cook until just opaque, about 4 minutes. Bring to a boil, add the cornstarch mixture, and cook, stirring constantly, until the soup is slightly thickened, about 1 minute. Divide the soup among 4 bowls and serve.

Helpful hint: The soup can be completed through step 1 up to 8 hours in advance. Return to a boil before proceeding.

FAT: 2G/7%
CALORIES: 267
SATURATED FAT: 0.3G
CARBOHYDRATE: 25G
PROTEIN: 36G
CHOLESTEROL: 73MG
SODIUM: 693MG

Lemony soups made with rice (or rice-like orzo pasta) are typically Greek. The fresh lemon taste is perfect with fish.

CHUNKY CHICKEN AND CORN CHILI

SERVES: 4
WORKING TIME: 15 MINUTES
TOTAL TIME: 25 MINUTES

To add rich flavor to this robust chili, we've first cooked the fragrant spices in a little oil. And, to reduce the sodium content, we've rinsed the beans and used no-salt-added tomato sauce. Dark meat chicken makes a particularly flavorful chili, but skinless white meat chicken may be substituted.

2 teaspoons vegetable oil
2 large onions, coarsely chopped
6 cloves garlic, minced
1½ tablespoons mild chili powder
1½ teaspoons dried oregano
1 teaspoon ground cumin
1 teaspoon ground coriander
1 teaspoon cinnamon
¾ teaspoon freshly ground black pepper
½ teaspoon salt
1 pound skinless, boneless chicken thighs, cut into ½-inch chunks
Two 8-ounce cans no-salt-added tomato sauce
Two 16-ounce cans kidney beans, rinsed and drained
2 cups frozen corn kernels
2 tablespoons light sour cream

1. In a nonstick Dutch oven, heat the oil until hot but not smoking over medium heat. Add the onions and garlic and cook, stirring frequently, until the onions begin to soften, about 5 minutes. Stir in the chili powder, oregano, cumin, coriander, cinnamon, pepper, and salt and cook, stirring constantly, for 30 seconds.

2. Add the chicken, stirring to coat thoroughly, and the tomato sauce. Bring to a boil over medium-high heat, reduce to a simmer, cover, and cook until the chicken is cooked through, about 5 minutes.

3. Stir in the kidney beans and corn and cook, uncovered, until the kidney beans and corn are heated through, about 3 minutes longer. Serve the chili in bowls and top with the sour cream.

Suggested accompaniments: Red-leaf lettuce salad with a Dijon mustard vinaigrette, followed by angel food cake with raspberry sauce.

FAT: 11G/20%
CALORIES: 505
SATURATED FAT: 2.1G
CARBOHYDRATE: 66G
PROTEIN: 41G
CHOLESTEROL: 97MG
SODIUM: 714MG

APPETIZERS & SIDE DISHES

Left, Tomato Bruschetta
Above, Lemon-Garlic Mushrooms

GUACAMOLE

SERVES: 4
WORKING TIME: 20 MINUTES
TOTAL TIME: 25 MINUTES

Four 6-inch corn tortillas, each cut into 6 wedges
Two 10-ounce packages frozen peas
1 large tomato, coarsely chopped
1 cup diced avocado
½ cup finely chopped red onion
⅓ cup chopped fresh cilantro
3 tablespoons fresh lime juice
¾ teaspoon ground cumin
½ teaspoon salt

1. Preheat the oven to 425°. Place the tortilla wedges on a baking sheet and bake for 5 minutes, turning once, or until lightly browned and crisp. Set aside.

2. Meanwhile, in a small saucepan of boiling water, cook the peas for 30 seconds to blanch. Drain well. Transfer the peas to a food processor and purée until smooth. Push the purée through a fine-mesh sieve into a large bowl.

3. Stir in the tomato, avocado, onion, cilantro, lime juice, cumin, and salt until the mixture is well combined but still slightly chunky. Spoon the guacamole into a small serving bowl and serve with the tortilla chips.

Helpful hints: This mild guacamole can be made spicier by stirring in a little medium-hot or hot prepared salsa. The nubby-textured black Haas avocado has a richer taste and meatier consistency than the larger, smooth-skinned green Fuerte type. Avoid buying a rock-hard avocado. To ripen, place the avocado in a loosely closed brown paper bag and store at room temperature.

Guacamole, once found only in Mexican restaurants, has become a national favorite. The hitch, however, is the high-fat avocado. Our trick is to replace some of the avocado with green peas—the color and texture remain the same, and no one will be the wiser. What's more, we've made our own tasty tortilla chips—corn tortilla wedges that are baked, not fried.

FAT: 7G/26%
CALORIES: 246
SATURATED FAT: 1.1G
CARBOHYDRATE: 39G
PROTEIN: 10G
CHOLESTEROL: 0MG
SODIUM: 483MG

CAULIFLOWER WITH CHEDDAR SAUCE

MAKES: 4 CUPS
WORKING TIME: 25 MINUTES
TOTAL TIME: 30 MINUTES

Our version of this vegetable classic tastes as good as the original, even though we've cut way back on the fat. Adding vinegar to the cauliflower cooking water lends a subtle flavor to the vegetable, and also helps to keep it white. For a simple embellishment, garnish with chopped fresh parsley or chives just before serving.

3 tablespoons flour
1½ cups low-fat (1%) milk
1 cup diced onion
1 teaspoon Dijon mustard
½ teaspoon salt
¼ teaspoon cayenne pepper
1 cup finely diced red bell pepper
¼ cup plus 2 tablespoons shredded Cheddar cheese
1 tablespoon distilled white vinegar or cider vinegar
1 head cauliflower, cut into florets

1. Place the flour in a large saucepan, and gradually whisk in the milk over medium heat until no lumps remain. Bring to a boil and stir in the onion, mustard, salt, and cayenne. Reduce to a simmer and cook, stirring frequently, until the sauce is slightly thickened, about 5 minutes.

2. Stir in the bell pepper and Cheddar and cook just until the cheese has melted, about 1 minute longer. Remove from the heat.

3. Meanwhile, bring a large pot of water to a boil, add the vinegar and cauliflower, and cook until the cauliflower is tender, about 5 minutes. Drain well and transfer to a medium serving bowl. Spoon the hot sauce over the cauliflower and serve.

Helpful hint: The sauce can be made earlier in the day and refrigerated. Gently reheat in a double boiler while you cook the cauliflower.

VALUES ARE PER ½ CUP
FAT: 2G/27%
CALORIES: 81
SATURATED FAT: 1.4G
CARBOHYDRATE: 11G
PROTEIN: 5G
CHOLESTEROL: 7MG
SODIUM: 220MG

GRILLED PEPPERS

SERVES: 4
WORKING TIME: 20 MINUTES
TOTAL TIME: 30 MINUTES

These fire-roasted peppers are one of the great pleasures of grilling. Excellent just as they are, they're even better when bathed in a savory herbed dressing as we do here. You can toss them with hot pasta, lavish them on chicken breasts or swordfish steaks, or heap them on toasted rolls. They can also be used in any recipe that calls for roasted peppers from a jar.

2 cloves garlic, unpeeled

4 bell peppers, mixed colors, halved lengthwise and seeded

2 anchovy fillets or ½ teaspoon anchovy paste (optional)

½ teaspoon firmly packed light or dark brown sugar

3 tablespoons balsamic vinegar

1 teaspoon olive oil

¼ cup chopped fresh basil

1. Preheat the grill to a medium heat. Spray the rack—off the grill—with nonstick cooking spray (see page 6). Wrap the garlic cloves in a piece of foil. Grill the garlic packet and the pepper halves, cut-sides up, covered, without turning, for 10 minutes or until the pepper skins are blackened. Remove the peppers from the grill. When cool enough to handle, peel the peppers and cut them into ½-inch-wide strips.

2. Continue grilling the garlic for 10 minutes or until softened. When cool enough to handle, snip the stem end of each clove of garlic and squeeze the garlic pulp into a large bowl. Add the anchovies, mashing until well combined. Whisk in the brown sugar, vinegar, and oil. Add the peppers and basil to the bowl, toss well, and serve warm, at room temperature, or chilled.

Helpful hint: If the wires of your grill are widely spaced, be sure to wrap the garlic cloves in a large enough piece of foil so that they won't fall through.

FAT: 1G/24%
CALORIES: 38
SATURATED FAT: .1G
CARBOHYDRATE: 7G
PROTEIN: 2G
CHOLESTEROL: 1MG
SODIUM: 76MG

RISI E BISI

Italians celebrate spring—and the accompanying advent of the first green peas—with a bowl of this soothing, delicately flavored dish of rice and peas. The frozen small peas sometimes labeled "petit pois" are best for this recipe. You could also use tiny fresh peas; add them to the pan along with the onion.

2 teaspoons olive oil

2 tablespoons chopped pancetta or Canadian bacon

1 small onion, finely chopped

1 cup long-grain rice

2 cups reduced-sodium chicken broth, defatted

2 tablespoons dry white wine

2 cups frozen peas, thawed

3 tablespoons chopped fresh parsley

3 tablespoons grated Parmesan cheese

½ teaspoon salt

⅛ teaspoon freshly ground black pepper

1. In a large nonstick skillet, heat the oil until hot but not smoking over medium heat. Add the pancetta and onion and cook until the onion is softened, about 5 minutes.

2. Stir the rice into the skillet and cook, stirring occasionally, until lightly golden, about 3 minutes. Add the broth and wine and bring to a boil. Reduce to a simmer, cover, and cook for 15 minutes. Remove from the heat and stir in the peas, parsley, Parmesan, salt, and pepper. Let stand, covered, for 5 minutes before serving.

Helpful hint: If you are substituting fresh peas for frozen, you'll need 2 pounds of peas in the pod, which will yield 2 cups. Depending on the size of the peas, you may have to cook them a few minutes extra in step 1.

FAT: 4G/12%
CALORIES: 294
SATURATED FAT: 1.2G
CARBOHYDRATE: 50G
PROTEIN: 12G
CHOLESTEROL: 5MG
SODIUM: 814MG

CAVIAR-STUFFED ENDIVE LEAVES

MAKES: 2 DOZEN
WORKING TIME: 30 MINUTES
TOTAL TIME: 30 MINUTES

½ cup low-fat (1%) cottage cheese

3 tablespoons finely snipped fresh chives or minced scallions

3 Belgian endives, separated into 24 leaves

2 tablespoons salmon caviar

⅓ cup assorted julienned vegetables (red bell pepper, carrot, and scallion)

1. In a mini-food processor or with a hand-held blender, purée the cottage cheese until smooth and creamy. Stir in 2 tablespoons of the chives.

2. Spread a little of the cottage cheese mixture in the base of each endive leaf, then top each mound of cheese with a dab of the caviar. Arrange the vegetables decoratively in the endive leaves. Garnish with the remaining 1 tablespoon chives, place on a platter, and serve.

Helpful hint: To save time, fill the endive leaves and decorate up to 2 hours before serving, omitting the salmon caviar and garnish. Keep refrigerated until ready to serve. Spoon on the caviar and garnish at the last minute, since any sooner and the caviar may "bleed" into the cottage cheese.

VALUES ARE PER STUFFED ENDIVE LEAF
FAT: 0.3G/29%
CALORIES: 8
SATURATED FAT: 0G
CARBOHYDRATE: 0G
PROTEIN: 1G
CHOLESTEROL: 8MG
SODIUM: 40MG

Just the tiniest dollop of salmon caviar makes these endive leaves special enough for the fanciest parties. And these hors d'oeuvres are everything you need to whet the appetite—they're crunchy, creamy, and savory all at once. Depending on your artistic temperament, be as simple or as elaborate as you wish in arranging the julienned vegetables and caviar.

WALDORF SALAD

SERVES: 4
WORKING TIME: 20 MINUTES
TOTAL TIME: 20 MINUTES

1 cup plain nonfat yogurt

2 tablespoons reduced-fat sour cream

2 tablespoons reduced-fat mayonnaise

1 teaspoon grated lemon zest

2 tablespoons fresh lemon juice

¼ teaspoon salt

¼ teaspoon freshly ground black pepper

2 Granny Smith apples, cored and cut into 1-inch chunks

1 Red Delicious apple, cored and cut into 1-inch chunks

2 ribs celery, thinly sliced

1 cup red seedless grapes, halved

1 small head romaine lettuce, cut crosswise into ¼-inch-wide shreds

1 tablespoon coarsely chopped walnuts

1. In a large bowl, combine the yogurt, sour cream, mayonnaise, lemon zest, lemon juice, salt, and pepper and stir to blend. Add the apples, celery, and grapes and toss well to coat.

2. Place the lettuce on 4 salad plates and spoon the apple mixture on top. Garnish with the walnuts and serve.

Helpful hint: To get a jump on the party, toss the apple mixture with the dressing earlier in the day and refrigerate. Just before serving, spoon over the shredded lettuce and then garnish with the walnuts.

Everyone will recognize this favorite, but they won't guess that we've lightened it for the holidays. The dressing is a creamy blend of nonfat yogurt, reduced-fat sour cream, and reduced-fat mayonnaise, sharpened with a touch of lemon juice and zest. Serve as a first course for a sit-down dinner, or in a beautiful wooden bowl as part of a buffet spread.

FAT: 5G/22%
CALORIES: 190
SATURATED FAT: 1.1G
CARBOHYDRATE: 34G
PROTEIN: 6G
CHOLESTEROL: 4MG
SODIUM: 266MG

ITALIAN GREEN BEANS WITH GARLIC AND TOMATOES

SERVES: 4
WORKING TIME: 20 MINUTES
TOTAL TIME: 30 MINUTES

1 teaspoon olive oil
1 onion, finely chopped
3 cloves garlic, slivered
1½ cups chopped tomatoes
½ cup chopped fresh basil
½ teaspoon salt
1 teaspoon hot pepper sauce
Two 10-ounce packages frozen Italian flat green beans

1. In a large nonstick skillet, heat the oil until hot but not smoking over medium heat. Add the onion and garlic and cook, stirring frequently, until the onion is softened, about 7 minutes.

2. Add the tomatoes, basil, salt, and hot pepper sauce and bring to a boil. Add the beans, reduce the heat to a simmer, and cook until the beans are tender, about 8 minutes.

Helpful hint: If you can get fresh Italian flat green beans, use them in place of the frozen. The cooking times will be approximately the same, depending on the size of the fresh beans. Test them after 8 minutes and if they are still too raw, continue cooking them, with the skillet covered.

FAT: 2G/19%
CALORIES: 96
SATURATED FAT: .3G
CARBOHYDRATE: 20G
PROTEIN: 4G
CHOLESTEROL: 0MG
SODIUM: 319MG

This colorful vegetable toss will brighten a meal centered on simple chicken breasts or pork cutlets. The flavors are as bright as the jade-green beans and crimson tomatoes: There's garlic, fresh basil, and peppery heat. Add the hot sauce in small increments to taste—half the amount called for here may be enough for some.

GRILLED MUSHROOMS, POTATOES, AND LEEKS

SERVES: 4
WORKING TIME: 15 MINUTES
TOTAL TIME: 30 MINUTES

Try this sesame-fragrant side dish in the fall, when leeks and potatoes are most abundant.

1 pound small red potatoes, halved

3 large leeks

½ cup reduced-sodium chicken broth, defatted

2 tablespoons reduced-sodium soy sauce

2 tablespoons ketchup

2 teaspoons red wine vinegar

1½ teaspoons dark Oriental sesame oil

¼ teaspoon salt

8 large mushrooms, stems removed

½ cup chopped fresh parsley

1. In a large pot of boiling water, cook the potatoes for 10 minutes to blanch. Trim the root ends off each leek, being careful to keep the leeks intact. Trim the dark green tops off, then split the leeks lengthwise up to but not through the root. Rinse the leeks thoroughly, easing the leaves apart to remove the grit.

2. In a large bowl, combine the broth, soy sauce, ketchup, vinegar, sesame oil, and salt. Add the potatoes, leeks, and mushrooms, tossing well to coat. Set aside to marinate while the grill preheats.

3. Preheat the grill with the grill topper to a medium heat. Spray the grill topper—off the grill—with nonstick cooking spray (see page 6). Reserving the marinade, place the vegetables on the grill topper and grill, covered, turning occasionally, for 7 minutes or until the potatoes are tender.

4. Thickly slice the mushrooms and cut the potatoes into quarters. Cut the leeks into 1½-inch lengths and return them to the bowl along with the mushrooms and potatoes. Add the chopped parsley, tossing to combine. Serve warm or at room temperature.

Helpful hint: You can marinate the vegetables for up to 5 hours in the refrigerator.

FAT: 3G/13%
CALORIES: 215
SATURATED FAT: .3G
CARBOHYDRATE: 44G
PROTEIN: 6G
CHOLESTEROL: 0MG
SODIUM: 644MG

CRANBERRY-POACHED HERBED APPLES

MAKES: 2½ CUPS
WORKING TIME: 15 MINUTES
TOTAL TIME: 30 MINUTES

6-ounce can frozen cranberry juice concentrate, thawed

¼ cup red currant jelly

2 bay leaves

½ teaspoon dried sage

½ teaspoon dried rosemary

½ teaspoon salt

½ teaspoon freshly ground black pepper

4 large Granny Smith or Empire apples, peeled, cored, and cut into 2-inch chunks

1. In a large saucepan, stir together the juice concentrate, jelly, bay leaves, sage, rosemary, salt, and pepper. Bring to a boil over medium heat, add the apples, and reduce to a very gentle boil. Cook, stirring frequently, until the apples are tender, about 10 minutes. With a slotted spoon, transfer the apples to a medium serving bowl and set aside.

2. Increase the heat to high and cook the juice mixture until it is reduced to a light syrup, about 5 minutes.

3. Strain the sauce, discarding the solids. Spoon the sauce over the apples and serve.

Helpful hints: This can also be chilled and served cold to accompany a platter of leftover sliced turkey or other meats. For a more relish-like appearance, cut the apple into small dice, and then reduce the initial cooking time slightly.

VALUES ARE PER ½ CUP
FAT: 1G/0.2%
CALORIES: 197
SATURATED FAT: 0.1G
CARBOHYDRATE: 51G
PROTEIN: 0G
CHOLESTEROL: 0MG
SODIUM: 227MG

This savory, chutney-like side dish is the perfect accompaniment to rich holiday meats, such as turkey and pork.

CLAMS WITH WHITE WINE AND GARLIC

SERVES: 4
WORKING TIME: 25 MINUTES
TOTAL TIME: 25 MINUTES

4 ounces Italian bread, cut into
8 slices
1 clove garlic, halved, plus
3 cloves garlic, minced
2 teaspoons olive oil
3 shallots, finely chopped, or
⅓ cup chopped scallions
¾ cup dry white wine
½ teaspoon dried oregano
¼ teaspoon red pepper flakes
24 littleneck clams
2 tablespoons chopped fresh
parsley

1. In a toaster oven or under the broiler, toast the bread on both
   sides. Rub both sides of the toast with the cut garlic.

2. In a large nonstick skillet, heat the oil until hot but not smoking
   over medium heat. Add the shallots and minced garlic and cook,
   stirring frequently, until the shallots are softened, about 2 minutes.
   Add the wine, oregano, and red pepper flakes. Bring to a boil and
   cook for 1 minute.

3. Add the clams to the skillet, cover, and cook just until the clams
   open up, about 4 minutes. With a slotted spoon, transfer the clams
   to 4 shallow soup bowls, discarding any clams that have not
   opened. Stir the parsley into the skillet and spoon the sauce over
   the clams. Place 2 slices of garlic toast in each bowl and serve.

*Helpful hint: When buying clams, be sure that the shells are tightly closed.
If any are slightly open, tap them with your fingertip: They should snap
shut. Use live clams within a day of buying them.*

FAT: 4G/18%
CALORIES: 200
SATURATED FAT: .6G
CARBOHYDRATE: 19G
PROTEIN: 14G
CHOLESTEROL: 29MG
SODIUM: 217MG

The northern coastal region of Liguria is home to disarmingly simple shellfish preparations like this one (when seafood is impeccably fresh, it doesn't need much in the way of dressing up). Here, clams are steamed with wine, garlic, shallots, and herbs. If all the clams do not open at once, cook the unopened ones a minute or two longer; if they still don't open, discard them.

*L*ike all chili peppers, jalapeños take on a whole new dimension when roasted over an open fire. Combine them with grilled bell peppers, tomatoes, and scallions and you're headed for the finest salsa ever. If you can save some before it's all scooped up (with low-fat tortilla chips or oven-baked tortilla triangles), try it on burgers and baked potatoes, too.

GRILLED TOMATO SALSA

SERVES: 4
WORKING TIME: 15 MINUTES
TOTAL TIME: 25 MINUTES

*2 green bell peppers, halved
lengthwise and seeded,
membranes removed*

*2 jalapeño peppers, halved
lengthwise and seeded (see tip)*

2 pounds firm-ripe tomatoes

4 scallions, trimmed

*⅓ cup chopped fresh cilantro or
parsley*

3 tablespoons red wine vinegar

1 teaspoon olive oil

1 teaspoon ground cumin

1 teaspoon salt

1. Preheat the grill with the grill topper to a medium heat. Spray the grill topper—off the grill—with nonstick cooking spray (see page 6). Grill the bell peppers and the jalapeños on the grill topper, cut-sides up, covered, for 10 minutes or until blackened. Remove from the grill and set aside. Grill the tomatoes, stem-sides up, on the grill topper, covered, for 8 minutes or until they blister, char, and soften. Remove from the grill and set aside. Grill the scallions on the grill topper, covered, for 2 minutes or until lightly browned.

2. Peel the bell peppers. Coarsely chop the bell peppers, jalapeños, and the tomatoes, with their skins, and transfer to a large bowl. Slice the scallions and add to the bowl along with the cilantro, vinegar, oil, cumin, and salt. Serve at room temperature.

Helpful hint: Use tomatoes that are firm-ripe—ripe so the flavor is at its peak, yet firm so the tomatoes won't fall apart on the grill.

TIP

Most of the heat from fresh chili peppers comes from the volatile oils found in the ribs (and to a lesser extent in the seeds). For a tamer dish, omit those parts. When working with chili peppers, fresh or grilled, use rubber gloves to protect your hands and keep your hands away from your face, especially the eyes. Wash your hands thoroughly with hot soapy water when you're done.

PROSCIUTTO AND MELON

SERVES: 4
WORKING TIME: 30 MINUTES
TOTAL TIME: 30 MINUTES

The city of Parma and its environs have given the world two great delicacies: Parmesan cheese and prosciutto di Parma, a painstakingly produced air-dried ham. Even with just half an ounce of prosciutto on each of these delicious honeydew melon wedges, the unique combination of flavors is sure to please. Garnish with two teaspoons of grated lime zest, if you like.

¼ cup sugar
¼ cup fresh lime juice
½ of a honeydew melon, chilled
2 ounces very thinly sliced prosciutto, cut into thin strips
¼ teaspoon freshly ground black pepper

1. In a small saucepan, combine the sugar, lime juice, and ¼ cup of water. Bring to a boil over medium heat, reduce to a simmer, and cook until syrupy, about 12 minutes. Set aside to cool slightly.

2. Cut the melon into 4 even wedges. With a sharp paring knife, score the melon wedges crosswise at ½-inch intervals, cutting to, but not through, the rind. Place the melon on a serving platter and spoon the lime syrup over each wedge. Sprinkle the prosciutto and pepper over the melon and serve.

Helpful hint: For a change, serve the prosciutto with cantaloupe quarters instead of honeydew wedges.

FAT: 2G/13%
CALORIES: 143
SATURATED FAT: .5G
CARBOHYDRATE: 29G
PROTEIN: 5G
CHOLESTEROL: 12MG
SODIUM: 279MG

PEAR AND ROQUEFORT SALAD

SERVES: 4
WORKING TIME: 20 MINUTES
TOTAL TIME: 20 MINUTES

1 cup canned pear nectar

2 tablespoons fresh lime juice

1 tablespoon honey

1 teaspoon minced fresh ginger

¼ teaspoon salt

¼ teaspoon freshly ground black pepper

4 Bartlett pears, cored and thinly sliced lengthwise

2 bunches watercress, thick stems trimmed

½ cup dried currants

2 ounces Roquefort cheese, crumbled (about ¼ cup)

2 tablespoons coarsely chopped pecans, toasted

1. In a large bowl, combine the nectar, lime juice, honey, ginger, salt, and pepper and stir to blend. Add the pears and toss well to coat.

2. Place the watercress on 4 salad plates, arrange the pears on top, and spoon any remaining dressing over. Garnish with the currants, Roquefort, and pecans and serve.

Helpful hints: You can toss the pear slices with the dressing earlier in the day and refrigerate, and then assemble the salads just before serving. If good-quality watercress is unavailable, substitute shredded romaine lettuce or curly endive.

The classic winter flavors of sweetly ripe pears and pungent Roquefort are nicely enhanced by peppery watercress and toasted pecans. Arrange the salads on individual plates, fanning the pear slices over the watercress, and offer them as a first course for roasted chicken or baked ham.

FAT: 7G/23%
CALORIES: 289
SATURATED FAT: 3G
CARBOHYDRATE: 55G
PROTEIN: 7G
CHOLESTEROL: 13MG
SODIUM: 431MG

HUMMUS

SERVES: 8
WORKING TIME: 10 MINUTES
TOTAL TIME: 20 MINUTES

J ust a little intensely flavored sesame oil goes a long way in our zesty version of the Middle Eastern chick-pea dip.

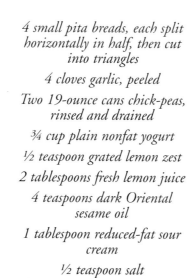

4 small pita breads, each split horizontally in half, then cut into triangles

4 cloves garlic, peeled

Two 19-ounce cans chick-peas, rinsed and drained

¾ cup plain nonfat yogurt

½ teaspoon grated lemon zest

2 tablespoons fresh lemon juice

4 teaspoons dark Oriental sesame oil

1 tablespoon reduced-fat sour cream

½ teaspoon salt

½ teaspoon ground coriander

¼ teaspoon cayenne pepper

⅛ teaspoon ground allspice

2 teaspoons chopped fresh parsley

1 cucumber, thinly sliced

1. Preheat the oven to 350°. Place the pita triangles on a baking sheet and bake for 5 to 7 minutes, or until lightly browned and crisp. Set aside.

2. Meanwhile, in a small saucepan of boiling water, cook the garlic for 3 minutes to blanch. Drain well. Transfer the garlic to a food processor. Add the chick-peas, yogurt, lemon zest, lemon juice, sesame oil, sour cream, salt, coriander, cayenne, and allspice and purée until smooth.

3. Spoon the hummus into a small serving bowl and sprinkle with the parsley. Serve with the toasted pita triangles and cucumber slices.

Helpful hints: The hummus will keep refrigerated for up to 3 days. Asian-style sesame oils get their dark color and rich flavor from toasted sesame seeds. Look for the oil in the Oriental foods section of your supermarket.

FAT: 5G/21%
CALORIES: 213
SATURATED FAT: 0.6G
CARBOHYDRATE: 33G
PROTEIN: 9G
CHOLESTEROL: 1MG
SODIUM: 456MG

GRILLED RED ONIONS

SERVES: 4
WORKING TIME: 15 MINUTES
TOTAL TIME: 20 MINUTES

2 tablespoons sugar

1½ teaspoons ground ginger

1 teaspoon dried oregano

1 teaspoon salt

½ teaspoon ground allspice

½ teaspoon freshly ground
black pepper

3 pounds large red onions, cut
into ½-inch-thick rounds

¾ cup orange juice

1 tablespoon olive oil

1. Preheat the grill with the grill topper to a medium heat. (When ready to cook, spray the grill topper—off the grill—with non-stick cooking spray; see page 6.)

2. In a large bowl, combine the sugar, ginger, oregano, salt, allspice, and pepper. Add the onion rings, tossing well to coat. Add the orange juice and oil and toss again. Place the onions on the grill topper and grill, covered, turning occasionally, for 18 minutes or until the onions are crisp-tender. Serve hot.

Helpful hint: Any type of mild-to-sweet onion, such as Bermuda, Spanish, Vidalia, or Walla Walla, would also work well in this recipe.

FAT: 4G/16%
CALORIES: 220
SATURATED FAT: .5G
CARBOHYDRATE: 44G
PROTEIN: 6G
CHOLESTEROL: 0MG
SODIUM: 587MG

Lean steaks are instantly transformed into a feast when you top them with these tangy spiced onions.

ASPARAGUS VINAIGRETTE

SERVES: 4
WORKING TIME: 10 MINUTES
TOTAL TIME: 15 MINUTES

1 pound asparagus, tough ends trimmed

2 tablespoons no-salt-added tomato paste

½ cup orange juice

2 tablespoons reduced-sodium chicken broth, defatted, or water

2 tablespoons red wine vinegar

1 teaspoon Dijon mustard

1 teaspoon olive oil, preferably extra-virgin

¼ teaspoon salt

1. In a large pot of boiling water, cook the asparagus until just crisp-tender, about 3 minutes. Drain well and pat dry on paper towels. Arrange the asparagus on a serving platter.

2. Place the tomato paste in a small bowl. Whisk in the orange juice, broth, vinegar, mustard, oil, and salt until well combined. Spoon the vinaigrette over the asparagus and serve.

Helpful hints: Although asparagus is available all year round, spring asparagus is still the most prized. Select spears with moist-looking, unwrinkled stems and tight tips. If the stems are very thick, you may want to peel the tough outer skin with a vegetable peeler. Refrigerate asparagus for no more than a day or two, wrapping the bases of the stems in moist paper towels and placing them in a plastic bag.

We've created a tomato-based vinaigrette scented with orange juice that showcases both the delicate flavor and the brilliant color of fresh asparagus. Be careful not to overcook the asparagus—the spears are at their best when they are still firm to the bite. Serve as part of a spring buffet menu, or as a prelude to a vegetable frittata.

FAT: 1G/26%
CALORIES: 47
SATURATED FAT: 0.2G
CARBOHYDRATE: 7G
PROTEIN: 2G
CHOLESTEROL: 0MG
SODIUM: 192MG

SICILIAN ORANGE SALAD

SERVES: 4
WORKING TIME: 20 MINUTES
TOTAL TIME: 20 MINUTES

Although this traditional Italian salad is sometimes served between courses to freshen the palate, it would also be welcome alongside a rich and savory entrée such as a stuffed beef roast. We've added the peppery bite of watercress for an even more refreshing dish; arugula would be a tasty alternative. Plump green Sicilian olives lend an authentic touch.

6 navel oranges

3 tablespoons honey

2 tablespoons red wine vinegar

1 tablespoon extra-virgin olive oil

2 teaspoons Dijon mustard

½ teaspoon salt

⅛ teaspoon red pepper flakes

2 bunches watercress, tough stems removed

1 red onion, halved and thinly sliced

¼ cup slivered green olives

1. With a small knife, remove the peel and trim away all the bitter white pith from the oranges. Working over a sieve set over a large bowl to catch the juices, cut between the membranes to release the orange segments. Squeeze the membranes to get a total of ½ cup of juice. Set the segments aside.

2. Add the honey, vinegar, oil, mustard, salt, and red pepper flakes to the orange juice, whisking to blend. Add the watercress, onion, orange segments, and olives, tossing well to combine.

Helpful hint: If you can't find Sicilian olives, you can use purple-black Greek Calamatas instead.

FAT: 5G/21%
CALORIES: 215
SATURATED FAT: .7G
CARBOHYDRATE: 43G
PROTEIN: 5G
CHOLESTEROL: 0MG
SODIUM: 580MG

HOLIDAY PEPPERS

MAKES: 4 CUPS
WORKING TIME: 25 MINUTES
TOTAL TIME: 25 MINUTES

1 teaspoon olive oil

*3 red bell peppers, cut into
1½-inch squares*

*2 green bell peppers, cut into
1½-inch squares*

3 cloves garlic, minced

½ teaspoon grated orange zest

⅓ cup orange juice

*1 tablespoon no-salt-added
tomato paste*

½ teaspoon salt

½ teaspoon dried oregano

*¼ teaspoon freshly ground black
pepper*

1. In a large nonstick skillet, heat the oil until hot but not smoking over medium heat. Add the bell peppers and cook, stirring frequently, until the peppers are almost tender, about 5 minutes.

2. Stir in the garlic and cook until the garlic is fragrant, about 1 minute. Add the orange zest, orange juice, tomato paste, salt, oregano, and black pepper and cook, stirring frequently, until the peppers are tender and glossy, about 3 minutes longer. Spoon the peppers into a medium bowl and serve.

Helpful hint: Finely chop any leftovers and stir into egg-white scrambled eggs for a quick and easy brunch dish.

What could be more holiday-spirited than these red and green peppers, brightly seasoned with orange? Garnish with long, thin strips of orange zest and a light sprinkling of finely ground toasted walnuts, if desired. This robust dish would deliciously enhance a roasted beef filet or loin of pork.

VALUES ARE PER ½ CUP
FAT: 1G/21%
CALORIES: 30
SATURATED FAT: 0.1G
CARBOHYDRATE: 6G
PROTEIN: 1G
CHOLESTEROL: 0MG
SODIUM: 140MG

LEMON-GARLIC MUSHROOMS

SERVES: 4
WORKING TIME: 30 MINUTES
TOTAL TIME: 30 MINUTES

2 slices (1 ounce each) white sandwich bread, torn into large pieces

2 pounds mushrooms, quartered

1 cup reduced-sodium chicken broth, defatted

2 cloves garlic, peeled

¼ cup fresh lemon juice

2 teaspoons olive oil

½ teaspoon salt

¼ teaspoon freshly ground black pepper

2 tablespoons chopped fresh parsley

1 teaspoon grated lemon zest

1. Preheat the broiler. In a food processor or blender, process the bread just until coarse crumbs form. Spread the bread crumbs on a baking sheet and broil for 30 seconds to lightly toast. Set aside.

2. In a medium saucepan, combine the mushrooms and broth. Bring to a boil over medium-high heat, reduce to a simmer, and cook until the mushrooms are tender, about 10 minutes. Reserving ¼ cup of the broth, drain the mushrooms and set aside to cool slightly.

3. Meanwhile, in a small pot of boiling water, cook the garlic for 2 minutes to blanch. Transfer the garlic to a cutting board and mince. In a large bowl, combine the reserved broth, the lemon juice, oil, half of the garlic, the salt, and pepper, whisking well to blend. Add the cooled mushrooms, stirring to coat thoroughly.

4. In a small bowl, combine the bread crumbs, parsley, lemon zest, and the remaining garlic. Spoon the mushrooms into a serving dish and sprinkle with the topping. Serve at room temperature.

Helpful hint: Slightly stale or very lightly toasted bread makes the best crumbs. If you don't have a food processor, you can use your fingers to tear the bread into fluffy crumbs.

FAT: 4G/29%
CALORIES: 126
SATURATED FAT: .5G
CARBOHYDRATE: 20G
PROTEIN: 7G
CHOLESTEROL: 0MG
SODIUM: 521MG

Stuffed mushroom caps are great for parties, but they can require a fair amount of fuss and fiddling. This mushroom salad captures the flavors of stuffed mushrooms—right down to the garlicky bread crumbs—without the time-consuming preparation. Try this dish as a component of a buffet centered around smoked turkey or ham.

POTATO-ONION ANTIPASTO

SERVES: 4
WORKING TIME: 30 MINUTES
TOTAL TIME: 30 MINUTES

In some ways, this first course resembles a classic American potato salad, with hard-cooked eggs and celery for textural contrast. But this Italian version is dressed with a mustardy red-wine vinaigrette and served on a bed of slivered onions and tomatoes. It's a great starter for your next al fresco meal—or even for a plain old American picnic.

1 pound small red potatoes, cut into ½-inch dice

1 egg

2 tablespoons red wine vinegar

1 tablespoon extra-virgin olive oil

2 teaspoons Dijon mustard

½ teaspoon salt

¼ teaspoon freshly ground black pepper

2 ribs celery, diced

2 tablespoons chopped fresh parsley

2 tomatoes, thinly sliced

½ cup slivered red onion

1. In a large pot of boiling water, cook the potatoes until firm-tender, about 9 minutes. Drain.

2. Meanwhile, place the egg in a saucepan, add cold water to cover by 1 inch, and bring to a boil over medium-high heat. As soon as the water comes to a boil, cover the pan, remove from the heat, and let stand for 17 minutes. Peel the egg under cold running water and coarsely chop.

3. In a large bowl, combine the vinegar, oil, mustard, salt, and pepper, whisking well. Stir in the potatoes, celery, and parsley.

4. Arrange the tomatoes and onion on a serving platter. Spoon the potato mixture on top, sprinkle with the egg, and serve.

Helpful hint: If you find the flavor of raw onions too sharp, drop the slivered onions into a bowl of cold water and place them in the freezer for 15 minutes. They'll emerge noticeably milder. Drain the onions and pat them dry before using.

FAT: 5G/27%
CALORIES: 169
SATURATED FAT: .9G
CARBOHYDRATE: 26G
PROTEIN: 5G
CHOLESTEROL: 53MG
SODIUM: 384MG

TOMATO BRUSCHETTA

SERVES: 4
WORKING TIME: 25 MINUTES
TOTAL TIME: 25 MINUTES

In its most basic form, bruschetta consists of slabs of coarse bread toasted over coals and drizzled generously with olive oil. In our version, we rub the bread with garlic and top it with basil and tomatoes, eliminating the need for so much oil—there's just one teaspoon of it in the tomato mixture.

4 ounces Italian bread, cut into 8 slices
2 cloves garlic, peeled
2 large tomatoes, diced
¼ cup chopped fresh basil
1 teaspoon extra-virgin olive oil
½ teaspoon salt
¼ teaspoon freshly ground black pepper

1. In a toaster oven or under the broiler, toast the bread on both sides. Cut 1 clove of garlic in half and rub both sides of the toast with it. Set aside.

2. In a small pot of boiling water, cook the remaining garlic clove for 2 minutes to blanch. Transfer the garlic to a cutting board and mince. In a medium bowl, combine the tomatoes, basil, oil, salt, pepper, and the minced garlic.

3. Arrange the toast on a plater. Dividing evenly, spoon the tomato mixture over the toast and serve.

Helpful hints: If the tomatoes you're using seem watery, halve them crosswise and squeeze out some of the juice before dicing them. Even with meaty tomatoes, the topping will tend to soak into and soften the toast, so don't make the bruschetta until right before you are ready to serve it.

FAT: 2G/17%
CALORIES: 108
SATURATED FAT: .5G
CARBOHYDRATE: 19G
PROTEIN: 3G
CHOLESTEROL: 0MG
SODIUM: 446MG

GREEN BEAN SALAD

SERVES: 4
WORKING TIME: 15 MINUTES
TOTAL TIME: 20 MINUTES

These deliciously toothsome green beans, enlivened with dill and lemon juice, are tossed with sliced water chestnuts for a bit of crunch.

The dressing is a flavorful mix of broth, lemon juice, and Dijon mustard—but not a bit of oil. This is an ideal dish for entertaining since it looks pretty on a buffet table and will hold up at room temperature.

1¼ pounds green beans

¼ cup reduced-sodium chicken broth, defatted, or reduced-sodium vegetable broth

2 tablespoons fresh lemon juice

1 tablespoon Dijon mustard

¼ teaspoon salt

⅛ teaspoon freshly ground black pepper

1 small red onion, finely chopped

½ cup canned sliced water chestnuts, well drained

⅓ cup snipped fresh dill

1. In a large pot of boiling water, cook the green beans until crisp-tender, about 4 minutes. (The time will vary depending on the age of the beans.) Drain, rinse under cold water, and drain again.

2. In a large serving bowl, whisk together the broth, lemon juice, mustard, salt, and pepper. Add the green beans, onion, water chestnuts, and dill, toss well to combine, and serve.

Helpful hints: This salad is equally good served at room temperature or chilled. If you do decide to serve it chilled, some of the bright green color of the beans will fade, but don't worry, the taste won't.

FAT: 0.2G/3%
CALORIES: 76
SATURATED FAT: 0G
CARBOHYDRATE: 17G
PROTEIN: 4G
CHOLESTEROL: 0MG
SODIUM: 282MG

ROASTED PEPPER AND TOMATO ANTIPASTO

SERVES: 4
WORKING TIME: 25 MINUTES
TOTAL TIME: 25 MINUTES

*I*n a traditional Italian meal, the appetite-honing delights that precede the pasta course—known as antipasti—must please the eye as well as the palate. These golden roasted peppers layered over lush ripe tomatoes certainly fill the bill. Accompany the peppers with sesame-seeded semolina bread. This first course could also be served as a side dish with meat or poultry.

2 red or yellow bell peppers, quartered lengthwise and seeded

2 large tomatoes, sliced

½ cup slivered red onion

2 tablespoons balsamic vinegar

½ teaspoon salt

¼ teaspoon freshly ground black pepper

3 tablespoons shredded part-skim mozzarella or smoked mozzarella cheese

1. Preheat the broiler. Place the bell peppers, cut-sides down, on the broiler rack. Broil the peppers 4 inches from the heat for 12 minutes, or until the skins are blackened. When the peppers are cool enough to handle, remove the skins.

2. On a serving platter, arrange the peppers, tomatoes, and onion. Sprinkle with the vinegar, salt, and black pepper, top with the mozzarella, and serve.

Helpful hint: Double or triple this recipe for a party, using a colorful mix of red and yellow peppers.

FAT: 1G/18%
CALORIES: 49
SATURATED FAT: .6G
CARBOHYDRATE: 8G
PROTEIN: 3G
CHOLESTEROL: 3MG
SODIUM: 308MG

The classic French rémoulade sauce mixes together mayonnaise, mustard, tarragon, and capers, among other ingredients. We follow suit in our version, but use only a small amount of reduced-fat mayonnaise, extended with evaporated low-fat milk. This crunchy salad is an ideal starter for a casual picnic or barbecue.

VEGETABLES RÉMOULADE

SERVES: 4
WORKING TIME: 30 MINUTES
TOTAL TIME: 30 MINUTES PLUS CHILLING TIME

⅓ cup evaporated low-fat milk

⅓ cup chopped fresh parsley

¼ cup fresh lemon juice

2 tablespoons reduced-fat mayonnaise

1 tablespoon Dijon mustard

¾ teaspoon salt

½ teaspoon dried tarragon

¼ teaspoon freshly ground black pepper

1 pound celery root, peeled and cut into 2-inch julienne strips (see tip)

2 carrots, cut into 2-inch julienne strips

1 Granny Smith apple, cored and diced

1 tablespoon capers, rinsed and drained

1. In a large serving bowl, whisk together the evaporated milk, parsley, lemon juice, mayonnaise, mustard, salt, tarragon, and pepper.

2. Add the celery root, carrots, apple, and capers and toss well to combine. Cover with plastic wrap and refrigerate until well chilled, about 1 hour.

Helpful hints: Celery root, also known as celeriac, is generally available from fall through early spring. If you can't find it, substitute white turnips for the crunchy texture and celery tops for the flavor. You can prepare this salad up to 8 hours ahead. The dressing is equally good on potato salad or, for that matter, any cold vegetable or pasta salad.

FAT: 2G/19%
CALORIES: 109
SATURATED FAT: 0.3G
CARBOHYDRATE: 20G
PROTEIN: 3G
CHOLESTEROL: 3MG
SODIUM: 707MG

TIP

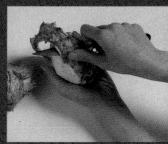

To prepare celery root, first peel off the thick, knobby skin with a paring knife. Cut the celery root into slices, and then cut the slices into 2-inch julienne strips. Since celery root quickly discolors when cut, place the strips in a bowl of water made acid with 2 tablespoons of lemon juice.

SAUTÉS & STIR-FRIES

Left, Chicken Stir-Fry with Broccoli, Garlic, and Basil
Above, Pork Sauté with Chive Cream Sauce

Stir-Fried Korean-Style Beef

Serves: 4
Working time: 30 minutes
Total time: 30 minutes

1 cup long-grain rice

½ teaspoon salt

4 teaspoons cornstarch

½ cup reduced-sodium chicken broth, defatted

3 tablespoons reduced-sodium soy sauce

2 tablespoons rice vinegar

2 teaspoons sesame seeds

1 teaspoon dark Oriental sesame oil

½ teaspoon sugar

½ pound well-trimmed beef sirloin, cut into 2 x ½-inch strips

2 teaspoons olive oil

4 scallions, cut into 1-inch lengths

4 cloves garlic, minced

1 green bell pepper, cut into 2 x ½-inch strips

1 red bell pepper, cut into 2 x ½-inch strips

½ pound sugar snap peas, strings removed

2 cups cherry tomatoes, halved

1. In a medium saucepan, bring 2¼ cups of water to a boil. Add the rice and ¼ teaspoon of the salt, reduce to a simmer, cover, and cook until the rice is tender, about 17 minutes.

2. Meanwhile, in a medium bowl, combine 1 teaspoon of the cornstarch, the broth, soy sauce, vinegar, sesame seeds, sesame oil, and sugar. Set aside.

3. Dredge the beef in the remaining 3 teaspoons cornstarch, shaking off the excess. In a large nonstick skillet, heat the oil until hot but not smoking over medium heat. Add the beef to the pan and cook, stirring frequently, until lightly browned, about 2 minutes. With a slotted spoon, transfer the beef to a plate.

4. Add the scallions and garlic to the pan and cook, stirring frequently, until crisp-tender, about 1 minute. Add the bell peppers, sugar snap peas, and tomatoes and cook, stirring frequently, until the tomatoes begin to collapse, about 3 minutes. Whisk the broth mixture to combine and pour into the skillet along with the remaining ¼ teaspoon salt. Bring to a boil and cook, stirring, until slightly thickened, about 1 minute. Return the beef to the pan and cook just until heated through, about 1 minute. Divide the rice among 4 plates, spoon the beef alongside, and serve.

Helpful hint: Fresh or frozen snow peas may be substituted for the sugar snap peas.

Fat: 7g/18%
Calories: 357
Saturated Fat: 1.5g
Carbohydrate: 52g
Protein: 19g
Cholesterol: 35mg
Sodium: 837mg

In Korea, beef is by far the favorite meat. It is typically cut into thin slices or narrow strips and stir-fried, grilled, or braised. Sesame seeds (and sesame oil) are among the signature seasonings of Korean cuisine; in this recipe, they are blended with other characteristic Korean flavorings—soy sauce, garlic, and scallions. As in most of Asia, rice completes the meal.

VEGETABLE FAJITAS

SERVES: 4
WORKING TIME: 30 MINUTES
TOTAL TIME: 30 MINUTES

These meatless fajitas—based on a mixture of vegetables, black beans, and spices rather than beef or chicken—are quite a departure from the original recipe, but are no less delicious. As always, fajitas can make an appealing "hands on" meal: Bring the skillet, warmed tortillas, and cheese to the table for do-it-yourself assembly. Offer extra salsa on the side.

2 teaspoons olive oil
4 scallions, thinly sliced
3 cloves garlic, finely chopped
2 zucchini, halved lengthwise and thinly sliced
2 yellow summer squash, halved lengthwise and thinly sliced
16-ounce can black beans, rinsed and drained
½ cup mild or medium-hot prepared salsa
1 tomato, coarsely chopped
1½ cups frozen corn kernels
2 tablespoons fresh lime juice
½ teaspoon dried oregano
½ teaspoon hot pepper sauce
Eight 8-inch flour tortillas
½ cup shredded Monterey jack cheese (2 ounces)

1. In a large nonstick skillet or wok, heat the oil until hot but not smoking over medium heat. Add the scallions and garlic and stir-fry until fragrant, about 1 minute. Add the zucchini and yellow squash and stir-fry until crisp-tender, about 4 minutes.

2. Add the beans, salsa, tomato, corn, lime juice, oregano, and hot pepper sauce and cook, stirring frequently, until just heated through, about 3 minutes.

3. Meanwhile, preheat the oven to 400°. Wrap the tortillas in foil and heat just until warm, about 5 minutes. Place 2 tortillas on each of 4 plates. Spoon the vegetables onto the tortillas, sprinkle with the cheese, and roll up the tortillas or serve open-face.

Helpful hint: Monterey jack is a semisoft, cream-colored cheese with a mildly tangy flavor. Dry jack, the aged version of the same cheese, is a grating cheese rather like a cross between Cheddar and Parmesan.

FAT: 13G/24%
CALORIES: 479
SATURATED FAT: 3.8G
CARBOHYDRATE: 74G
PROTEIN: 18G
CHOLESTEROL: 15MG
SODIUM: 941MG

THAI-STYLE SALMON

SERVES: 4
WORKING TIME: 25 MINUTES
TOTAL TIME: 30 MINUTES

1 cup jasmine or long-grain rice

½ teaspoon salt

4 salmon steaks (about 5 ounces each), any visible bones removed

1 tablespoon fresh lime juice

2 tablespoons flour

1 tablespoon olive oil

1 red bell pepper, cut into julienne strips

1 green bell pepper, cut into julienne strips

1 small red onion, halved and thinly sliced

1 tablespoon finely chopped fresh ginger

1 cup bottled clam juice, or reduced-sodium chicken broth, defatted

3 tablespoons chili sauce

½ teaspoon grated lime zest

⅛ teaspoon red pepper flakes

⅓ cup chopped fresh basil

¼ cup chopped fresh mint

1. In a medium saucepan, bring 2¼ cups of water to a boil. Add the rice and ¼ teaspoon of the salt, reduce to a simmer, cover, and cook until the rice is tender, about 17 minutes.

2. Meanwhile, sprinkle the salmon on both sides with the lime juice. Place the flour on a sheet of waxed paper. Dredge the salmon in the flour, shaking off the excess. In a large nonstick skillet, heat the oil until hot but not smoking over medium heat. Add the salmon and cook until lightly crisped and just opaque, about 3 minutes per side. With a slotted spoon or spatula, transfer the salmon to a plate and cover loosely with foil to keep warm.

3. Add the bell peppers, onion, and ginger to the pan and cook, stirring, until the bell peppers are crisp-tender, about 3 minutes. Stir in the clam juice, chili sauce, lime zest, red pepper flakes, and the remaining ¼ teaspoon salt. Bring to a boil and cook until slightly thickened, about 3 minutes. Stir in the basil and mint. Divide the rice among 4 plates. Serve the salmon alongside, topped with the sauce.

Helpful hint: If you can't find jasmine rice (now grown in the United States as well as Thailand), look for Texmati, a reasonably priced Texas-grown rice similar to basmati.

FAT: 12G/25%
CALORIES: 433
SATURATED FAT: 1.8G
CARBOHYDRATE: 50G
PROTEIN: 30G
CHOLESTEROL: 69MG
SODIUM: 635MG

Salmon is often treated gently—poached and served with a creamy sauce. The Thai way with fish is bolder, using tart flavors like citrus juice and zest, hot chilies, and aromatic herbs. Here, the salmon is topped with peppers and onion cooked with ginger, lime, and chili sauce. Jasmine rice, a fragrant Thai variety, tastes much like Indian basmati rice but costs less.

A light coating of seasoned flour keeps these pork tenderloin cutlets flavorful and juicy as they're sautéed. The coating is seasoned with fennel seeds and red pepper flakes, a fine complement to the accompanying corn relish, which boasts a tangy honey-mustard dressing. Serve roasted or oven-fried potatoes to round out the main dish.

FENNEL-CRUSTED PORK WITH CORN-PEPPER RELISH

SERVES: 4
WORKING TIME: 20 MINUTES
TOTAL TIME: 20 MINUTES

2 tablespoons red wine vinegar

4 teaspoons olive oil

2 teaspoons Dijon mustard

1 teaspoon honey

¾ teaspoon salt

2 cups frozen corn kernels, thawed

2 scallions, thinly sliced

1 red bell pepper, cut into ¼-inch dice

1 green bell pepper, cut into ¼-inch dice

3 tablespoons flour

¾ teaspoon fennel seeds, crushed

¼ teaspoon red pepper flakes

1 egg white beaten with 2 teaspoons water

¾ pound well-trimmed pork tenderloin, cut into 4 slices and pounded (see page 8) ½ inch thick

1. In a medium bowl, combine the vinegar, 1 teaspoon of the oil, the mustard, honey, and ¼ teaspoon of the salt. Add the corn, scallions, and bell peppers, stirring to combine. Set aside.

2. In a pie plate or shallow bowl, combine the remaining ½ teaspoon salt, the flour, fennel, and red pepper flakes. Place the egg white mixture in a shallow bowl. Dip the pork in the egg white (see tip; top photo), then dredge in the flour mixture, pressing the mixture into the meat (bottom photo).

3. In a large nonstick skillet, heat the remaining 3 teaspoons oil until hot but not smoking over medium heat. Add the pork and cook until browned, crisped, and cooked through, about 2 minutes per side. Transfer the pork to 4 plates, spoon the corn relish over, and serve.

Helpful hint: The corn-pepper relish can be prepared up to 24 hours in advance. Refrigerate it in a covered bowl.

FAT: 8G/27%
CALORIES: 263
SATURATED FAT: 1.7G
CARBOHYDRATE: 27G
PROTEIN: 22G
CHOLESTEROL: 55MG
SODIUM: 533MG

TIP

Dip each pork cutlet in the egg white mixture, turning it to coat completely. Then dredge the cutlet in the seasoned flour, patting and pressing the coating so that it adheres to the meat.

VEGETARIAN CHEESEBURGERS

SERVES: 4
WORKING TIME: 20 MINUTES
TOTAL TIME: 30 MINUTES PLUS SOAKING TIME

V*eggie burgers made from nuts are high in fat. Our bean-based burger has a meaty flavor and impressively healthy "numbers."*

2 cups boiling water
½ cup bulghur (cracked wheat)
Two 16-ounce cans pinto beans, rinsed and drained
2 tablespoons fresh lime juice
1½ teaspoons ground coriander
½ teaspoon cayenne pepper
1 red bell pepper, finely chopped
1 yellow bell pepper, finely chopped
4 scallions, thinly sliced
¼ cup ketchup
4 teaspoons olive oil
¼ cup flour
¾ cup shredded Monterey jack cheese (3 ounces)
4 hamburger buns
8 leaves of Boston lettuce

1. In a medium bowl, combine the boiling water and bulghur and set aside to soften for 30 minutes. Drain. In a large bowl, combine the beans with the drained bulghur. With a potato masher, mash the beans and bulghur until almost smooth with some lumps remaining. Add the lime juice, coriander, and cayenne, stirring to combine. Add ½ cup of the red bell pepper, ½ cup of the yellow bell pepper, and ¼ cup of the scallions. Shape into 4 patties 4 inches in diameter.

2. In a small bowl, combine the ketchup, and the remaining bell peppers and scallions. Set aside.

3. In a large nonstick skillet, heat the oil until hot but not smoking over medium heat. Dredge the patties in the flour, shaking off the excess. Sauté the patties until crisp on the outside and heated through, about 4 minutes per side. Sprinkle the cheese on top, cover, and cook until the cheese is melted, about 1 minute. Divide the buns among 4 plates. Place 2 lettuce leaves on each of the buns, top with a patty and the ketchup mixture, and serve.

Helpful hints: If you're not used to cayenne, start with just ¼ teaspoon (or even less) and gradually add more if necessary. Brighten the plate with a garnish of red radishes or cherry tomatoes.

FAT: 15G/27%
CALORIES: 495
SATURATED FAT: 5G
CARBOHYDRATE: 71G
PROTEIN: 21G
CHOLESTEROL: 23MG
SODIUM: 908MG

Sautéed Pork and Summer Squash

SERVES: 4
WORKING TIME: 25 MINUTES
TOTAL TIME: 30 MINUTES

1 cup long-grain rice

¾ teaspoon salt

2 tablespoons flour

½ teaspoon freshly ground black pepper

10 ounces well-trimmed pork tenderloin, cut into 8 slices and pounded (see page 8) ½ inch thick

1 tablespoon olive oil

4 cloves garlic, minced

1 yellow summer squash, quartered lengthwise and thinly sliced

1 zucchini, quartered lengthwise and thinly sliced

½ cup chopped fresh basil

¾ cup reduced-sodium chicken broth, defatted

1. In a medium saucepan, bring 2¼ cups of water to a boil. Add the rice and ¼ teaspoon of the salt, reduce to a simmer, cover, and cook until the rice is tender, about 17 minutes.

2. Meanwhile, on a sheet of waxed paper, combine the flour, the remaining ½ teaspoon salt, and the pepper. Dredge the pork in the flour mixture, shaking off the excess. In a large nonstick skillet, heat the oil until hot but not smoking over medium-high heat. Add the pork and cook until lightly browned, about 1 minute per side. Transfer the pork to a plate.

3. Reduce the heat to medium, add the garlic, and cook, stirring frequently, until softened, about 2 minutes. Add the yellow squash, zucchini, and basil and cook, stirring frequently, until the squash is crisp-tender, about 3 minutes. Add the broth and cook until the squash is very tender, about 3 minutes.

4. Return the pork to the pan and cook just until cooked through, about 1 minute. Divide the rice among 4 plates, spoon the pork and vegetables alongside, and serve.

Helpful hint: Thin-skinned summer squashes are not as sturdy as their winter counterparts. Whereas acorn or Hubbard squash will keep in a cool place for months, zucchini and yellow squash should be refrigerated in plastic bags for no longer than one week.

FAT: 6G/17%
CALORIES: 323
SATURATED FAT: 1.4G
CARBOHYDRATE: 45G
PROTEIN: 21G
CHOLESTEROL: 46MG
SODIUM: 558MG

Slices of summer squash, like translucent petals of green and gold, complement these delicate pork scallops.

Steak coated with cracked black peppercorns is a French bistro classic. The steak is usually topped with a knob of butter and flambéed with brandy; we've cut the fat (and toned down the performance) by making a brandy sauce in the pan after the steak is done. Creamy yet low in fat, the sauce gets its body from cornstarch and evaporated low-fat milk.

STEAK AU POIVRE WITH PEPPERS AND POTATOES

SERVES: 4
WORKING TIME: 25 MINUTES
TOTAL TIME: 30 MINUTES

1½ pounds small red potatoes, quartered

2 teaspoons coarsely cracked black pepper

½ teaspoon salt

¾ pound well-trimmed beef sirloin, cut into 4 steaks

4 teaspoons olive oil

3 bell peppers, mixed colors, cut into 2 x ¼-inch strips

¼ cup brandy

1 cup reduced-sodium beef broth, defatted

¼ cup evaporated low-fat (1%) milk

½ teaspoon dried thyme

1 teaspoon cornstarch mixed with 1 tablespoon water

1. In a medium pot of boiling water, cook the potatoes until firm-tender, about 12 minutes. Drain. Meanwhile, on a sheet of waxed paper, combine the cracked pepper and ¼ teaspoon of the salt. Coat both sides of the steaks with the pepper mixture (see tip). In a medium nonstick skillet, heat the oil until hot but not smoking over medium-high heat. Add the steaks and cook until well browned and crusty, about 2 minutes per side. Transfer the steaks to a plate.

2. Add the bell peppers to the skillet, reduce the heat to medium, and cook, stirring frequently, until crisp-tender, about 4 minutes. Remove the pan from the heat, add the brandy, and return to the heat. Cook until the brandy has almost evaporated, about 1 minute. Add the broth and cook until reduced by one-third, about 4 minutes.

3. Add the evaporated milk, thyme, and the remaining ¼ teaspoon salt to the pan and bring to a boil. Stir in the cornstarch mixture and cook, stirring, until slightly thickened, about 1 minute. Return the steaks to the pan and gently cook until heated through, about 2 minutes. Divide among 4 plates and serve with the potatoes.

Helpful hint: If evaporated low-fat milk isn't available, substitute evaporated skimmed milk.

FAT: 9G/22%
CALORIES: 362
SATURATED FAT: 1.9G
CARBOHYDRATE: 37G
PROTEIN: 24G
CHOLESTEROL: 54MG
SODIUM: 512MG

TIP

Place each steak in the cracked-pepper mixture and press the steak onto the pepper so that it adheres; then turn the steak and press the pepper into the other side.

Lamb with Spring Vegetables

SERVES: 4
WORKING TIME: 20 MINUTES
TOTAL TIME: 30 MINUTES

We've taken a classic French lamb stew and turned it into an innovative stir-fry with a distinct American twist. The lamb is marinated in steak sauce before being stir-fried, and mint jelly (often served with roast lamb) is stirred into the sauce as a finishing-touch flavoring. There are no potatoes in this stir-fry as there would be in a stew, so the lamb and vegetables are served with orzo.

8 ounces orzo pasta

1 tablespoon steak sauce or Worcestershire sauce

2 tablespoons fresh lemon juice

¾ pound well-trimmed boneless leg of lamb, cut into 1-by-¼-inch strips

2 teaspoons olive oil

3 carrots, thinly sliced

½ pound asparagus, tough ends trimmed, cut on the diagonal into ¾-inch lengths

1 zucchini, quartered lengthwise and cut into ½-inch slices

1 red bell pepper, cut into ¾-inch squares

½ cup reduced-sodium chicken broth, defatted

3 tablespoons mint jelly

1 teaspoon salt

¼ pound snow peas

2 teaspoons cornstarch mixed with 1 tablespoon water

1. In a large pot of boiling water, cook the pasta until just tender. Drain well.

2. Meanwhile, in a medium bowl, combine the steak sauce and lemon juice. Add the lamb, tossing to coat well. Let stand at room temperature for 10 minutes.

3. In a large nonstick skillet or wok, heat 1 teaspoon of the oil until hot but not smoking over medium-high heat. Reserving the marinade, add the lamb and stir-fry until no longer pink, 2 to 3 minutes. With a slotted spoon, transfer the lamb to a plate.

4. Add the remaining 1 teaspoon oil to the skillet. Add the carrots, asparagus, zucchini, and bell pepper and stir-fry until the vegetables are crisp-tender, about 5 minutes. Add the reserved marinade, the broth, mint jelly, and salt. Add the snow peas and bring to a boil. Stir in the cornstarch mixture and cook, stirring, until slightly thickened, about 2 minutes. Return the lamb to the pan and cook until heated through, about 1 minute. Divide the orzo among 4 plates, spoon the lamb mixture alongside, and serve.

Helpful hint: You can substitute sugar snap peas for the snow peas, if you like.

FAT: 7G/14%
CALORIES: 447
SATURATED FAT: 1.9G
CARBOHYDRATE: 67G
PROTEIN: 29G
CHOLESTEROL: 55MG
SODIUM: 778MG

Asian Vegetable Rolls

SERVES: 4
WORKING TIME: 30 MINUTES
TOTAL TIME: 30 MINUTES

2 tablespoons reduced-sodium soy
sauce

2 tablespoons fresh lime juice

1 tablespoon minced fresh ginger

2½ teaspoons dark Oriental
sesame oil

2 teaspoons honey

⅛ teaspoon ground cloves

1 whole egg

2 egg whites

¾ teaspoon sugar

1 red bell pepper, cut into thin
slivers

1 cup shredded carrots

2 cups bean sprouts

1 cup canned black beans, rinsed
and drained

3 scallions, slivered

8 large soft lettuce leaves, such as
Boston or Bibb

1. In a small bowl, combine 4 teaspoons of the soy sauce, the lime juice, ginger, 1 teaspoon of the oil, the honey, and cloves.

2. In a small bowl, whisk together the whole egg, egg whites, sugar, and the remaining 2 teaspoons soy sauce. Spray an 8-inch nonstick skillet with nonstick cooking spray and preheat over medium-low heat. Add the egg mixture and cook until it is almost set on top, about 4 minutes. Flip the egg pancake over and cook until it is set, about 30 seconds. Transfer the pancake to a cutting board and when cool enough to handle, cut into thin strips.

3. In a large nonstick skillet, heat the remaining 1½ teaspoons oil until hot but not smoking over medium heat. Add the bell pepper and cook until softened, about 6 minutes. Stir in the carrots and bean sprouts and cook, stirring, for 1 minute. Stir in the egg strips, black beans, scallions, and 1 tablespoon of the soy-lime sauce. Cook until the beans are heated through, about 1 minute. Divide the lettuce leaves among 4 plates. Spoon the vegetables over and drizzle each with 1 teaspoon of the soy-lime sauce. Roll up the lettuce leaves, securing each with a toothpick. Serve the rolls with the remaining sauce on the side.

Helpful hint: You'll need 1 to 1½ heads of Boston or Bibb lettuce for 8 large leaves.

FAT: 5G/28%
CALORIES: 161
SATURATED FAT: 0.8G
CARBOHYDRATE: 22G
PROTEIN: 9G
CHOLESTEROL: 53MG
SODIUM: 491MG

The tender lettuce leaves in this Cantonese-style dish make a pleasant contrast to the warm stir-fried egg and vegetable mixture. Though ground beef is a more traditional filling, you'll find the protein-rich beans and crunchy vegetables deliciously satisfying. Lettuce leaves with a natural "cup" shape work well here; they're easy to wrap and then lift to your mouth without mishaps.

HAM AND SWEET POTATO SAUTÉ

SERVES: 4
WORKING TIME: 20 MINUTES
TOTAL TIME: 30 MINUTES

This homey weeknight supper is enlivened with mango chutney and Dijon mustard, and for a hint of delicate sweetness and texture, we've slipped in wedges of Bartlett pears. If you'd like, press your microwave oven into service for preparing the sweet potatoes: Cook, covered, in a microwave-safe casserole on high power for four to five minutes.

1 pound sweet potatoes, peeled and cut into 1-inch chunks

2 teaspoons olive oil

¾ cup diced onion

2 Bartlett pears, peeled, cored, and cut into 8 wedges each

3 tablespoons chopped mango chutney

1 tablespoon fresh lemon juice

2 teaspoons Dijon mustard

3 cups broccoli florets

½ pound boneless ham steak, cut into 1-inch chunks

1. In a large saucepan of boiling water, cook the sweet potatoes until almost tender, about 5 minutes. Drain well and set aside.

2. Meanwhile, in a large nonstick skillet, heat the oil until hot but not smoking over medium heat. Add the onion and cook, stirring frequently, until the onion is lightly browned, about 5 minutes.

3. Add the pears to the skillet, stirring to coat. Stir in the chutney, ¼ cup of water, the lemon juice, and mustard. Bring to a boil, reduce to a simmer, cover, and cook until the pears are almost tender, about 5 minutes (cooking time will vary depending on the ripeness of the pears).

4. Stir in the sweet potatoes and broccoli and cook, uncovered, until the broccoli is tender, about 5 minutes. Stir in the ham and cook until the ham is just heated through, about 4 minutes longer.

Suggested accompaniments: Escarole salad with a parsley vinaigrette. For dessert, fruit sorbet topped with a drizzle of chocolate syrup and a few slivered toasted almonds.

FAT: 6G/18%
CALORIES: 305
SATURATED FAT: 1.2G
CARBOHYDRATE: 50G
PROTEIN: 16G
CHOLESTEROL: 26MG
SODIUM: 947MG

SWEET AND SOUR VEGETABLES

SERVES: 4
WORKING TIME: 25 MINUTES
TOTAL TIME: 30 MINUTES

Enjoy a colorful Chinese stir-fry without leaving home. Our recipe is considerably lower in fat than the restaurant version, too.

1 cup long-grain rice

¾ teaspoon salt

1 tablespoon vegetable oil

½ pound mushrooms, halved

2 green bell peppers, cut into ½-inch-wide strips

1 red bell pepper, cut into ½-inch-wide strips

4 scallions, cut into 1-inch lengths

2 tablespoons grated fresh ginger

2 cloves garlic, minced

1 cup canned baby corn, cut into 1-inch lengths if large

1 cup cherry tomatoes

½ cup canned sliced water chestnuts

20-ounce can juice-packed pineapple chunks, drained, juice reserved

⅓ cup chili sauce

1½ teaspoons cornstarch

¼ cup chopped peanuts

1. In a medium saucepan, bring 2¼ cups of water to a boil. Add the rice and ¼ teaspoon salt, reduce to a simmer, cover, and cook until the rice is tender, about 17 minutes.

2. Meanwhile, in a large nonstick skillet, heat the oil until hot but not smoking over medium heat. Add the mushrooms and bell peppers and cook, stirring frequently, until the peppers are crisp-tender, about 5 minutes. Add the scallions, ginger, and garlic and cook until the scallions are softened, about 2 minutes.

3. Add the corn, tomatoes, water chestnuts, and pineapple chunks to the pan and cook until heated through, about 4 minutes. In a small bowl, combine the chili sauce, ½ cup of the reserved pineapple juice, the cornstarch, and the remaining ½ teaspoon salt. Stir into the vegetable mixture, bring to a boil, and cook, stirring constantly, until slightly thickened, about 1 minute. Divide the rice among 4 plates. Spoon the vegetable mixture over, sprinkle with the peanuts, and serve.

Helpful hint: If the fresh ginger you are using has thin skin, you don't need to peel it before grating. If the skin is thick and leathery, however, it's best to remove it with a vegetable peeler or paring knife.

FAT: 10G/21%
CALORIES: 440
SATURATED FAT: 1.2G
CARBOHYDRATE: 83G
PROTEIN: 11G
CHOLESTEROL: 0MG
SODIUM: 742MG

PORK CUTLETS IN BASIL AND RED WINE SAUCE

SERVES: 4
WORKING TIME: 30 MINUTES
TOTAL TIME: 30 MINUTES

8 ounces orzo

¼ cup chopped fresh basil

¾ pound well-trimmed center-cut pork loin, cut into 8 slices

2 tablespoons flour

¾ teaspoon salt

½ teaspoon freshly ground black pepper

2 teaspoons olive oil

½ cup dry red wine

¾ cup reduced-sodium chicken broth, defatted

1 tablespoon fresh lemon juice

⅔ cup frozen peas

1 teaspoon cornstarch mixed with 1 tablespoon water

1. In a large pot of boiling water, cook the orzo until just tender. Drain well, transfer to a medium bowl, and toss with 1 tablespoon of the basil.

2. Meanwhile, place the pork slices between two sheets of waxed paper, and with the flat side of a small skillet or meat pounder, pound the pork to a ¼-inch thickness. On another sheet of waxed paper, combine the flour, ¼ teaspoon of the salt, and ¼ teaspoon of the pepper. Dredge the pork in the flour mixture, shaking off the excess. In a large nonstick skillet, heat the oil until hot but not smoking over medium-high heat. Add the pork and cook until golden brown and cooked through, about 2 minutes per side. With a spatula, transfer the pork to a plate.

3. Add the wine to the pan, stirring to scrape up any browned bits that cling to the bottom of the pan, and cook for 2 minutes. Add the broth, lemon juice, the remaining ½ teaspoon salt, and remaining ¼ teaspoon pepper and cook until slightly reduced, about 2 minutes. Stir in the peas and bring to a boil. Stir in the cornstarch mixture and cook, stirring, until slightly thickened, about 1 minute. Stir in 2 tablespoons of the remaining basil. Place the pork on 4 plates, top with the sauce, and sprinkle with the remaining 1 tablespoon basil. Spoon the orzo alongside and serve.

FAT: 8G/17%
CALORIES: 414
SATURATED FAT: 1.9G
CARBOHYDRATE: 51G
PROTEIN: 29G
CHOLESTEROL: 54MG
SODIUM: 622MG

Pork, cooked in the manner of scallopini, is dressed up with wine sauce and peas here and served with orzo.

Indian-Style Sautéed Cod Steaks

SERVES: 4
WORKING TIME: 20 MINUTES
TOTAL TIME: 30 MINUTES

We tend to think of curry powder as the quintessential Indian seasoning, but in fact there is actually a myriad of styles and variations of Indian spice mixtures—some are hot, others mild—each suited to different foods. Here, a mildly hot mixture of paprika, ginger, cumin, and cayenne pepper is rubbed onto the cod steaks and then is used to season the tangy yogurt sauce.

2 teaspoons paprika

1¼ teaspoons ground cumin

½ teaspoon ground ginger

¼ teaspoon cayenne pepper

1 cup plain nonfat yogurt

1 cup small cherry tomatoes, halved

½ cup frozen baby peas, thawed

3 scallions, thinly sliced

1 tablespoon fresh lemon juice

½ teaspoon salt

4 cod steaks (about 6 ounces each), any visible bones removed

2 tablespoons flour

1 tablespoon olive oil

1. In a medium bowl, combine the paprika, cumin, ginger, and cayenne. Remove 2 teaspoons of the mixture and set aside. Add the yogurt, tomatoes, peas, scallions, lemon juice, and salt to the spice mixture in the bowl. Stir to combine.

2. Rub the reserved spice mixture onto both sides of the cod steaks. Place the flour on a sheet of waxed paper. Dredge the cod in the flour, shaking off the excess. In a large nonstick skillet, heat the oil until hot but not smoking over medium heat. Add the cod and cook until lightly browned and just opaque, about 4 minutes per side. Place on 4 plates, spoon the yogurt sauce over, and serve.

Helpful hint: Haddock or pollock steaks can be substituted for cod; these fish may be slightly softer than cod, so be extra careful when turning the steaks.

FAT: 5G/20%
CALORIES: 231
SATURATED FAT: 0.8G
CARBOHYDRATE: 13G
PROTEIN: 32G
CHOLESTEROL: 66MG
SODIUM: 435MG

*T*his Chinese-American classic was reputedly created by Chinese cooks in California in the 19th century. The dish became an American family favorite in the 1940s and '50s—but without real Chinese ingredients, which were hard to get back then. Our version, made with Napa cabbage, fresh ginger, and soy sauce, restores some of its Asian authenticity.

Pork Chop Suey

SERVES: 4
WORKING TIME: 25 MINUTES
TOTAL TIME: 30 MINUTES

1 cup long-grain rice

¾ teaspoon salt

4 teaspoons cornstarch

½ pound well-trimmed pork tenderloin, cut into 2 x ¼-inch strips

1 tablespoon vegetable oil

3 ribs celery, thinly sliced on the diagonal

½ pound mushrooms, thinly sliced

1 cup reduced-sodium chicken broth, defatted

3 scallions, thinly sliced

2 tablespoons finely chopped fresh ginger

2 cups shredded Napa cabbage (see tip) or green cabbage

8-ounce can sliced bamboo shoots, rinsed and drained

2 tablespoons reduced-sodium soy sauce

1 teaspoon sugar

1. In a medium saucepan, bring 2¼ cups of water to a boil. Add the rice and ¼ teaspoon of the salt, reduce to a simmer, cover, and cook until the rice is tender, about 17 minutes.

2. Meanwhile, on a sheet of waxed paper, combine 3 teaspoons of the cornstarch and ¼ teaspoon of the salt. Dredge the pork in the cornstarch mixture, shaking off the excess. In a large nonstick skillet, heat the oil until hot but not smoking over medium-high heat. Add the pork and cook, stirring frequently, until lightly browned, about 2 minutes. With a slotted spoon, transfer the pork to a plate.

3. Add the celery, mushrooms, and ¼ cup of the broth to the pan and cook until the celery is crisp-tender, about 4 minutes. Add the scallions and ginger and cook, stirring frequently, until the scallions are tender, about 2 minutes. Add the cabbage and bamboo shoots and cook until the cabbage is just wilted, about 2 minutes.

4. In a small bowl, combine the remaining 1 teaspoon cornstarch with the remaining ¾ cup broth, the soy sauce, sugar, and the remaining ¼ teaspoon salt. Pour into the skillet, bring to a boil, and cook, stirring, until slightly thickened, about 1 minute. Return the pork to the pan and cook just until heated through, about 1 minute. Divide the rice among 4 plates, spoon the pork chop suey over, and serve.

FAT: 6G/17%
CALORIES: 327
SATURATED FAT: 1.2G
CARBOHYDRATE: 49G
PROTEIN: 19G
CHOLESTEROL: 37MG
SODIUM: 919MG

TIP

To shred Napa cabbage, first remove each leaf individually. Stack three to four leaves at a time and, with a large chef's knife, trim off and discard the tough ends. Then cut the stacked leaves crosswise into thin shreds about ¼ inch wide.

SCALLOPS WITH ORANGE SAUCE

SERVES: 4
WORKING TIME: 30 MINUTES
TOTAL TIME: 30 MINUTES

While scallops may seem like something of a luxury, they justify their cost by their convenience (there's nothing to shuck, clean, or fillet) and, of course, by their inimitable flavor. Here, bay scallops are dredged with flour to give them a crisp coating when stir-fried; the tarragon-scented sauce is based on orange juice and vermouth.

1 cup long-grain rice
¾ teaspoon salt
2 tablespoons flour
1 pound bay scallops or quartered sea scallops
4 teaspoons olive oil
2 red bell peppers, slivered
3 shallots, finely chopped, or ¼ cup chopped scallions
½ cup dry vermouth
½ teaspoon grated orange zest
1 cup orange juice
¾ teaspoon dried tarragon
2 teaspoons cornstarch mixed with 1 tablespoon water
¼ cup chopped fresh parsley

1. In a medium saucepan, bring 2¼ cups of water to a boil. Add the rice and ¼ teaspoon of the salt, reduce to a simmer, cover, and cook until the rice is tender, about 17 minutes.

2. In a sturdy plastic bag, combine the flour and ¼ teaspoon of the salt. Add the scallops to the bag, shaking to coat with the flour mixture. In a large nonstick skillet or wok, heat the oil until hot but not smoking over medium heat. Add the scallops and stir-fry until not quite opaque in the center, about 1 minute. With a slotted spoon, transfer the scallops to a plate.

3. Add the bell peppers and shallots to the skillet and stir-fry until softened, about 3 minutes. Add the vermouth, increase the heat to high, and cook, stirring, until reduced by half, about 1 minute. Add the orange zest, orange juice, tarragon, and the remaining ¼ teaspoon salt and bring to a boil. Add the cornstarch mixture and cook, stirring, until slightly thickened, about 1 minute. Reduce the heat to low, return the scallops to the pan, and cook just until the scallops are opaque throughout, about 1 minute. Divide the rice among 4 plates. Spoon the scallop mixture over, sprinkle with the parsley, and serve.

Helpful hint: Vermouth is a fortified wine made aromatic by infusion with herbs, spices, barks, and flowers. You can substitute dry white wine, if you like.

FAT: 6G/13%
CALORIES: 411
SATURATED FAT: 0.8G
CARBOHYDRATE: 56G
PROTEIN: 24G
CHOLESTEROL: 38MG
SODIUM: 604MG

SPICY STIR-FRIED PORK WITH WATERCRESS

SERVES: 4
WORKING TIME: 30 MINUTES
TOTAL TIME: 30 MINUTES

*T*he richness of pork is set off by peppery watercress and the tang of tomatoes here. Make the dish as hot (or mild) as you like.

1 cup long-grain rice

¾ teaspoon salt

½ pound well-trimmed pork loin, cut into 2 x ¼-inch strips

4 teaspoons cornstarch

2 teaspoons olive oil

1 red onion, halved and thinly sliced

3 cloves garlic, minced

6 cups watercress, tough stems removed

½ teaspoon sugar

½ teaspoon hot pepper sauce

½ cup reduced-sodium chicken broth, defatted

2 cups cherry tomatoes, halved

1. In a medium saucepan, bring 2¼ cups of water to a boil. Add the rice and ¼ teaspoon of the salt, reduce to a simmer, cover, and cook until the rice is tender, about 17 minutes. Meanwhile, dredge the pork in 3 teaspoons of the cornstarch, shaking off the excess. In a large skillet, heat the oil until hot but not smoking over medium heat. Add the pork and cook, stirring frequently, until lightly browned and just cooked through, about 2 minutes. With a slotted spoon, transfer the pork to a plate.

2. Add the onion and garlic to the pan and cook, stirring frequently, until the onion is crisp-tender, about 4 minutes. Add the watercress, sprinkle with the sugar, hot pepper sauce, and the remaining ½ teaspoon salt and cook, stirring frequently, until the watercress is wilted, about 3 minutes. Add the broth, bring to a boil, and stir in the tomatoes. Cook until the tomatoes begin to collapse, about 2 minutes.

3. In a small bowl, combine the remaining 1 teaspoon cornstarch and 1 tablespoon of water. Add to the skillet along with the pork and cook, stirring, until the sauce is slightly thickened and the pork is heated through, about 1 minute. Divide the rice among 4 plates, spoon the pork mixture alongside, and serve.

Helpful hint: If you're not sure that ½ teaspoon of hot pepper sauce will suit your taste buds, start with a few drops and add more as desired.

FAT: 6G/17%
CALORIES: 321
SATURATED FAT: 1.5G
CARBOHYDRATE: 48G
PROTEIN: 18G
CHOLESTEROL: 34MG
SODIUM: 561MG

Pan-Fried Chicken with Pepper-Garlic Sauce

Serves: 4
Working time: 20 minutes
Total time: 30 minutes

6 ounces all-purpose potatoes, peeled and thinly sliced

12 cloves garlic, peeled

¾ teaspoon salt

¾ cup jarred roasted red peppers, rinsed and drained

1 teaspoon chili powder

2 tablespoons flour

¼ teaspoon freshly ground black pepper

4 skinless, boneless chicken breast halves (about 1 pound total)

1 tablespoon olive oil

½ cup reduced-sodium chicken broth, defatted

½ cup evaporated low-fat milk

1 tablespoon no-salt-added tomato paste

½ teaspoon dried rosemary

1. In a medium saucepan of boiling water, cook the potatoes and garlic with ¼ teaspoon of the salt until tender, about 10 minutes. Reserving ¼ cup of the cooking liquid, drain the potatoes and garlic and transfer to a medium bowl. Mash with the reserved cooking liquid until smooth. In a food processor, process the peppers to a smooth purée. Stir the pepper purée and the chili powder into the mashed potatoes; set aside.

2. Meanwhile, on a sheet of waxed paper, combine the flour, ¼ teaspoon of the salt, and the black pepper. Dredge the chicken in the flour mixture, shaking off the excess.

3. In a large nonstick skillet, heat the oil until hot but not smoking over medium heat. Add the chicken and cook until golden brown and cooked through, about 5 minutes per side. With a slotted spoon, transfer the chicken to a plate.

4. Add the broth, evaporated milk, tomato paste, rosemary, and the remaining ¼ teaspoon salt to the skillet and bring to a boil. Add the roasted pepper mixture and cook, stirring occasionally, until slightly thickened, about 3 minutes. Return the chicken to the pan and cook until just heated through, about 1 minute. Divide the chicken among 4 plates, top with the sauce, and serve.

Fat: 6g/21%
Calories: 256
Saturated Fat: 0.8g
Carbohydrate: 19g
Protein: 31g
Cholesterol: 71mg
Sodium: 666mg

Serve this chicken sauté and its lush (but light) pepper-garlic sauce with steamed Italian green beans.

ZUCCHINI AND GREEN PEA FRITTATA

SERVES: 4
WORKING TIME: 20 MINUTES
TOTAL TIME: 20 MINUTES

A frittata is an Italian dish consisting of beaten eggs and a filling—such as vegetables, leftover pasta, or cheese. Although it's similar to an omelete, a frittata is easier to prepare since the tricky step of folding the omelete over the other ingredients is eliminated. This frittata is filled with zucchini, peas, and herbs and is topped with Parmesan cheese.

2 whole eggs
5 egg whites
1 cup canned white kidney beans (cannellini), rinsed and drained
2 scallions, cut into 1-inch pieces
¾ teaspoon salt
¼ teaspoon hot pepper sauce
2 teaspoons olive oil
2 zucchini, quartered lengthwise and thinly sliced
2 tablespoons chopped fresh mint
½ teaspoon dried basil
1½ cups frozen peas
1 tablespoon balsamic vinegar
3 tablespoons grated Parmesan cheese

1. Preheat the broiler. In a blender or food processor, combine the whole eggs, egg whites, beans, scallions, salt, and hot pepper sauce and process until smooth.

2. In a medium broilerproof skillet, heat the oil until hot but not smoking over medium heat. Add the zucchini and cook until crisp-tender, about 5 minutes. Add the mint, basil, peas, and vinegar and cook until fragrant, about 1 minute.

3. Reduce the heat to low, add the egg mixture to the skillet, cover, and cook until the frittata is set around the edges but still liquid in the center, 6 to 8 minutes.

4. Place the skillet under the broiler 3 inches from the heat and cook for 2 to 5 minutes, or until golden brown and set in the center. Sprinkle the Parmesan over and broil for 1 minute, or until the cheese is golden. Cut into wedges, divide among 4 plates, and serve.

Helpful hint: If your skillet doesn't have a broilerproof handle, wrap the handle in a double layer of foil.

FAT: 7G/29%
CALORIES: 202
SATURATED FAT: 1.9G
CARBOHYDRATE: 19G
PROTEIN: 17G
CHOLESTEROL: 109MG
SODIUM: 741MG

PORK SAUTÉ WITH CHIVE CREAM SAUCE

SERVES: 4
WORKING TIME: 25 MINUTES
TOTAL TIME: 25 MINUTES

This upscale one-pot main dish combines delicately browned pork tenderloin cutlets with an appealing mix of tender vegetables.

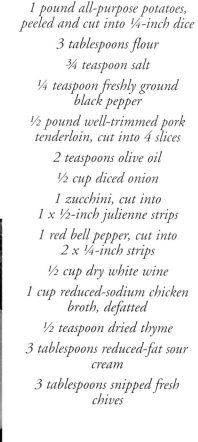

1 pound all-purpose potatoes, peeled and cut into ¼-inch dice

3 tablespoons flour

¾ teaspoon salt

¼ teaspoon freshly ground black pepper

½ pound well-trimmed pork tenderloin, cut into 4 slices

2 teaspoons olive oil

½ cup diced onion

1 zucchini, cut into 1 x ½-inch julienne strips

1 red bell pepper, cut into 2 x ¼-inch strips

½ cup dry white wine

1 cup reduced-sodium chicken broth, defatted

½ teaspoon dried thyme

3 tablespoons reduced-fat sour cream

3 tablespoons snipped fresh chives

1. In a large pot of boiling water, cook the potatoes until firm-tender, about 5 minutes. Drain.

2. Meanwhile, on a sheet of waxed paper, combine 2 tablespoons of the flour, ¼ teaspoon of the salt, and the black pepper. Dredge the pork in the flour mixture, shaking off the excess. In a large nonstick skillet, heat the oil until hot but not smoking over medium-high heat. Add the pork and cook until lightly browned, about 1 minute per side. Transfer the pork to a plate.

3. Add the onion to the skillet and cook, stirring frequently, until softened, about 2 minutes. Add the zucchini and bell pepper, stirring to coat. Add the wine and cook until reduced by one-third, about 2 minutes. Add the broth, thyme, potatoes, and the remaining ½ teaspoon salt. Bring to a boil, reduce to a simmer, and cook until the vegetables are tender, about 2 minutes.

4. In a small bowl, combine the sour cream and the remaining 1 tablespoon flour. Stir into the skillet along with the pork and cook, stirring occasionally, until the pork is just cooked through, the sauce is slightly thickened, and no floury taste remains, about 2 minutes. Place the pork on 4 plates. Stir the chives into the sauce, spoon over the pork, and serve.

Helpful hint: If you can't get fresh chives, substitute scallion greens.

FAT: 6G/23%
CALORIES: 239
SATURATED FAT: 1.7G
CARBOHYDRATE: 25G
PROTEIN: 17G
CHOLESTEROL: 41MG
SODIUM: 596MG

RED SNAPPER WITH CHILI-CORN SALSA

SERVES: 4
WORKING TIME: 20 MINUTES
TOTAL TIME: 25 MINUTES

2 teaspoons chili powder

1 teaspoon ground cumin

1 teaspoon ground coriander

½ teaspoon salt

1½ cups frozen corn kernels, thawed

1 tomato, diced

3 scallions, thinly sliced

1 pickled jalapeño pepper, seeded and finely chopped

2 tablespoons balsamic or red wine vinegar

4 skinless red snapper fillets (about 6 ounces each), any visible bones removed

2 tablespoons flour

1 tablespoon olive oil

1. In a medium bowl, combine the chili powder, cumin, coriander, and salt. Remove 2 teaspoons of the mixture and set aside. Stir the corn, tomato, scallions, jalapeño, and vinegar into the mixture remaining in the bowl.

2. Rub the reserved spice mixture onto both sides of the red snapper fillets. Place the flour on a sheet of waxed paper. Dredge the snapper in the flour, shaking off the excess. In a large nonstick skillet, heat the oil until hot but not smoking over medium heat. Add the snapper and cook until lightly browned and just opaque, about 3 minutes per side. Divide the snapper among 4 plates, spoon the salsa over, and serve.

Helpful hints: You can substitute any firm-fleshed white fish, such as flounder or sole, for the red snapper. If you like the blend of chili powder, cumin, and coriander, try mixing up some extra to rub on chicken breasts, turkey cutlets, and other meats and poultry before sautéing, broiling, or grilling.

FAT: 7G/22%
CALORIES: 286
SATURATED FAT: 1G
CARBOHYDRATE: 19G
PROTEIN: 38G
CHOLESTEROL: 63MG
SODIUM: 458MG

Toss a salad to serve with this zesty Mexican-style dish. The snapper is rubbed with chili, cumin, and coriander.

MOROCCAN SPICED PORK SAUTÉ

SERVES: 4
WORKING TIME: 25 MINUTES
TOTAL TIME: 30 MINUTES

1 cup long-grain rice

5 cloves garlic, minced

¾ teaspoon salt

¾ cup chopped fresh cilantro or basil

½ cup dried apricots, diced

2 tablespoons sliced almonds

2 tablespoons flour

½ pound well-trimmed center-cut pork loin, cut into 4 slices and pounded (see page 8) ½ inch thick

2 teaspoons olive oil

¾ teaspoon grated orange zest

¾ cup orange juice

1 teaspoon ground coriander

¾ teaspoon ground cumin

1¼ cups reduced-sodium chicken broth, defatted

1½ teaspoons cornstarch mixed with 1 tablespoon water

1. In a medium saucepan, bring 2¼ cups of water to a boil. Add the rice, 2 cloves of the garlic, and ¼ teaspoon of the salt, reduce to a simmer, cover, and cook until the rice is tender, about 17 minutes. Stir in the cilantro, apricots, and almonds; set the pilaf aside.

2. Meanwhile, on a sheet of waxed pepper, combine the flour and ¼ teaspoon of the salt. Dredge the pork in the flour mixture, shaking off the excess. In a large nonstick skillet, heat the oil until hot but not smoking over medium-high heat. Add the pork and cook until lightly browned, about 2 minutes per side. Transfer the pork to a plate.

3. Reduce the heat to medium, add the remaining 3 cloves of garlic, and cook, stirring frequently, until softened, about 2 minutes. Add the orange zest, orange juice, coriander, cumin, and the remaining ¼ teaspoon salt and cook, scraping up any browned bits that cling to the pan, until slightly reduced, about 2 minutes.

4. Add the broth to the pan and bring to a boil. Stir in the cornstarch mixture and cook, stirring, until sightly thickened, about 1 minute. Return the pork to the pan and cook just until cooked through, about 1 minute. Divide the pilaf among 4 plates. Place the pork alongside, spoon the sauce over, and serve.

Helpful hint: You'll need 2 to 3 oranges for ¾ cup juice.

FAT: 7G/17%
CALORIES: 376
SATURATED FAT: 1.5G
CARBOHYDRATE: 58G
PROTEIN: 19G
CHOLESTEROL: 36MG
SODIUM: 632MG

W e've based this pork sauté on the Moroccan way of cooking lamb, with aromatic spices, such as cumin and coriander, and garlic. The colorful pilaf also draws from traditional Moroccan ingredients; fresh cilantro, sliced almonds, dried apricots, oranges, and yet more heady garlic. Serve a mixed green salad alongside to complete the meal.

CHICKEN STIR-FRY WITH BROCCOLI, GARLIC, AND BASIL

SERVES: 4
WORKING TIME: 20 MINUTES
TOTAL TIME: 20 MINUTES

Tomato-vegetable juice adds a rich undertone to this intriguing dish—be sure to keep some on hand since it's a great flavor shortcut. As with all stir-fries, cooking is very quick so it's important to have all the ingredients cut and measured beforehand. Also, remember to cut meats and vegetables into small, uniform pieces to ensure even cooking.

2 teaspoons vegetable oil

1 pound skinless, boneless chicken breasts, cut into 2-inch chunks

3 cloves garlic, minced

¼ cup finely chopped scallions

1 tablespoon minced fresh ginger

3 cups broccoli florets

1 cup peeled, thinly sliced broccoli stems

1 cucumber, halved lengthwise and thinly sliced

1 cup cherry tomatoes

5½-ounce can reduced-sodium tomato-vegetable juice

¾ teaspoon salt

3 tablespoons chopped fresh basil

1. In a large nonstick skillet, heat the oil until hot but not smoking over medium heat. Add the chicken and cook, stirring frequently, until the chicken is no longer pink, about 2 minutes.

2. Add the garlic, scallions, and ginger and cook, stirring constantly, until fragrant, about 30 seconds. Add the broccoli florets and stems, the cucumber, tomatoes, tomato-vegetable juice, and salt. Cook, stirring frequently, until the chicken is cooked through and the broccoli is crisp-tender, about 5 minutes longer.

3. Stir in the basil. Spoon the chicken and vegetables onto 4 plates and serve.

Suggested accompaniments: Steamed white rice, followed by fresh cherries marinated in red wine.

FAT: 4G/18%
CALORIES: 201
SATURATED FAT: .7G
CARBOHYDRATE: 11G
PROTEIN: 30G
CHOLESTEROL: 66MG
SODIUM: 545MG

BEEF AND MUSHROOM BURGERS

SERVES: 4
WORKING TIME: 20 MINUTES
TOTAL TIME: 30 MINUTES

For these thick, juicy burgers, you chop the beef yourself, adding garlic, shallots, capers, and Worcestershire sauce for robust flavor.

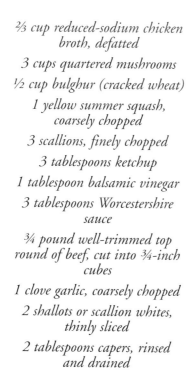

⅔ cup reduced-sodium chicken broth, defatted

3 cups quartered mushrooms

½ cup bulghur (cracked wheat)

1 yellow summer squash, coarsely chopped

3 scallions, finely chopped

3 tablespoons ketchup

1 tablespoon balsamic vinegar

3 tablespoons Worcestershire sauce

¾ pound well-trimmed top round of beef, cut into ¾-inch cubes

1 clove garlic, coarsely chopped

2 shallots or scallion whites, thinly sliced

2 tablespoons capers, rinsed and drained

2 teaspoons olive oil

4 hamburger rolls

1. In a medium saucepan, bring the broth to a boil. Add the mushrooms and cook for 1 minute to blanch. With a slotted spoon, transfer the mushrooms to a food processor. Add the bulghur to the hot broth in the saucepan and set aside, off the heat, until the broth is absorbed, about 15 minutes.

2. Meanwhile, in a small bowl, combine the summer squash, scallions, ketchup, vinegar, and 1 tablespoon of the Worcestershire sauce. Set the relish aside.

3. Add the beef, garlic, shallots, capers, bulghur (drained if necessary), and the remaining 2 tablespoons Worcestershire sauce to the mushrooms in the food processor. With on/off pulses, process until the meat is finely chopped and the other ingredients are well combined. Form the mixture into 4 patties about 3½ inches in diameter (about 1 inch thick).

4. In a large nonstick skillet, heat 1 teaspoon of the oil until hot but not smoking over medium-high heat. Add the burgers and cook for 3 minutes. Add the remaining 1 teaspoon oil, turn the burgers, and cook until medium, about 3 minutes. Place the hamburger rolls on 4 plates, top with the burgers and relish, and serve.

Helpful hint: Try toasted English muffins instead of the hamburger rolls.

FAT: 8G/20%
CALORIES: 366
SATURATED FAT: 1.9G
CARBOHYDRATE: 47G
PROTEIN: 28G
CHOLESTEROL: 49MG
SODIUM: 769MG

TURKEY AND GINGERED NAPA CABBAGE

SERVES: 4
WORKING TIME: 20 MINUTES
TOTAL TIME: 30 MINUTES

*1 large sweet potato
(10 ounces), peeled and cut
into ½-inch cubes*

1 tablespoon olive oil

*3 scallions, cut into 1-inch
pieces*

3 cloves garlic, minced

*1 Granny Smith apple, cored
and cut into 1-inch chunks*

3 cups shredded Napa cabbage

¼ cup red wine vinegar

*¼ cup reduced-sodium chicken
broth, defatted*

¾ teaspoon ground ginger

½ teaspoon salt

¼ teaspoon dried sage

*¾ pound cooked turkey breast,
cut into 1-inch chunks*

1. In a large pot of boiling water, cook the sweet potato until tender, about 8 minutes. Drain well.

2. Meanwhile, in a large nonstick skillet, heat the oil until hot but not smoking over medium heat. Add the scallions and garlic and cook until the garlic is fragrant, about 1 minute. Stir in the apple, cabbage, vinegar, broth, ginger, salt, and sage. Cover and cook until the cabbage is wilted, about 5 minutes. Add the sweet potato and turkey and cook just until warmed through, about 2 minutes.

3. Spoon the turkey and vegetable mixture onto 4 plates and serve.

Helpful hints: You can cook the turkey in the microwave for this recipe. Place 1 pound of uncut turkey breast in a shallow microwave-safe dish. Loosely cover the dish with plastic wrap and cook on high power for 7 to 8 minutes. When cool enough to handle, cut into chunks. The sweet potato can be microwaved, too: Scrub the potato and prick it in several places with a fork. Cook on high power for 3 to 5 minutes, turning once. The potato should be firm-tender, not mushy. Let the potato stand for 2 minutes before peeling and cutting.

FAT: 4G/15%
CALORIES: 239
SATURATED FAT: 0.7G
CARBOHYDRATE: 22G
PROTEIN: 28G
CHOLESTEROL: 71MG
SODIUM: 372MG

U*sing
cooked turkey breast in
this warm, flavorful
sauté makes it
especially easy to
prepare.*

*T*here's
nothing humdrum
about the chunky
sauce—virtually
a side dish in itself—
that surrounds these
pork cutlets. The
combination of
broccoli, oranges, and
peanuts seems to
suggest an Asian dish,
but the seasonings are
oregano and cayenne
rather than soy sauce
and ginger. Orzo pasta
is the simple backdrop
for the flavorful sauce.

PORK MEDALLIONS WITH ORANGES AND PEANUTS

SERVES: 4
WORKING TIME: 25 MINUTES
TOTAL TIME: 25 MINUTES

8 ounces orzo pasta

¾ teaspoon dried oregano

¾ teaspoon salt

¼ teaspoon cayenne pepper

10 ounces well-trimmed pork loin, cut into 4 slices

4¼ teaspoons cornstarch

2½ teaspoons olive oil

1 red bell pepper, cut into 2 x ¼-inch strips

1 onion, halved and thinly sliced

3 cloves garlic, slivered

1½ cups reduced-sodium chicken broth, defatted

2 cups small broccoli florets

½ teaspoon grated orange zest

2 navel oranges, peeled and sectioned, juices reserved (see tip)

4 teaspoons coarsely chopped peanuts

1. In a large pot of boiling water, cook the pasta until just tender. Drain well.

2. Meanwhile, in a small bowl, combine the oregano, salt, and cayenne. Sprinkle the pork with 1 teaspoon of the mixture, rubbing it into the meat (set the remaining spice mixture aside). Dredge the pork in 3 teaspoons of the cornstarch, shaking off the excess. In a large nonstick skillet, heat the oil until hot but not smoking over medium-high heat. Add the pork and cook until lightly browned and almost cooked through, about 1 minute per side. Transfer the pork to a plate.

3. Add the bell pepper, onion, and garlic to the skillet, reduce the heat to medium, and cook, stirring frequently, until the bell pepper is crisp-tender, about 3 minutes. Add the broth, broccoli, orange zest, and the reserved spice mixture. Bring to a boil, reduce to a simmer, and cook until the vegetables are tender, about 2 minutes.

4. In a small bowl, combine the remaining 1¼ teaspoons cornstarch and 1 tablespoon of water. Return the vegetable mixture in the skillet to a boil, stir in the cornstarch mixture, and cook, stirring, until slightly thickened, about 1 minute. Return the pork to the pan along with the oranges and their juices and the peanuts and cook just until heated through, about 1 minute. Divide the pasta among 4 plates, spoon the pork and sauce alongside, and serve.

FAT: 10G/20%
CALORIES: 449
SATURATED FAT: 2.1G
CARBOHYDRATE: 63G
PROTEIN: 28G
CHOLESTEROL: 42MG
SODIUM: 694MG

TIP

To prepare the oranges, remove the peel and, using a small knife, trim away all the bitter white pith. Working over a sieve set over a bowl to catch the juices, cut between the membranes to release the orange sections.

TEX-MEX SOFT VEGETABLE TACOS

SERVES: 4
WORKING TIME: 25 MINUTES
TOTAL TIME: 25 MINUTES

The filling for these generously stuffed tacos is a satisfying mixture of black beans, corn, mushrooms, zucchini, and onion in a spicy salsa sauce. There's Cheddar cheese and sour cream inside, too. Accompany the tacos with your favorite fixings, such as tomato wedges, chopped onion, and shredded lettuce—even some extra salsa, if you like.

Four 8-inch low-fat flour tortillas

1½ teaspoons olive oil

1 red onion, slivered

1 zucchini, quartered lengthwise and thinly sliced

1½ cups sliced mushrooms

2 teaspoons chili powder

1 teaspoon ground cumin

1½ cups frozen corn kernels

2 tablespoons no-salt-added tomato paste

¾ cup mild or medium-hot prepared salsa

15-ounce can black beans, rinsed and drained

3 tablespoons chopped fresh cilantro or parsley

¼ cup shredded Cheddar cheese

¼ cup reduced-fat sour cream

1. Preheat the oven to 350°. Wrap the tortillas in foil and place in the oven for 10 minutes, or until heated through.

2. Meanwhile, in a large nonstick skillet, heat the oil until hot but not smoking over medium-high heat. Add the onion, zucchini, and mushrooms and cook, stirring occasionally, until the onion is tender and the mushrooms have released their juices, about 8 minutes. Stir in the chili powder, cumin, and corn and cook until fragrant, about 2 minutes. Stir in the tomato paste, salsa, black beans, and cilantro and cook until heated through, about 2 minutes.

3. Divide the tortillas among 4 plates. Spoon the vegetables down the center of the tortillas, sprinkle with the Cheddar, and top with a dollop of sour cream. Roll up the tortillas, cut them in half if desired, and serve.

Helpful hint: For easy cleanup, spray the grater with nonstick cooking spray before shredding the cheese.

FAT: 9G/23%
CALORIES: 357
SATURATED FAT: 3G
CARBOHYDRATE: 59G
PROTEIN: 14G
CHOLESTEROL: 12MG
SODIUM: 717MG

A definite for lemon-lovers, our easy take on the classic veal dish is complete down to the caper and parsley finish. Once you've prepared the ingredients, the cooking is done in a flash. Steamed sliced carrots and zucchini and a colorful salad of greens and radicchio are deliciously light accompaniments.

CHICKEN PICCATA

SERVES: 4
WORKING TIME: 25 MINUTES
TOTAL TIME: 30 MINUTES

1 cup orzo

2 tablespoons flour

½ teaspoon salt

¼ teaspoon freshly ground black pepper

4 skinless, boneless chicken breast halves (about 1 pound total)

Half a lemon, plus ¼ cup fresh lemon juice (see tip)

⅓ cup dry white wine

¼ cup reduced-sodium chicken broth, defatted

1 tablespoon olive oil

2 cloves garlic, minced

½ pound mushrooms, halved

4 teaspoons capers, rinsed and drained

2 tablespoons chopped fresh parsley

1. In a large pot of boiling water, cook the orzo until just tender. Drain well.

2. Meanwhile, on a sheet of waxed paper, combine the flour, salt, and pepper. Dredge the chicken in the flour mixture, shaking off and reserving the excess. Thinly slice the lemon half and set the slices aside. In a jar with a tight-fitting lid, combine the lemon juice, wine, broth, and reserved flour mixture and shake until smooth.

3. In a large nonstick skillet, heat the oil until hot but not smoking over medium heat. Add the chicken and cook until lightly browned, about 2 minutes per side. Add the garlic and mushrooms and cook, stirring frequently, until the mushrooms are slightly softened, about 2 minutes.

4. Shake the lemon juice mixture and add it to the pan, stirring to combine. Bring to a boil, reduce to a simmer, and cook until the chicken is cooked through, about 5 minutes. Add the lemon slices and cook for 1 minute. Divide the orzo among 4 plates and spoon the chicken mixture on top. Sprinkle with the capers and parsley and serve.

Helpful hint: Even though the orzo, a smooth, rice-shaped pasta, is a pleasant change, you can serve this with white rice or noodles, if desired.

FAT: 6G/13%
CALORIES: 393
SATURATED FAT: 1G
CARBOHYDRATE: 47G
PROTEIN: 35G
CHOLESTEROL: 66MG
SODIUM: 469MG

TIP

To juice a lemon: first let it sit at room temperature for about 30 minutes, then roll it on a flat surface such as a countertop while pressing on it, to loosen the pulp and release more juice. It may be helpful to use a juicer attached to a small cup or bowl that catches the juices and strains out any seeds. Generally, you will get 2 to 3 tablespoons of juice from 1 medium lemon.

*S*ummer suppers in Provence often include ratatouille, a colorful meatless "stew" of fresh tomatoes, eggplant, peppers, and squash. Topped with goat cheese and accompanied with pasta, this ratatouille is a meal in itself. You don't have to serve the ratatouille straight from the stove; it's quite delicious at room temperature and makes tempting picnic fare.

Ratatouille Stir-Fry with Goat Cheese

Serves: 4
Working time: 30 minutes
Total time: 30 minutes

TIP

6 ounces orzo pasta

1 tablespoon olive oil

1 red onion, coarsely diced

4 cloves garlic, finely chopped

1 red bell pepper, cut into thin strips

1 zucchini, cut into 2-by-½-inch strips

1 yellow summer squash, cut into 2-by-½-inch strips

1 small eggplant, cut into 2-by-½-inch strips (see tip)

5½-ounce can low-sodium tomato-vegetable juice

1½ cups cherry tomatoes, halved

2 teaspoons capers, rinsed and drained

¾ teaspoon dried tarragon

¾ teaspoon salt

¼ cup chopped fresh basil

3 ounces goat cheese or feta cheese, crumbled

1. In a large pot of boiling water, cook the pasta until just tender. Drain well.

2. Meanwhile, in a large nonstick skillet or wok, heat the oil until hot but not smoking over medium heat. Add the onion and garlic and stir-fry until the onion is slightly softened, about 2 minutes. Add the bell pepper, zucchini, and yellow squash and stir-fry until crisp-tender, about 4 minutes.

3. Add the eggplant and stir-fry until lightly browned, about 4 minutes. Add the tomato-vegetable juice, tomatoes, capers, tarragon, and salt and cook until the tomatoes are softened, about 4 minutes. Stir in the basil. Divide the orzo among 4 plates. Spoon the vegetables over the orzo, sprinkle the cheese on top, and serve.

Helpful hint: If you can't get low-sodium tomato-vegetable juice, use regular tomato-vegetable juice and reduce the salt in the recipe to ½ teaspoon.

To cut an eggplant into strips, first cut it crosswise into ½-inch-thick slices. Stack several slices, and then cut through the stack to create ½-inch-wide strips.

Fat: 11g/29%
Calories: 347
Saturated Fat: 5g
Carbohydrate: 51g
Protein: 14g
Cholesterol: 17mg
Sodium: 606mg

BROILED & GRILLED DISHES

Left, Shrimp Kebabs with Lime-Basil Orzo
Above, Classic Fajitas

DELUXE CHEESEBURGERS

SERVES: 4
WORKING TIME: 20 MINUTES
TOTAL TIME: 30 MINUTES

½ cup reduced-sodium chicken broth, defatted

1 small onion, finely chopped

1 clove garlic, minced

½ pound well-trimmed top round, cut into large chunks

¼ pound lean ground turkey

¼ cup plain dried bread crumbs

¼ cup chili sauce

¼ teaspoon freshly ground black pepper

¼ cup shredded Swiss cheese (1 ounce)

4 hamburger rolls, split

1 cup shredded romaine lettuce

4 thick slices of tomato

1. In a small saucepan, combine the broth, onion, and garlic. Bring to a simmer over medium heat and cook until the onion is very soft and all the liquid is absorbed, about 5 minutes. Set aside to cool slightly.

2. Meanwhile, preheat the broiler. In a food processor, process the beef until coarsely ground. In a medium bowl, combine the ground beef, turkey, bread crumbs, 2 tablespoons of the chili sauce, the pepper, and the cooled onion. Blend thoroughly and form into 4 patties. Broil the burgers 3 to 4 inches from the heat, turning once, for 8 minutes, or until cooked through. Sprinkle the Swiss cheese on top and broil for 30 seconds to melt the cheese.

3. Broil the hamburger buns for 30 seconds to lightly toast. Place the buns on 4 plates and top with the lettuce, tomato, and a burger. Top the burgers with the remaining 2 tablespoons chili sauce and serve.

Helpful hint: You can customize these burgers with your favorite cheese. Cheddar, Monterey jack, Gouda, and blue cheese can all be substituted for the Swiss.

FAT: 9G/25%
CALORIES: 325
SATURATED FAT: 3.1G
CARBOHYDRATE: 35G
PROTEIN: 26G
CHOLESTEROL: 60MG
SODIUM: 686MG

Can a thick, juicy burger on a bun, crowned with melted cheese be a healthy meal? Definitely. The patty is made from lean top round plus ground turkey; bread crumbs bulk up the burgers, while braised onions and chili sauce keep them juicy. And there's just one-quarter ounce of cheese on each burger. Add a slice of raw onion, if you like, and a side order of potato salad.

Sweet and Sour Halibut

Serves: 4
Working time: 15 minutes
Total time: 30 minutes

Despite its exotic flavor, the piquant marinade for the fish in this recipe is made with ingredients that you may already have on hand. If you don't already have rice vinegar, it's worth buying—it's extremely mild, allowing you to make dressings and marinades with very little oil. Serve the halibut with rice seasoned with lemon zest and fresh herbs, and a green salad.

¼ cup firmly packed light brown sugar

3 tablespoons rice vinegar or cider vinegar

3 tablespoons ketchup

1 tablespoon reduced-sodium soy sauce

1 clove garlic, minced

¾ teaspoon ground ginger

4 halibut steaks (about 1½ pounds total)

1 red bell pepper, halved lengthwise and seeded

1 green bell pepper, halved lengthwise and seeded

2 scallions, cut into 2-inch julienne strips

1. Preheat the grill to a medium heat. (When ready to cook, spray the rack—off the grill—with nonstick cooking spray; see page 6.)

2. In a nonaluminum pan or large shallow bowl, combine the brown sugar, ¼ cup of water, the vinegar, ketchup, soy sauce, garlic, and ginger. Measure out ¼ cup of the mixture and set aside. Add the halibut to the mixture remaining in the pan, turning to coat.

3. Grill the bell pepper halves, cut-sides up, for 5 minutes, or until the skin is blackened. When cool enough to handle, peel the peppers and cut them into thin strips.

4. Grill the halibut, covered, turning once, for 5 minutes or until the halibut is just opaque. Place the halibut on 4 plates, top with the reserved brown sugar mixture, the bell pepper strips, and the scallions, and serve.

Helpful hint: Keep brown sugar in an airtight jar or tin and it will stay spoonably soft. You can also tuck a piece of fresh bread into the container to help keep the sugar moist.

Fat: 3g/12%
Calories: 234
Saturated Fat: .5g
Carbohydrate: 21g
Protein: 30g
Cholesterol: 44mg
Sodium: 366mg

TANGY BARBECUED CHICKEN

SERVES: 4
WORKING TIME: 15 MINUTES
TOTAL TIME: 25 MINUTES

*T*o keep the dinner down-home, serve this open-face sandwich with corn on the cob and a lettuce and tomato salad.

8-ounce can no-salt-added tomato sauce

2 tablespoons red wine vinegar

2 teaspoons Worcestershire sauce

2 cloves garlic, minced

¼ teaspoon hot pepper sauce

¼ teaspoon salt

1 pound skinless, boneless chicken breasts

6 ounces French or Italian bread, halved lengthwise then crosswise to make 4 equal pieces

1. In a small saucepan, stir together the tomato sauce, vinegar, Worcestershire sauce, garlic, hot pepper sauce, and salt. Bring to a boil over medium heat, reduce to a simmer, and cook for 2 minutes to blend the flavors. Measure out ½ cup of the sauce and set aside. Place the remaining sauce in a shallow nonaluminum pan or dish and let cool to room temperature. Add the chicken, toss to coat, and set aside to marinate for 10 minutes.

2. Preheat the broiler or prepare the grill. Broil or grill the chicken 6 inches from the heat, turning once, for 8 minutes, or until cooked through. Remove the chicken and set aside. Place the bread on the broiler or grill rack and toast for 30 seconds, or until lightly browned.

3. Cut the chicken into thin diagonal slices and toss with the reserved ½ cup sauce. Place the toasted bread on 4 plates, top with the chicken, and serve.

Helpful hints: Double or triple the amount of barbecue sauce and keep some on hand in the refrigerator for impromptu barbecues. You can even try just a few drops to dress up a plate of steamed vegetables or a green salad.

FAT: 3G/10%
CALORIES: 267
SATURATED FAT: 0.6G
CARBOHYDRATE: 28G
PROTEIN: 31G
CHOLESTEROL: 66MG
SODIUM: 516MG

HERBED FLOUNDER ROLLS

SERVES: 4
WORKING TIME: 15 MINUTES
TOTAL TIME: 25 MINUTES

¼ cup plain nonfat yogurt

1 tablespoon reduced-fat mayonnaise

1 red bell pepper, finely diced

3 tablespoons chopped fresh parsley

1 teaspoon dried tarragon

¾ teaspoon grated lemon zest

Four 6-ounce flounder fillets, any visible bones removed

2 tablespoons fresh lemon juice

½ teaspoon salt

¼ teaspoon freshly ground black pepper

3 tablespoons plain dried bread crumbs

1. In a small bowl, combine the yogurt, mayonnaise, bell pepper, 1 tablespoon of the parsley, ¼ teaspoon of the tarragon, and ¼ teaspoon of the lemon zest. Cover and refrigerate until serving time.

2. Preheat the grill with the grill topper to a medium heat. (When ready to cook, spray the grill topper—off the grill—with non-stick cooking spray; see page 6.)

3. Lay the flounder fillets flat, skinned-side up. Season with the lemon juice, salt, and black pepper. In a small bowl, combine the bread crumbs, the remaining 2 tablespoons parsley, remaining ¾ teaspoon tarragon, and remaining ½ teaspoon lemon zest. Sprinkle the mixture over the flounder, and starting from a short side, neatly roll up each fillet.

4. Grill the flounder rolls on the grill topper, seam-side down, covered, turning once, for 5 minutes or until the fish is just opaque in the center of the roll. Place the rolls on 4 plates, top with the bell pepper-tartar sauce, and serve.

Helpful hint: For a more traditional flavor, add 2 teaspoons of minced dill pickle to the tartar sauce.

FAT: 3G/13%
CALORIES: 204
SATURATED FAT: .7G
CARBOHYDRATE: 8G
PROTEIN: 34G
CHOLESTEROL: 82MG
SODIUM: 497MG

A flavor-packed tartar sauce tops these lemon-herb seasoned flounder rolls. Asparagus is the perfect accompaniment.

GRILLED MUSTARD-COATED BEEF

SERVES: 4
WORKING TIME: 15 MINUTES
TOTAL TIME: 30 MINUTES

The light, tangy seasonings rubbed into the flank steak here also flavor the accompanying corn and bean salad. Flank steak (sometimes sold as London broil) is lean and relatively tender, but when broiled or grilled it should not be cooked beyond medium-rare, or it may become tough. Slicing the steak on the diagonal helps enhance its tenderness.

3 tablespoons Dijon mustard

3 tablespoons red wine vinegar

1 teaspoon dried tarragon

¼ teaspoon salt

¾ pound well-trimmed flank steak

2 cloves garlic, minced

1 tablespoon honey

1 cucumber, peeled, halved lengthwise, seeded, and diced

15¼-ounce can red kidney beans, rinsed and drained

2 cups frozen corn kernels, thawed

1 cup cherry tomatoes, quartered

3 scallions, thinly sliced

1. In a medium bowl, combine the mustard, vinegar, tarragon, and salt. Remove 2 tablespoons of the mixture and rub it into the steak along with the garlic. Let the meat stand at room temperature while you make the corn and bean salad and preheat the grill.

2. Preheat the grill to medium heat. Add the honey, cucumber, kidney beans, corn, tomatoes, and scallions to the mustard mixture remaining in the bowl. Refrigerate until serving time.

3. Spray the rack—off the grill—with nonstick cooking spray. Place the steak on the rack, cover, and grill for 7 minutes, or until medium-rare. Let stand for 10 minutes before thinly slicing on the diagonal. Divide the corn and bean salad among 4 plates, place the beef slices alongside, and serve.

Helpful hints: The vegetable mixture can be prepared up to 4 hours in advance; keep it covered in the refrigerator until serving time. The steak may be marinated for several hours or overnight: After rubbing the seasoning mixture and garlic into the steak, put it on a plate, cover with plastic wrap, and refrigerate it until ready to grill.

FAT: 8G/22%
CALORIES: 329
SATURATED FAT: 2.9G
CARBOHYDRATE: 38G
PROTEIN: 26G
CHOLESTEROL: 43MG
SODIUM: 603MG

HAWAIIAN CHICKEN KEBABS

SERVES: 4
WORKING TIME: 25 MINUTES
TOTAL TIME: 30 MINUTES

This is a festive dish that will brighten any table, regardless of the season. If weather permits, use the grill or hibachi—this dish will only improve with that outdoor barbecue flavor. For a side dish, blanch thick slices of sweet potato, coat with the basting sauce, and broil or grill along with the kebabs.

7-ounce can juice-packed pineapple chunks, drained, juice reserved

¼ cup ketchup

2 tablespoons reduced-sodium soy sauce

2 tablespoons firmly packed light brown sugar

3 cloves garlic, minced

¼ teaspoon red pepper flakes

1 pound skinless, boneless chicken breasts, cut into 16 pieces

1 large red onion, cut into 16 chunks

16 cherry tomatoes

1. In a large bowl, stir together ⅓ cup of the reserved pineapple juice, the ketchup, soy sauce, brown sugar, garlic, and red pepper flakes. Add the chicken and onion, stirring to coat.

2. Preheat the broiler or prepare the grill. Alternately thread the chicken, onion, pineapple, and cherry tomatoes onto 8 skewers. Reserve the marinade. Broil or grill the kebabs 6 inches from the heat, turning the skewers and basting with the reserved marinade, for 8 minutes, or until the chicken and vegetables are cooked through. Divide the skewers among 4 plates and serve.

Helpful hint: You can assemble the kebabs up to 8 hours in advance and refrigerate them in the marinade. Bring them to room temperature and cook as directed.

FAT: 2G/6%
CALORIES: 261
SATURATED FAT: 0.4G
CARBOHYDRATE: 32G
PROTEIN: 29G
CHOLESTEROL: 66MG
SODIUM: 573MG

GRILLED BEEF WITH TOMATO SALSA

SERVES: 4
WORKING TIME: 20 MINUTES
TOTAL TIME: 30 MINUTES PLUS MARINATING TIME

*T*op *round is one of the leanest cuts of beef, but it's delectably juicy when properly cooked. Here, the steak benefits from a lime juice marinade: The acid in the citrus tenderizes the meat. A fresh, chunky jalapeño salsa adds a lively counterpoint. Serve with a salad of Bibb or Boston lettuce, tomatoes, and radishes.*

¼ cup fresh lime juice
½ teaspoon salt
¾ pound well-trimmed top round of beef, in one piece
¾ pound plum tomatoes, diced
½ cup chopped fresh cilantro or parsley
2 scallions, thinly sliced
1 pickled jalapeño pepper, finely chopped
Four 8-inch flour tortillas

1. In a sturdy plastic bag, combine 3 tablespoons of the lime juice and ¼ teaspoon of the salt. Add the beef, squeeze the air out of the bag, seal, and marinate at room temperature for 30 minutes or up to 2 hours in the refrigerator.

2. Meanwhile, in a medium bowl, stir together the tomatoes, cilantro, scallions, jalapeño, the remaining 1 tablespoon lime juice, and remaining ¼ teaspoon salt. Refrigerate until serving time.

3. Preheat the grill to a high heat. Spray the rack—off the grill—with nonstick cooking spray (see page 6). Grill the beef, covered, turning once, for 10 minutes or until browned. Let the meat stand 5 minutes before thinly slicing. Divide the steak and tomato salsa evenly among 4 plates. Serve with the flour tortillas.

Helpful hint: Plum tomatoes were used for this recipe because they tend to be dense and meaty. If plum tomatoes are not available, use round tomatoes: but halve them crosswise and squeeze out the seeds before chopping them.

FAT: 6G/21%
CALORIES: 254
SATURATED FAT: 1.5G
CARBOHYDRATE: 26G
PROTEIN: 24G
CHOLESTEROL: 54MG
SODIUM: 544MG

BROILED SHRIMP WITH LEMON AND BASIL

SERVES: 4
WORKING TIME: 25 MINUTES
TOTAL TIME: 30 MINUTES PLUS MARINATING TIME

Italian cooks season many foods with the simple and elegant combination of lemon, garlic, and olive oil. Here, this traditional blend of flavors— enhanced by the addition of fresh basil and a hint of vermouth—serves as a marinade for broiled shrimp. In the summer, skewer the shrimp and grill them outdoors.

¼ cup chopped fresh basil

2 cloves garlic, minced

2 tablespoons dry vermouth or vodka

1 tablespoon olive oil

1 teaspoon grated lemon zest

2 tablespoons fresh lemon juice

½ teaspoon dried oregano

¼ teaspoon salt

¼ teaspoon freshly ground black pepper

1 pound large shrimp, shelled and deveined

4 ounces Italian bread, cut into 8 slices

1. In a large bowl, combine the basil, garlic, vermouth, oil, lemon zest, lemon juice, oregano, salt, and pepper. Add the shrimp, tossing to coat. Set aside to marinate for at least 30 minutes at room temperature or for up to 4 hours in the refrigerator.

2. Preheat the broiler or grill. Under the broiler or on the grill, toast the bread on one side. Set aside. Broil or grill the shrimp 6 inches from the heat, turning once, for 3 minutes, or until just opaque.

3. Place 2 slices of toast on each of 4 plates. Top with the shrimp and serve.

Helpful hint: For extra flavor, rub the bread slices with a halved clove of peeled garlic before toasting them.

FAT: 6G/24%
CALORIES: 222
SATURATED FAT: 1G
CARBOHYDRATE: 17G
PROTEIN: 22G
CHOLESTEROL: 140MG
SODIUM: 438MG

PORK BURGERS WITH SWEET POTATO RELISH

SERVES: 4
WORKING TIME: 20 MINUTES
TOTAL TIME: 30 MINUTES

8 ounces sweet potato, peeled and cut into ½-inch cubes

½ cup frozen corn kernels, thawed

1 tomato, coarsely chopped

⅓ cup plus 2 tablespoons chili sauce

2 scallions, thinly sliced

2 tablespoons red wine vinegar

1 teaspoon olive oil

1¼ pounds well-trimmed pork tenderloin, cut into chunks

2 slices (1 ounce each) firm-textured white bread, crumbled

½ cup seltzer or club soda

2 tablespoons chopped pickled jalapeño pepper

¾ teaspoon freshly ground black pepper

¼ teaspoon dried sage

4 hamburger buns

1. In a medium pot of boiling water, cook the sweet potato until firm-tender, about 7 minutes. Drain well. Transfer to a medium bowl and add the corn, tomato, 2 tablespoons of the chili sauce, the scallions, vinegar, and oil. Toss to combine and refrigerate until serving time.

2. Meanwhile, in a food processor, process the pork until finely ground. Transfer the pork to a large bowl and stir in the bread, seltzer, jalapeño, black pepper, sage, and the remaining ⅓ cup chili sauce. Shape the mixture into 4 patties.

3. Preheat the grill to medium heat. Spray the rack—off the grill—with nonstick cooking spray. Place the burgers on the rack, cover, and grill, turning once, for 8 minutes, or until cooked through but still juicy. Place the buns, cut-sides down, on the grill and cook until lightly browned and toasted, about 30 seconds.

4. Divide the buns among 4 plates, top with the burgers and relish, and serve.

Helpful hint: The chilied sweet potato relish would be equally delicious on turkey burgers or sliced turkey sandwiches.

FAT: 11G/21%
CALORIES: 475
SATURATED FAT: 3.2G
CARBOHYDRATE: 53G
PROTEIN: 40G
CHOLESTEROL: 100MG
SODIUM: 883MG

Move over, turkey burger—here's another contender for the title of "leanest, juiciest burger." Here, we've ground pork tenderloin and combined it with fresh crumbled bread and seltzer—a tried-and-true "secret ingredient" for tender burgers and meatballs. Serve the burgers on toasted buns, topped with the chunky sweet potato relish and accompanied by a summery salad.

GRILLED HALIBUT WITH FRESH TOMATO-HERB SAUCE

SERVES: 4
WORKING TIME: 15 MINUTES
TOTAL TIME: 20 MINUTES

Halibut is great for grilling, and our tomato-basil sauce, along with green beans and a salad make this a quick and delicious meal.

½ cup orange juice
⅓ cup dry white wine
1 clove garlic, crushed and peeled
¼ teaspoon red pepper flakes
4 halibut steaks (about 1½ pounds total)
1 tomato, diced
2 scallions, thinly sliced
¼ cup chopped fresh parsley
¼ cup chopped fresh basil
1 teaspoon olive oil
½ teaspoon salt

1. In a nonaluminum pan, combine ¼ cup of the orange juice, the wine, garlic, and red pepper flakes. Add the halibut, turning to coat. Set aside to marinate at room temperature while you make the tomato-herb sauce and preheat the grill.

2. In a medium bowl, combine the tomato, scallions, parsley, basil, oil, salt, and the remaining ¼ cup orange juice.

3. Preheat the grill to a medium heat. Spray the rack—off the grill—with nonstick cooking spray (see page 6). Grill the halibut, covered, turning once, for 6 minutes or until the halibut is just opaque. Place the halibut on 4 plates, top with the tomato-herb sauce, and serve.

Helpful hint: You can marinate the halibut for up to 4 hours in the refrigerator. Bring the fish to room temperature before grilling.

FAT: 5G/22%
CALORIES: 204
SATURATED FAT: .6G
CARBOHYDRATE: 7G
PROTEIN: 30G
CHOLESTEROL: 44MG
SODIUM: 355MG

Soft Turkey Tacos

SERVES: 4
WORKING TIME: 15 MINUTES
TOTAL TIME: 20 MINUTES

2 teaspoons olive oil

¾ pound turkey cutlets, cut into ½-inch-wide strips

½ teaspoon salt

½ teaspoon chili powder

½ teaspoon ground cumin

1¾ pounds plum tomatoes, coarsely chopped

4½-ounce can chopped mild green chilies with their juice

3 scallions, thinly sliced

1 tablespoon fresh lime juice

Eight 6-inch flour tortillas

2 cups shredded romaine lettuce

2 tablespoons reduced-fat sour cream

1. Preheat the oven to 400°. In a large nonstick skillet, heat the oil until hot but not smoking over medium heat. Add the turkey, sprinkle with ¼ teaspoon of the salt, ¼ teaspoon of the chili powder, and ¼ teaspoon of the cumin and cook, stirring frequently, until just cooked through, about 2 minutes per side. With a slotted spoon, transfer the turkey to a plate.

2. Add the tomatoes, chilies, scallions, the remaining ¼ teaspoon salt, remaining ¼ teaspoon chili powder, and remaining ¼ teaspoon cumin to the skillet. Cook until the sauce is slightly reduced, about 4 minutes. Return the turkey to the pan and cook just until warmed through, about 1 minute. Remove from the heat and stir in the lime juice.

3. Meanwhile, wrap the tortillas in foil and bake until hot but not crisp, about 4 minutes. Divide the tortillas among 4 plates. Spoon the turkey mixture onto the warm tortillas, top with the lettuce and a dollop of the sour cream. Roll up the tortillas or leave open and serve.

Helpful hint: You can serve the tacos with a variety of accompaniments, such as minced scallions, shredded cilantro, extra chopped chilies, or salsa.

FAT: 8G/23%
CALORIES: 318
SATURATED FAT: 1.5G
CARBOHYDRATE: 36G
PROTEIN: 28G
CHOLESTEROL: 55MG
SODIUM: 731MG

Roll 'em up and dig in: These soft tacos are overflowing with flavor, and are easier to eat than crisp tacos.

Rich-
*fleshed bluefish calls
for a tart counterpoint:
Plain lemon juice
would serve the
purpose, but instead,
we opt for this
fascinating blend of
lime juice, honey,
cumin, and coriander.
The same mixture
becomes a dressing for
bright cubes of mango,
bell pepper, red onion,
and jalapeño.*

BROILED BLUEFISH WITH MANGO RELISH

SERVES: 4
WORKING TIME: 15 MINUTES
TOTAL TIME: 25 MINUTES

¼ cup fresh lime juice

2 tablespoons honey

1 teaspoon olive oil

¾ teaspoon ground cumin

½ teaspoon ground coriander

½ teaspoon salt

Four bluefish fillets, with skin,
any visible bones removed (about
1½ pounds total)

1 mango, peeled and diced
(see tip)

1 red bell pepper, diced

1 red onion, diced

1 small pickled jalapeño pepper,
finely chopped

1. Preheat the broiler. In a large bowl, combine the lime juice, honey, oil, cumin, coriander, and salt. Place the fish, skin-side down, on the rack and sprinkle with 4 teaspoons of the lime juice mixture. Broil 6 inches from the heat for 6 minutes, or until the fish is lightly browned and just opaque.

2. Meanwhile, add the mango, bell pepper, onion, and jalapeño to the lime mixture remaining in the bowl, tossing to combine. Place the fish on 4 plates, spoon the relish on top, and serve.

Helpful hint: Because the skin is left on the bluefish, it's easy to grill, should you prefer it. A nonstick grill basket or a smooth grill topper will help ensure that the fish doesn't break when you remove it from the fire.

FAT: 9G/26%
CALORIES: 316
SATURATED FAT: 1.7G
CARBOHYDRATE: 24G
PROTEIN: 35G
CHOLESTEROL: 100MG
SODIUM: 427MG

HERBED BEEF KEBABS

SERVES: 4
WORKING TIME: 15 MINUTES
TOTAL TIME: 30 MINUTES

K ebabs are easy to grill and, if you use handsome skewers like these, very impressive to serve as well. Note that the skewers have flat (rather than round) blades to help keep the food from slipping and twisting as it grills. For these kebabs, the steak, squash, potatoes, and tomatoes are bathed in a pesto-like marinade. Serve a tossed green salad alongside.

1½ pounds red potatoes, cut into 16 wedges

1¼ cups reduced-sodium chicken broth, defatted

1 tablespoon olive oil

⅔ cup packed fresh basil leaves

3 cloves garlic, peeled

¾ teaspoon salt

¾ pound well-trimmed beef sirloin, cut into 16 chunks

1 zucchini, halved lengthwise and cut crosswise into 16 pieces

1 yellow summer squash, halved lengthwise and cut crosswise into 16 pieces

16 cherry tomatoes

1. In a medium pot of boiling water, cook the potatoes until firm-tender, about 10 minutes. Drain well.

2. Meanwhile, in a food processor, combine the broth, oil, basil, garlic, and salt and process until smooth. Transfer the mixture to a large bowl and add the beef, zucchini, yellow squash, tomatoes, and the potatoes, tossing to coat.

3. Preheat the grill to medium heat. Reserving the marinade, alternately thread the beef, zucchini, yellow squash, tomatoes, and potatoes onto 8 skewers.

4. Spray the rack—off the grill—with nonstick cooking spray. Place the skewers on the rack, cover, and grill, turning and basting the skewers with the reserved marinade, for 7 minutes, or until the potatoes are golden brown and the beef is medium-rare.

Helpful hint: You can marinate the beef and vegetables up to 2 hours in advance; cover the bowl and place it in the refrigerator.

FAT: 9G/25%
CALORIES: 329
SATURATED FAT: 2.3G
CARBOHYDRATE: 37G
PROTEIN: 26G
CHOLESTEROL: 57MG
SODIUM: 650MG

BROILED ORANGE CHICKEN

SERVES: 4
WORKING TIME: 10 MINUTES
TOTAL TIME: 20 MINUTES

A spice rub and a fruity glaze combine to give these skinless chicken breasts a lovely finish and a fabulous flavor. If you have some extra time, you could intensify the ginger taste by adding a tablespoon of grated fresh ginger to the orange juice mixture. Serve this with a tossed salad, along with rice or roasted potatoes, for a simple, yet elegant meal.

1 teaspoon paprika
1 teaspoon dried tarragon
½ teaspoon ground ginger
4 skinless, boneless chicken breast halves (about 1 pound total)
½ cup orange juice
2 tablespoons red wine vinegar
1 tablespoon firmly packed light brown sugar
½ teaspoon salt
½ teaspoon olive oil
2 cloves garlic, minced
1 green bell pepper, cut into 1-inch squares
1 teaspoon cornstarch mixed with 1 tablespoon water

1. Preheat the broiler. In a small bowl, combine the paprika, tarragon, and ginger. Rub the mixture onto the chicken. Place the chicken on the broiler rack and sprinkle with 2 tablespoons of the orange juice. Broil the chicken 6 inches from the heat, turning once, for 8 minutes, or until just cooked through.

2. Meanwhile, in a medium saucepan, combine the remaining 6 tablespoons orange juice, the vinegar, brown sugar, salt, oil, garlic, and bell pepper. Bring to a boil over medium heat and cook until the bell pepper is crisp-tender, about 2 minutes. Stir in the cornstarch mixture and cook, stirring, until slightly thickened, about 1 minute. Place the chicken on 4 plates, spoon the sauce over, and serve.

Helpful hint: If you have any leftover chicken, use it for sandwiches the next day. Slice the chicken and serve it on French bread with Boston lettuce; add a little chutney, if you have it on hand.

FAT: 2G/11%
CALORIES: 171
SATURATED FAT: 0.5G
CARBOHYDRATE: 10G
PROTEIN: 27G
CHOLESTEROL: 66MG
SODIUM: 350MG

It's fun to have fajitas as a "serve yourself" meal: Prepare the lettuce, salsa, and the pepper-and-onion and yogurt mixtures in separate bowls, then bring out the sizzling steak strips and warm tortillas at the last moment. Fajitas can be finger food for the dexterous, but some people prefer to eat them with a knife and fork. Either way, supply plenty of napkins.

CLASSIC FAJITAS

Serves: 4
Working time: 30 minutes
Total time: 30 minutes

¼ cup fresh lime juice

1 tablespoon chili powder

3 bell peppers, mixed colors, cut into thin strips

1 red onion, thinly sliced

¾ pound well-trimmed flank steak

Eight 6-inch flour tortillas

¼ cup plain nonfat yogurt

2 tablespoons reduced-fat sour cream

1 cup mild or medium-hot prepared salsa

2 cups shredded romaine lettuce

1. Preheat the broiler. In a medium bowl, combine the lime juice, chili powder, bell peppers, and onion. With a slotted spoon, transfer the bell peppers and onion to a broiler pan. Broil 4 to 5 inches from the heat, turning occasionally, for 10 minutes.

2. Meanwhile, brush the steak with the remaining lime juice mixture. Push the vegetables to the outer edges of the broiler pan and place the steak in the center. Broil, turning once, for 10 minutes, or until medium-rare. Transfer the steak to a cutting board and with a sharp knife, cut the steak into two pieces. Then slice it into strips (see tip).

3. Place the tortillas under the broiler for 30 seconds to warm through. In a small bowl, combine the yogurt and sour cream. Place 2 tortillas on each of 4 plates. Dividing evenly, top the tortillas with the steak strips, pepper and onion mixture, salsa, lettuce, and yogurt mixture.

Helpful hint: If you have a grill topper, you can cook both the vegetables and the steak on the barbecue rather than under the broiler.

FAT: 11G/28%
CALORIES: 349
SATURATED FAT: 3.7G
CARBOHYDRATE: 38G
PROTEIN: 24G
CHOLESTEROL: 45MG
SODIUM: 926MG

TIP

Flank steak tends to be tough; for tender fajitas, cook the steak just until it is medium-rare, then carve it this way: Cut the steak in half, with the grain. Then carve it across the grain at an acute angle into ¼-inch-thick slices.

181

Barbecued Red Snapper with Corn Relish

SERVES: 4
WORKING TIME: 20 MINUTES
TOTAL TIME: 30 MINUTES

A Mexican-style corn medley with roasted peppers and scallions is the vibrant accompaniment for these snapper fillets brushed with a zesty barbecue sauce. If you have some extra time, you can marinate the fish in the refrigerator for up to eight hours. Roasted potatoes—or a yogurt-dressed new potato salad—round out the meal nicely.

¼ cup ketchup

2 tablespoons balsamic vinegar

5½ teaspoons honey

½ teaspoon dried sage

¼ teaspoon hot pepper sauce

⅛ teaspoon ground allspice

4 red snapper fillets, any visible bones removed (about 1½ pounds total)

2 cups frozen corn kernels, thawed

3 scallions, thinly sliced

½ cup diced jarred roasted red peppers

2 tablespoons fresh lime juice

½ teaspoon salt

1. In a small bowl, combine the ketchup, vinegar, 1½ teaspoons of the honey, the sage, hot pepper sauce, and allspice. Brush the snapper with half of the sauce and set aside to marinate while you make the relish and preheat the broiler.

2. Preheat the broiler. In a medium bowl, combine the corn, scallions, roasted red peppers, lime juice, salt, and the remaining 4 teaspoons honey. Set aside.

3. Broil the snapper 5 inches from the heat, brushing with the remaining sauce, for 8 minutes, or until just opaque. Divide among 4 plates and serve.

Helpful hint: For a deeper barbecue flavor, cook the marinated snapper fillets on the grill over medium heat, using a grill topper sprayed with nonstick cooking spray.

FAT: 3G/9%
CALORIES: 300
SATURATED FAT: 0.6G
CARBOHYDRATE: 32G
PROTEIN: 38G
CHOLESTEROL: 63MG
SODIUM: 611MG

VEGETABLE AND BEAN QUESADILLAS

SERVES: 4
WORKING TIME: 20 MINUTES
TOTAL TIME: 30 MINUTES

Layered tortillas, beans, corn, cheese, and salsa transform traditional quesadillas into this satisfying (and healthy) main course.

19-ounce can black beans, rinsed and drained

4 scallions, thinly sliced

1 tablespoon fresh lime juice

¾ teaspoon chili powder

½ teaspoon ground cumin

¾ teaspoon ground coriander

Twelve 6-inch low-fat flour tortillas

2 cups frozen corn kernels, thawed

1 cup shredded Monterey jack cheese (4 ounces)

½ cup mild to medium-hot prepared salsa

1. Preheat the grill. In a small bowl, mash the beans with the scallions, lime juice, chili powder, cumin, and coriander. Spread the bean mixture on 8 of the tortillas.

2. Tear off four 24-inch lengths of heavy-duty foil, fold each in half to form a 12 x 18-inch rectangle, and spray with nonstick cooking spray. Place a bean-topped tortilla, topping-side up, in the center of each rectangle. Sprinkle half of the corn, cheese, and salsa over. Top with another bean-topped tortilla, topping-side up, and sprinkle the remaining corn, cheese, and salsa over. Top each with one of the remaining tortillas and seal the packets (see hint).

3. Place the packets on the grill, cover, and grill at medium, or 6 inches from the heat, for about 12 minutes, or until the cheese has melted and the tortillas are lightly crisped. Remove the quesadillas from their packets, divide among 4 plates, and serve.

Helpful hint: Grilling packets should be made of double layers of heavy-duty foil to prevent tearing. To seal the packets, draw the short ends of the foil together; then roll the edges together, making a series of ½-inch folds. Leave the final fold up to act as a handle. Last, fold in or crimp the sides of the packet.

FAT: 13G/25%
CALORIES: 476
SATURATED FAT: 5.1G
CARBOHYDRATE: 73G
PROTEIN: 21G
CHOLESTEROL: 30MG
SODIUM: 960MG

GRILLED BUFFALO CHICKEN SANDWICHES

SERVES: 4
WORKING TIME: 20 MINUTES
TOTAL TIME: 30 MINUTES

⅓ cup plain nonfat yogurt

2 tablespoons reduced-fat sour cream

2 tablespoons reduced-fat mayonnaise

1 ounce blue cheese, crumbled

½ teaspoon Worcestershire sauce

⅓ cup jarred roasted red peppers, drained and diced

1 rib celery, diced

1 carrot, diced

1 scallion, thinly sliced

2 teaspoons paprika

1 teaspoon dried thyme

¼ teaspoon salt

¼ teaspoon freshly ground black pepper

⅛ teaspoon cayenne pepper

1 pound skinless, boneless chicken breasts

2 tablespoons fresh lime juice

Four 6-inch pita breads

2 cups shredded romaine lettuce

1. In a medium bowl, combine the yogurt, sour cream, mayonnaise, and blue cheese. Stir in the Worcestershire sauce, red peppers, celery, carrot, and scallion. Cover and refrigerate until serving time.

2. In a small bowl, combine the paprika, thyme, salt, black pepper, and cayenne. Rub the mixture onto the chicken breasts, sprinkle the lime juice over, and set aside to marinate while the grill preheats.

3. Preheat the grill to a medium heat. Spray the rack—off the grill—with nonstick cooking spray (see page 6). Grill the chicken, covered, turning once, for 8 minutes or until cooked through. Slice the pita breads open along one edge. Place the pitas on the grill for 1 minute to lightly toast them.

4. Cut the chicken into thin diagonal slices. Dividing evenly, spoon half of the vegetable mixture into the pitas, top with the chicken and the lettuce, and spoon the remaining vegetable mixture on top. Place the sandwiches on 4 plates and serve.

Helpful hint: You can marinate the chicken for up to 12 hours in the refrigerator. Bring it to room temperature before grilling.

FAT: 7G/16%
CALORIES: 384
SATURATED FAT: 2.6G
CARBOHYDRATE: 43G
PROTEIN: 36G
CHOLESTEROL: 74MG
SODIUM: 757MG

Based on the famous "hot wings" created in Buffalo, New York, these sandwiches pair well with a cool salad.

Jamaican Jerked Shrimp with Pineapple

Serves: 4
Working time: 25 minutes
Total time: 30 minutes

The Caribbean spice blend called "jerk" adds an intriguing mixture of hot (cayenne) and sweet (cinnamon and allspice) flavors to barbecued chicken, meat, and seafood. Jerk works deliciously on this shrimp—and a minty pineapple relish is the perfect Caribbean way to cool the fire.

5 scallions, thinly sliced
2 tablespoons minced fresh ginger
3 cloves garlic, minced
2 teaspoons olive oil
½ teaspoon ground allspice
½ teaspoon freshly ground black pepper
¼ teaspoon cinnamon
⅛ teaspoon cayenne pepper
¾ teaspoon salt
1 tablespoon firmly packed dark brown sugar
24 large shrimp (about 1 pound), shelled and deveined
20-ounce can juice-packed pineapple wedges, drained
1 large red bell pepper, diced
2 tablespoons fresh lime juice
2 tablespoons chopped fresh mint

1. In a large bowl, combine 4 of the scallions, 1 tablespoon plus 2 teaspoons of the ginger, the garlic, oil, allspice, black pepper, cinnamon, cayenne, ½ teaspoon of the salt, and 1 teaspoon of the brown sugar. Add the shrimp, tossing well to coat. Set aside to marinate at room temperature while the grill preheats.

2. Preheat the grill with the grill topper to a medium heat. (When ready to cook, spray the grill topper—off the grill—with nonstick cooking spray; see page 6.)

3. Meanwhile, in a medium bowl, combine the pineapple, bell pepper, lime juice, the remaining scallion, remaining 1 teaspoon ginger, remaining ¼ teaspoon salt, and remaining 2 teaspoons brown sugar. Stir in the mint and set aside.

4. Place the shrimp on the grill topper and grill, covered, turning once, for 4 minutes or until just opaque. Divide the shrimp among 4 plates and serve with the pineapple mixture on the side.

Helpful hint: You can marinate the shrimp for up to 12 hours in the refrigerator.

Fat: 4g/15%
Calories: 240
Saturated Fat: .6g
Carbohydrate: 32g
Protein: 20g
Cholesterol: 140mg
Sodium: 555mg

This recipe is so quick you'll want to start your side dish before putting the turkey under the broiler. Julienned carrots and zucchini, steamed until tender and sprinkled with lemon juice and fresh herbs, are an appetizing partner for the crumb-crusted turkey cutlets. Green beans, asparagus, or broiled tomatoes would partner well, too.

BROILED TURKEY BREAST DIJONNAISE

SERVES: 4
WORKING TIME: 5 MINUTES
TOTAL TIME: 15 MINUTES

3 tablespoons reduced-fat mayonnaise

1 tablespoon Dijon mustard

1 tablespoon fresh lemon juice

½ teaspoon dried sage

½ teaspoon salt

¼ teaspoon freshly ground black pepper

4 turkey cutlets (about 1 pound total)

⅓ cup plain dried bread crumbs

1. Preheat the broiler. In a small bowl, combine the mayonnaise, mustard, lemon juice, sage, salt, and pepper.

2. Spread the mayonnaise mixture over one side of the cutlets. Broil the turkey cutlets, topping-side up, 6 inches from the heat for 4 minutes, or until the cutlets are cooked through. Sprinkle with the bread crumbs and cook for 30 seconds to lightly brown the topping. Place the cutlets on 4 plates and serve.

Helpful hint: You can prepare the mayonnaise mixture up to 1 day in advance and refrigerate it in a covered container until needed.

TIP

Turkey cutlets, available from your butcher or grocery store, are convenient single-portion pieces cut crosswise from a boneless turkey breast half. They usually weigh about 4 ounces each. They may be cooked as is, or pounded like scallopini.

FAT: 4G/18%
CALORIES: 196
SATURATED FAT: 0.7G
CARBOHYDRATE: 9G
PROTEIN: 29G
CHOLESTEROL: 70MG
SODIUM: 586MG

STRIPED BASS WITH GREEN CURRY SAUCE

SERVES: 4
WORKING TIME: 15 MINUTES
TOTAL TIME: 25 MINUTES

Indian food is not the only cuisine that takes advantage of curry. Thai curries—like this one—are blended from ingredients such as fresh chilies, scallions, cilantro, lime juice, and a range of spices from sweet to hot; coconut cream stirred into curry sauces serves to tame the fire. Here, flaked coconut adds flavor but little fat to this lively sauce. Serve with a salad.

½ cup packed fresh cilantro or parsley leaves

2 scallions, cut into large pieces

2 tablespoons fresh lime juice

3 tablespoons flaked coconut

1 jalapeño pepper, seeded and sliced

1½ teaspoons ground cumin

¾ teaspoon salt

½ teaspoon freshly ground black pepper

1 cup long-grain rice

1 teaspoon turmeric

4 striped bass fillets, skin on, any visible bones removed (about 1½ pounds total)

1. In a food processor or blender, combine the cilantro, scallions, lime juice, coconut, jalapeño, cumin, ½ teaspoon of the salt, and the black pepper. Add ¼ cup of water and process until the green curry paste is smooth and well combined, about 30 seconds.

2. In a medium saucepan, combine the rice, 2 tablespoons of the green curry paste, 2½ cups of water, the turmeric, and the remaining ¼ teaspoon salt. Bring to a boil, reduce to a simmer, cover, and cook until the rice is tender, about 17 minutes.

3. Preheat the grill to a medium heat. Spread the remaining green curry paste on the skinless side of the fish. Spray the rack—off the grill—with nonstick cooking spray (see page 6). Grill the fish, skin-side down, for 5 minutes or until the fish is just opaque. Divide the fish and rice among 4 plates and serve.

Helpful hint: In place of the striped bass, you can substitute another lean, flavorful fish, such as sea bass, red snapper, or tilefish.

FAT: 5G/13%
CALORIES: 355
SATURATED FAT: 1.9G
CARBOHYDRATE: 41G
PROTEIN: 33G
CHOLESTEROL: 130MG
SODIUM: 540MG

MEXICAN FLANK STEAK WITH RICE AND BEAN SALAD

SERVES: 4
WORKING TIME: 15 MINUTES
TOTAL TIME: 25 MINUTES

ost Mexican restaurant meals come with "sides" of rice and beans. These extra carbohydrates improve the nutrient balance, but unfortunately the beans are usually fried in fat. Our lightened interpretation is a mixture of rice and pinto beans, tossed with fresh tomato, salsa, and fragrant herbs. The warm rice-and-bean salad accompanies salsa-marinated flank steak.

1 cup long-grain rice

½ teaspoon salt

19-ounce can pinto beans, rinsed and drained

1 tomato, coarsely chopped

¼ cup chopped fresh cilantro or basil

¼ cup plus 2 tablespoons mild to medium-hot prepared salsa

2 tablespoons fresh lime juice

1 teaspoon olive oil

1 pound well-trimmed flank steak

Four 6-inch flour tortillas

1. In a medium saucepan, bring 2¼ cups of water to a boil. Add the rice and ¼ teaspoon of the salt, reduce to a simmer, cover, and cook until the rice is tender, about 17 minutes.

2. Meanwhile, in a medium bowl, combine the remaining ¼ teaspoon salt, the beans, tomato, cilantro, and 2 tablespoons of the salsa. In another medium bowl, combine the remaining ¼ cup salsa, the lime juice, and oil. Add the flank steak and let stand while you preheat the grill.

3. Preheat the grill to medium heat. Spray the rack—off the grill—with nonstick cooking spray. Reserving the marinade, place the steak on the rack, cover, and grill, turning once and basting with some of the reserved marinade, for 7 minutes, or until medium-rare. Let the steak stand for 10 minutes before thinly slicing on the diagonal. In a large bowl, combine the rice and beans.

4. Place the tortillas on the grill for 30 seconds, turning once, to warm them. Divide the rice and bean mixture among 4 plates and place the beef slices alongside. Serve with the tortillas on the side.

Helpful hint: You can use red beans, kidney beans, or black beans in place of the pinto beans, if you like.

FAT: 12G/21%
CALORIES: 511
SATURATED FAT: 4.2G
CARBOHYDRATE: 64G
PROTEIN: 33G
CHOLESTEROL: 57MG
SODIUM: 768MG

SHRIMP KEBABS WITH LIME-BASIL ORZO

SERVES: 4
WORKING TIME: 15 MINUTES
TOTAL TIME: 20 MINUTES

Shrimp is a snap to cook, and it always finds an appreciative audience. The lime slices flavor the shrimp; discard them before eating. To serve this meal in a slightly more formal fashion, use fettuccine instead of orzo, remove the shrimp and vegetables from the skewers, and arrange them over the hot pasta.

3 tablespoons fresh lime juice
¼ cup chopped fresh parsley
1 tablespoon olive oil
2 cloves garlic, minced
½ teaspoon dried oregano
¾ teaspoon salt
24 large shrimp (about 1 pound), shelled and deveined
1 large onion, cut into 16 chunks
8 ounces orzo pasta
½ teaspoon grated lime zest
¼ cup chopped fresh basil
16 cherry tomatoes
16 very thin lime slices
1 green bell pepper, cut into 16 pieces

1. In a large bowl, combine the lime juice, parsley, 2 teaspoons of the oil, the garlic, oregano, and ¼ teaspoon of the salt. Add the shrimp and onion, tossing to coat. Set aside to marinate while you preheat the grill and prepare the orzo.

2. Preheat the grill to a medium heat. (When ready to cook, spray the rack—off the grill—with nonstick cooking spray; see page 6.)

3. In a medium pot of boiling water, cook the orzo until just tender. Drain, transfer to a large bowl, and stir in the remaining 1 teaspoon oil, the lime zest, remaining ½ teaspoon salt, and the basil. Cover loosely to keep warm.

4. Alternately thread the shrimp, onion, tomatoes, lime slices, and bell pepper onto 8 skewers. Grill the kebabs, covered, turning once, for 4 minutes or until the shrimp are just opaque. Divide the orzo among 4 plates, place 2 skewers on each plate, and serve.

Helpful hints: You can marinate the shrimp for up to 1 hour, if you like. To shell fresh shrimp, pull apart the shell at the belly end of the shrimp with your fingers, splitting the shell, and remove. We've left the tails on, but you can remove them if you prefer.

FAT: 6G/14%
CALORIES: 393
SATURATED FAT: .9G
CARBOHYDRATE: 57G
PROTEIN: 28G
CHOLESTEROL: 140MG
SODIUM: 560MG

CHICKEN REUBEN SANDWICHES

SERVES: 4
WORKING TIME: 20 MINUTES
TOTAL TIME: 20 MINUTES

Corned beef and Russian dressing go into the classic Reuben; chicken and a flavorful yogurt dressing transform it into lighter fare.

2 tablespoons ketchup

2 tablespoons plain nonfat yogurt

2 tablespoons mango chutney

1 tablespoon Dijon mustard

1 tablespoon fresh lemon juice

8 slices (1 ounce each) rye bread

10 ounces cooked, skinned chicken breasts, cut crosswise into thin slices

1 cup sauerkraut, rinsed and drained

¾ cup shredded Swiss cheese (3 ounces)

1. Preheat the broiler. In a small bowl, combine the ketchup, yogurt, chutney, mustard, and lemon juice. Transfer half of the the ketchup mixture to another small bowl and set aside. Spread the remaining ketchup mixture on one side of each slice of bread. Place the chicken on top of the bread and broil 6 inches from the heat for 1 minute to warm the chicken through.

2. Spoon the reserved ketchup mixture over the chicken. Top each sandwich with sauerkraut and cheese and cook until the sauerkraut is hot and the cheese is melted, about 1 minute. Place 2 open-face sandwiches on each of 4 plates and serve.

Helpful hints: You can buy the chicken for this recipe at a supermarket deli or you can use leftover roast chicken. To cook it quickly yourself, use the microwave: Place 1 pound of skinless, boneless chicken breasts in a shallow microwave-safe dish. Loosely cover the dish with plastic wrap and cook on high power for 5 minutes, rotating the dish once. Let stand for 5 minutes before slicing.

FAT: 10G/23%
CALORIES: 391
SATURATED FAT: 4.9G
CARBOHYDRATE: 38G
PROTEIN: 34G
CHOLESTEROL: 80MG
SODIUM: 890MG

CHILI BURGERS

SERVES: 4
WORKING TIME: 20 MINUTES
TOTAL TIME: 30 MINUTES

1 pound well-trimmed top round of beef, cut into chunks

½ cup canned kidney beans, rinsed and drained

½ cup frozen corn kernels, thawed

½ cup chili sauce

2 tablespoons plain dried bread crumbs

1 egg white

2 teaspoons chili powder

¾ teaspoon ground cumin

½ teaspoon dried oregano

¼ teaspoon salt

4 hamburger buns, split

4 leaves of leaf lettuce

1. Preheat the grill to a medium heat. (When ready to cook, spray the rack—off the grill—with nonstick cooking spray; see page 6.)

2. In a food processor, process the beef until coarsely ground, about 30 seconds. Transfer to a large bowl. Add the beans to the processor and process until coarsely ground, about 30 seconds. Transfer the beans to the bowl and add the corn, ¼ cup of the chili sauce, the bread crumbs, egg white, chili powder, cumin, oregano, and salt, mixing to combine. Shape into 4 patties.

3. Grill the burgers, covered, turning occasionally, for 10 minutes or until cooked through. Grill the buns, cut-sides down, for 30 seconds to lightly toast. Place the buns on 4 plates and top with lettuce and a burger. Dividing evenly, top the burgers with the remaining ¼ cup of chili sauce and serve.

Helpful hint: Kidney beans have a "beefy" flavor, but you can use the same amount of another type of bean—pintos, for instance—if you have some on hand.

FAT: 7G/17%
CALORIES: 379
SATURATED FAT: 2G
CARBOHYDRATE: 42G
PROTEIN: 36G
CHOLESTEROL: 71MG
SODIUM: 986MG

Adding beans to ground beef gives you a deliciously thick but low-fat burger. Serve with a yogurt-dressed slaw.

197

BROILED SWORDFISH WITH SPICY HONEY SAUCE

SERVES: 4
WORKING TIME: 10 MINUTES
TOTAL TIME: 15 MINUTES

½ teaspoon grated lemon zest

¼ cup fresh lemon juice

¼ cup honey

1 teaspoon turmeric

¾ teaspoon ground cumin

½ teaspoon ground ginger

½ teaspoon salt

½ teaspoon hot pepper sauce

Four swordfish steaks (about 1½ pounds total)

1 small red bell pepper, finely diced

2 tablespoons chopped fresh parsley

1. Preheat the broiler. In a small bowl, combine the lemon zest, lemon juice, honey, turmeric, cumin, ginger, salt, and hot pepper sauce.

2. Place the swordfish on the rack and sprinkle with 2 tablespoons of the lemon-honey mixture. Broil the swordfish 6 inches from the heat, turning once, for 6 minutes, or until lightly colored and just opaque. Stir the bell pepper and parsley into the remaining honey-lemon mixture. Divide the fish among 4 plates, spoon the sauce over the fish, and serve.

Helpful hint: Depending on the fish's diet, swordfish flesh when raw can vary from pale beige to rosy pink; whatever its original shade, it will turn a cream color when cooked.

FAT: 6G/21%
CALORIES: 261
SATURATED FAT: 1.7G
CARBOHYDRATE: 21G
PROTEIN: 31G
CHOLESTEROL: 59MG
SODIUM: 430MG

A welcome change from steak, swordfish is just as meaty and satisfying. Turmeric in the honey-lemon basting sauce turns the fish a lovely golden color. As a side dish, lightly sauté some pre-shredded coleslaw mix, then toss it with a light, tangy rice-vinegar dressing—or serve store-bought slaw if you're pressed for time.

*C*orn, one of the focal points of Mexican cuisine, is partnered with zucchini and tomatoes in this meatless adaptation of a Mexican favorite. The vegetables are layered over a hearty tomato-basil paste and a low-fat cheese sauce, and are then topped with part-skim mozzarella. Heating the tostadas on a covered grill imparts a hint of smoky flavor.

ZUCCHINI AND CORN TOSTADAS

SERVES: 4
WORKING TIME: 25 MINUTES
TOTAL TIME: 25 MINUTES

½ cup low-fat (1%) cottage
cheese

2 tablespoons nonfat cream
cheese

¼ cup grated Parmesan cheese

¼ cup no-salt-added tomato
paste

2 tablespoons chopped fresh basil

Eight 6-inch flour tortillas

2 cups frozen corn kernels,
thawed

1 zucchini, coarsely grated

½ cup chopped scallions

4 plum tomatoes, thinly sliced

1 cup shredded part-skim
mozzarella cheese (4 ounces)

1. In a blender or food processor, combine the cottage cheese, cream cheese, and Parmesan and process to a smooth purée. Set aside. In a small bowl, combine the tomato paste and basil.

2. Preheat the grill with a grill topper (see tip). Spray the grill topper—off the grill—with nonstick cooking spray. Place the tortillas on the grill topper and grill at medium, or 6 inches from the heat, turning once, for 1 minute, or until lightly browned and crisp.

3. Dividing evenly, spread the tortillas first with the tomato paste mixture, then the cottage cheese mixture, then with the corn, zucchini, scallions, tomato slices, and mozzarella. Return the tortillas to the grill topper, cover, and cook for 2 minutes, or until the cheese is melted and the topping is heated through. Divide the tostadas among 4 plates and serve.

Helpful hint: A grill topper is a flat sheet of metal perforated at regular intervals with small, round holes. It works much better than a regular wire grill rack when you're cooking delicate foods. If you don't have a grill topper, see the tip at right for how to make one from foil.

FAT: 10G/25%
CALORIES: 357
SATURATED FAT: 4.6G
CARBOHYDRATE: 49G
PROTEIN: 21G
CHOLESTEROL: 22MG
SODIUM: 585MG

SKILLET & OVEN DISHES

Left, Buffalo Chicken Strips
Above, Chicken Milanese

CHICKEN AND APPLES NORMANDY

SERVES: 4
WORKING TIME: 20 MINUTES
TOTAL TIME: 30 MINUTES

2 Granny Smith apples, cored
and chopped

2 red bell peppers, cut into
½-inch chunks

1 large onion, chopped

1½ cups apple cider or natural
apple juice

¼ cup cider vinegar

¾ teaspoon salt

1 tablespoon flour

¼ teaspoon freshly ground
black pepper

4 skinless, boneless chicken
breast halves (about 1 pound
total)

2 teaspoons olive oil

3 tablespoons light sour cream

1. In a medium saucepan, combine the apples, bell peppers, onion, apple cider, vinegar, and ½ teaspoon of the salt. Bring to a boil over high heat, reduce to a simmer, and cook, partially covered, until the apples and vegetables begin to soften, about 7 minutes.

2. Meanwhile, on a plate, combine the flour, black pepper, and the remaining ¼ teaspoon salt. Dredge the chicken in the flour mixture, shaking off the excess. In a large nonstick skillet, heat the oil until hot but not smoking over medium heat. Add the chicken and cook, turning once, until golden brown, about 5 minutes. Add the apple mixture and bring to a boil over medium-high heat. Reduce to a simmer, cover, and cook until the chicken is cooked through, about 10 minutes longer.

3. With a slotted spoon, transfer the chicken to 4 serving plates. Stir the sour cream into the apple mixture, spoon over the chicken, and serve.

Suggested accompaniments: Wide noodles. For dessert, a reduced-calorie lemon pudding garnished with chopped crystallized ginger.

Tart apples and silky sour cream create a richly mellow sauce for this chicken. To make the dish nutritionally sensible without affecting the luscious flavor, we've used light sour cream and skinless chicken breasts. Be sure to serve over noodles or rice to soak up every bit of this delectable sauce.

FAT: 6G/19%
CALORIES: 284
SATURATED FAT: 1.5G
CARBOHYDRATE: 31G
PROTEIN: 28G
CHOLESTEROL: 70MG
SODIUM: 491MG

BRAISED PORK WITH TOMATOES AND ROSEMARY

SERVES: 4
WORKING TIME: 20 MINUTES
TOTAL TIME: 25 MINUTES

*A*n herb with a bold personality, rosemary announces its presence with a compelling fragrance and a robust flavor. So it's best matched with foods that can also hold their own—in this case, thick cutlets of pork loin, tomatoes, red wine, garlic, and mushrooms. The pasta (you could substitute rice for a change) serves as a foil for all that flavor.

8 ounces orzo pasta

2 tablespoons flour

¾ teaspoon salt

½ teaspoon freshly ground black pepper

10 ounces well-trimmed center-cut pork loin, cut into 4 slices

1 tablespoon olive oil

3 cloves garlic, slivered

¼ pound mushrooms, thickly sliced

⅔ cup dry red wine

2 cups no-salt-added canned tomatoes, chopped with their juices

½ teaspoon dried rosemary, crumbled

⅛ teaspoon red pepper flakes

1 teaspoon cornstarch mixed with 1 tablespoon water

¼ cup chopped fresh parsley

1. In a large pot of boiling water, cook the pasta until just tender. Drain well.

2. Meanwhile, on a sheet of waxed paper, combine the flour, ¼ teaspoon of the salt, and the black pepper. Dredge the pork in the flour mixture, shaking off the excess. In a large nonstick skillet, heat the oil until hot but not smoking over high heat. Add the pork and cook, stirring frequently, until lightly browned, about 1 minute per side. Transfer the pork to a plate.

3. Add the garlic to the skillet and cook, stirring frequently, until softened, about 3 minutes. Add the mushrooms and cook, stirring frequently, until tender, about 4 minutes. Add the wine, increase the heat to high, and cook until the liquid has reduced by half, about 4 minutes.

4. Stir the tomatoes, rosemary, red pepper flakes, and the remaining ½ teaspoon salt into the pan. Bring to a boil, reduce to a simmer, and return the pork to the pan. Cook until the pork is just cooked through and the sauce is flavorful, about 2 minutes. Add the cornstarch mixture and cook, stirring, until slightly thickened, about 1 minute. Stir in the parsley. Divide the pasta among 4 bowls, spoon the pork mixture alongside, and serve.

Helpful hint: Chilling the pork in the freezer will make it easier to slice.

FAT: 8G/18%
CALORIES: 396
SATURATED FAT: 1.9G
CARBOHYDRATE: 54G
PROTEIN: 25G
CHOLESTEROL: 45MG
SODIUM: 483MG

CHEESEBURGER PIZZAS

SERVES: 4
WORKING TIME: 15 MINUTES
TOTAL TIME: 30 MINUTES

Maybe you thought the only way to "slim down" pizza was to leave off the cheese. But these individual pizzas, topped with ground beef and two cheeses, have an impressively low total fat content. Cheddar and Parmesan have more flavor impact than mozzarella, so you can use less. Pair the pizzas with a big green salad; season the vinaigrette with a pinch of oregano.

3 tablespoons yellow cornmeal

1 pound store-bought pizza dough

6 ounces well-trimmed top round of beef, cut into chunks

15-ounce can no-salt-added whole tomatoes, coarsely chopped and drained

3 tablespoons ketchup

2 cloves garlic, minced

½ teaspoon dried thyme

¼ teaspoon red pepper flakes

2 scallions, sliced

¾ cup shredded Cheddar cheese (3 ounces)

3 tablespoons grated Parmesan cheese

1. Preheat the oven to 475°. Spray 2 baking sheets with nonstick cooking spray. Sprinkle each sheet evenly with the cornmeal. Divide the dough into 4 pieces and roll each piece into a 7-inch circle. Place 2 circles of dough on each of the prepared baking sheets. Bake for 6 minutes, or until cooked but not browned (the dough will puff up, but will collapse when removed from the oven). Leave the oven on.

2. Meanwhile, in a food processor, process the beef until finely ground. In a medium bowl, combine the tomatoes, ketchup, garlic, thyme, and red pepper flakes.

3. Spread the tomato mixture onto the cooked pizza bases. Crumble the beef evenly over the tops of the pizzas. Sprinkle with the scallions, Cheddar, and Parmesan. Bake for 8 minutes, or until the beef is cooked through and the cheeses are melted and bubbling. Remove and let stand for 5 minutes before dividing among 4 plates and serving.

Helpful hints: You can buy ready-to-use pizza dough from many pizzerias and Italian specialty stores; you may also find it in the dairy case in the supermarket. Or, you can use the refrigerated dough that comes in a roll.

FAT: 14G/25%
CALORIES: 507
SATURATED FAT: 6.5G
CARBOHYDRATE: 67G
PROTEIN: 28G
CHOLESTEROL: 50MG
SODIUM: 997MG

BUFFALO CHICKEN STRIPS

SERVES: 4
WORKING TIME: 15 MINUTES
TOTAL TIME: 25 MINUTES

½ cup low-fat (1%) milk

½ teaspoon honey

1 pound skinless, boneless chicken breasts, cut into 1-inch-wide strips

1 cup crushed cornflakes (about 2 cups uncrushed)

¼ teaspoon ground ginger

¼ teaspoon dried thyme

¼ teaspoon dried rosemary

1 cup plain nonfat yogurt

2 ounces blue cheese, crumbled

½ cup minced scallions

6 drops hot pepper sauce

2 carrots, cut into sticks

2 ribs celery with leaves, cut into sticks

1. Preheat the oven to 400°. Line a baking sheet with foil and spray with nonstick cooking spray. In a shallow bowl, combine the milk and honey and stir to blend. Add the chicken strips, stir to coat, and let stand for 10 minutes.

2. Meanwhile, on a plate, combine the cornflakes, ginger, thyme, and rosemary. Dip the chicken strips into the cornflake mixture to coat thoroughly, gently pressing cornflakes into the chicken. Place the chicken on the prepared baking sheet and bake for 8 minutes, or until the chicken is crisp, golden, and cooked through.

3. In a medium bowl, combine the yogurt, blue cheese, scallions, and hot pepper sauce and stir to blend. Place the chicken and the carrot and celery sticks on 4 plates and serve with the blue cheese dip.

Suggested accompaniments: Iced herbal tea, and a dessert of raspberry sorbet served with miniature nonfat cookies.

FAT: 6G/15%
CALORIES: 357
SATURATED FAT: 3.3G
CARBOHYDRATE: 37G
PROTEIN: 37G
CHOLESTEROL: 79MG
SODIUM: 716MG

For this popular finger food, we've substituted lean chicken breast for the usual wings and then soaked the strips in low-fat milk and honey for extra tenderness. The creamy base for the dip is nonfat yogurt rather than sour cream. To crush cornflakes, place them in a resealable plastic bag, seal, and run a rolling pin or heavy glass over the bag.

MEXICAN-STYLE PIZZA

SERVES: 4
WORKING TIME: 10 MINUTES
TOTAL TIME: 25 MINUTES

Ten 6-inch corn tortillas

4 ounces Monterey jack cheese, shredded (about 1 cup)

1¾ cups canned black beans, rinsed and drained

2 tablespoons fresh lime juice

½ teaspoon ground coriander

½ teaspoon dried oregano

½ cup minced scallions

½ cup chopped fresh cilantro

1 green bell pepper, cut into thin strips

2 plum tomatoes, thinly sliced

1. Preheat the oven to 400°. Spray a baking sheet with nonstick cooking spray. Arrange the tortillas in a circle on the prepared baking sheet, overlapping them slightly. Sprinkle ¾ cup of the cheese on top. Set aside.

2. In a medium bowl, stir together the beans, lime juice, 1 tablespoon of water, the coriander, and oregano. With a potato masher or the back of a spoon, mash the mixture until smooth. Add the scallions and cilantro and stir well to combine.

3. Spread the bean mixture over the cheese on the tortillas. Scatter half of the bell pepper over, arrange the tomatoes on top, and scatter the remaining pepper over. Sprinkle the remaining ¼ cup cheese on top and bake for 10 minutes, or until the tortillas are crisp and the cheese is melted.

Suggested accompaniments: Lemonade, and a green salad with chopped black olives drizzled with a citrus vinaigrette. Follow with fat-free pound cake slices topped with warm apricot jam.

FAT: 11G/29%
CALORIES: 341
SATURATED FAT: 5.3G
CARBOHYDRATE: 46G
PROTEIN: 16G
CHOLESTEROL: 30MG
SODIUM: 485MG

This eye-catching pizza takes practically no time to assemble since the crust is simply corn tortillas. You just layer on the cheese, black beans, and other flavorful ingredients. The meaty plum tomatoes hold their shape particularly well during the baking. To serve, cut the pizza into wedges with kitchen scissors or a pizza wheel cutter.

Hidden inside these Italian-style involtini (rolled cutlets) is a delicious bread-and-Parmesan filling and a hint of mustard. The sauce is bright with cubes of carrot and zucchini, along with the luxurious surprise of velvety pine nuts. To do the dish justice, be sure to use a good-quality Parmesan (preferably imported), freshly grated.

Braised Pork with Pine Nuts and Parmesan

Serves: 4
Working time: 20 minutes
Total time: 30 minutes

8 ounces orzo pasta

½ pound well-trimmed pork loin, cut into 8 slices and pounded (see page 8) ⅛ inch thick

4 teaspoons Dijon mustard

½ teaspoon salt

2 slices (2 ounces total) firm-textured white bread, finely crumbled

¼ cup grated Parmesan cheese

2 tablespoons flour

2 teaspoons olive oil

2 carrots, finely diced

1 zucchini, finely diced

1¼ cups reduced-sodium chicken broth, defatted

¾ teaspoon grated lemon zest

2 tablespoon fresh lemon juice

⅓ cup chopped fresh mint

½ teaspoon dried rosemary, crumbled

¼ teaspoon freshly ground black pepper

2 tablespoons pine nuts

1. In a large pot of boiling water, cook the pasta until just tender. Drain well.

2. Meanwhile, brush the tops of the pork slices with the mustard. Sprinkle ¼ teaspoon of the salt over. Sprinkle the bread crumbs and Parmesan over, lightly pressing down (see tip; top photo). Roll up the pork from one short end and secure with toothpicks (bottom photo).

3. Dredge the pork rolls in the flour, shaking off and reserving the excess. In a large nonstick skillet, heat the oil until hot but not smoking over medium heat. Cook the pork, turning frequently, until lightly browned, about 3 minutes. Transfer the pork rolls to a plate. Add the carrots and zucchini to the skillet. Stir in 1 cup of the broth, the lemon zest, lemon juice, mint, rosemary, pepper, and the remaining ¼ teaspoon salt. Bring to a boil, reduce to a simmer, and return the pork rolls to the pan. Cover, and cook until the pork is tender and the sauce is flavorful, about 10 minutes.

4. In a small bowl, combine the remaining ¼ cup broth and the reserved flour mixture. Stir the broth mixture into the skillet along with the pine nuts and cook, stirring, until the sauce is slightly thickened, about 2 minutes. Divide the pasta among 4 plates. Remove the toothpicks from the pork rolls and serve the pork rolls and vegetable mixture alongside the pasta.

Fat: 11g/22%
Calories: 444
Saturated Fat: 3g
Carbohydrate: 59g
Protein: 26g
Cholesterol: 38mg
Sodium: 786mg

TIP

After brushing the tops of the pork slices with mustard and seasoning them with salt, press the crumbs and Parmesan into the surface of the meat. Starting at one short end, roll up the pork with the breading inside. Secure the rolls with toothpicks.

CHICKEN AND BASMATI RICE

SERVES: 4
WORKING TIME: 15 MINUTES
TOTAL TIME: 30 MINUTES

1 teaspoon olive oil

3 scallions, thinly sliced

2 cloves garlic, minced

1⅓ cups basmati rice

2 cups reduced-sodium chicken broth, defatted

½ teaspoon salt

½ pound skinless, boneless chicken thighs, cut into ½-inch cubes

2 carrots, shredded

¼ cup raisins

2 tablespoons sliced almonds

2 tablespoons chopped fresh cilantro or parsley

1. In a large saucepan, heat the oil until hot but not smoking over medium heat. Add the scallions and garlic and cook until the garlic is fragrant, about 30 seconds. Add the rice, stirring to coat. Stir in the broth, 1½ cups of water, and the salt and bring to a boil. Reduce to a simmer, cover, and cook until the rice is almost tender, about 10 minutes.

2. Stir in the chicken, carrots, and raisins. Cover and cook until the chicken is cooked through and the rice is tender, about 7 minutes. Stir in the almonds and cilantro, divide among 4 plates, and serve.

Helpful hint: Chicken thighs are particularly flavorful and juicy, but if you prefer white meat, substitute ½ pound of skinless, boneless chicken breasts and slightly reduce the cooking time in step 2.

FAT: 5G/14%
CALORIES: 332
SATURATED FAT: 0.7G
CARBOHYDRATE: 61G
PROTEIN: 17G
CHOLESTEROL: 29MG
SODIUM: 669MG

Here's the quick version of an Indian biryani, which is an elaboration on rice pilaf. For the classic biryani—a celebratory dish—the chicken is marinated for several hours, then combined with rice and baked for another hour. This dish requires just 15 minutes of attention but offers an equally satisfying combination of aromas and flavors.

Ham and Potato Hash

SERVES: 4
WORKING TIME: 30 MINUTES
TOTAL TIME: 30 MINUTES

A splendid homestyle supper, this sage-scented hash would also make a terrific brunch dish, with or without eggs.

1½ pounds all-purpose potatoes, peeled and cut into ¼-inch dice

4 teaspoons olive oil

2 onions, finely chopped

2 green bell peppers, cut into ¼-inch dice

2 Granny Smith apples, cored and cut into ¼-inch dice

5 ounces thinly sliced baked ham, slivered

⅔ cup reduced-sodium chicken broth, defatted

1 tablespoon Dijon mustard

½ teaspoon sage

¼ teaspoon salt

¼ teaspoon freshly ground black pepper

1. In a large pot of boiling water, cook the potatoes until firm-tender, about 5 minutes. Drain.

2. Meanwhile, in a large nonstick skillet, heat the oil until hot but not smoking over medium heat. Add the onions and cook, stirring frequently, until lightly browned, about 5 minutes.

3. Add the bell peppers, apples, and potatoes to the pan and cook, stirring frequently, until the apples have softened, about 5 minutes. Add the ham and cook, stirring frequently, until crisped, about 4 minutes.

4. Stir the broth, mustard, sage, salt, and black pepper into the skillet and cook, stirring frequently, until the hash is richly flavored and slightly crusty, about 5 minutes. Divide among 4 plates and serve.

Helpful hint: You can cook the potatoes up to 12 hours in advance; drain them and refrigerate in a covered bowl. Bring the potatoes to room temperature before making the hash, and allow a little extra time for them to heat up in step 3.

FAT: 7G/23%
CALORIES: 280
SATURATED FAT: 1.3G
CARBOHYDRATE: 43G
PROTEIN: 12G
CHOLESTEROL: 19MG
SODIUM: 756MG

CREAMY SOLE WITH POTATOES AND MUSHROOMS

SERVES: 4
WORKING TIME: 15 MINUTES
TOTAL TIME: 25 MINUTES

1 baking potato, peeled and
thinly sliced

½ teaspoon dried marjoram

½ teaspoon paprika

4 sole or flounder fillets, any
visible bones removed (about
1½ pounds total)

2 teaspoons olive oil

2 cloves garlic, slivered

½ pound mushrooms, trimmed
and thinly sliced

1 cup reduced-sodium chicken
broth, defatted

½ teaspoon salt

2 tablespoons flour

⅔ cup evaporated low-fat milk

6 tablespoons shredded
Cheddar cheese (1½ ounces)

1. In a medium pot of boiling water, cook the potato until almost tender, about 5 minutes. Drain well. Meanwhile, sprinkle the marjoram and paprika over the sole fillets and roll the fillets up. Set aside.

2. In a large nonstick skillet, heat the oil until hot but not smoking over medium heat. Add the garlic and mushrooms and cook until the mushrooms are almost tender, about 4 minutes.

3. Stir in the potato slices, broth, and salt and bring to a boil. Whisk in the flour and evaporated milk and return to a boil. Reduce the heat to a simmer, place the fish on top of the vegetables, cover, and cook until the fish rolls are just opaque in the center, about 7 minutes. Sprinkle the cheese over the fish and cook, uncovered, until just melted, about 1 minute. Divide the fish rolls and potato mixture among 4 plates and serve.

Helpful hint: If you're in a real hurry, you can buy sliced mushrooms from a supermarket salad bar, but don't buy them more than a day in advance or they'll turn dark brown.

FAT: 9G/25%
CALORIES: 323
SATURATED FAT: 3.1G
CARBOHYDRATE: 18G
PROTEIN: 41G
CHOLESTEROL: 100MG
SODIUM: 687MG

H*ere's
a wonderfully soothing
meal of skillet-
scalloped potatoes,
herbed steamed fish,
and a cheese topping.*

*T*he
aroma of the sweet
Middle Eastern
mixture of ginger and
cinnamon will perfume
the kitchen as the
chicken simmers in its
savory broth. For this
simple twist on the
classic Moroccan stew,
we've used quick-
cooking couscous, a
pasta that requires just
a few minutes of
steeping in the
hot broth or other
liquid.

220

Spiced Chicken Couscous

SERVES: 4
WORKING TIME: 15 MINUTES
TOTAL TIME: 20 MINUTES

3 cups reduced-sodium chicken
broth, defatted

1½ teaspoons ground cumin

1 teaspoon turmeric

1 teaspoon ground ginger

1 teaspoon cinnamon

½ teaspoon freshly ground
black pepper

8 drops hot pepper sauce

1⅓ cups couscous

1½ teaspoons fresh lemon juice

1 pound skinless, boneless
chicken thighs, cut into
1½-inch chunks

3 zucchini, cut into 3-inch-
long strips

2 carrots, cut into 3-inch-long
strips

¼ cup dark raisins

3 tablespoons blanched slivered
almonds, toasted

1. In a large saucepan, combine the broth, 1½ cups of water, the cumin, turmeric, ginger, cinnamon, black pepper, and hot pepper sauce. Bring to a boil over high heat and cook for 3 minutes.

2. In a medium bowl, combine the couscous and lemon juice. Transfer 1 cup of the boiling broth to the bowl, cover, and let stand until the couscous has softened, about 5 minutes.

3. Meanwhile, add the chicken, zucchini, carrots, and more water to cover, if necessary, to the remaining broth. Return to a boil, reduce to a simmer, cover, and cook until the chicken is cooked through, about 5 minutes.

4. Fluff the couscous with a fork (see tip) and spoon onto 4 serving plates. With a slotted spoon, remove the chicken and vegetables from the broth, place on top of the couscous, and sprinkle with the raisins and almonds. Pour the broth into a sauceboat and serve along with the stew.

Suggested accompaniments: Toasted pita bread, and a Bibb lettuce salad with a citrus vinaigrette.

TIP

Traditional North African couscous is fine-grained cracked semolina, which takes a long time and quite a bit of fussing to prepare. But the couscous found in supermarkets is a precooked semolina pasta that requires only steeping. Use a fork to fluff the softened couscous, which will separate the grains without crushing them.

FAT: 9G/17%
CALORIES: 488
SATURATED FAT: 1.6G
CARBOHYDRATE: 66G
PROTEIN: 35G
CHOLESTEROL: 94MG
SODIUM: 609MG

SHRIMP ALL'ARRABBIATA

SERVES: 4
WORKING TIME: 25 MINUTES
TOTAL TIME: 25 MINUTES

In Italian, arrabbiata means "angry," and appropriately, the shrimp in this dish are bathed in a fiery tomato sauce. The sauce, seasoned with red pepper flakes, oregano, ginger, and rosemary, is brightened with bits of bell pepper and olives. For a colorful side dish, toss together a salad of radicchio, baby spinach, and other tender greens.

1 teaspoon olive oil

1 red bell pepper, diced

2 cloves garlic, minced

¾ cup bottled clam juice

1 tomato, chopped

¼ cup Calamata or other brine-cured black olives, pitted and slivered

¾ teaspoon dried oregano

½ teaspoon ground ginger

½ teaspoon dried rosemary

¼ teaspoon red pepper flakes

¼ teaspoon salt

1 pound medium shrimp, shelled and deveined

¾ teaspoon cornstarch mixed with 1 teaspoon water

1. In a large nonstick skillet, heat the oil until hot but not smoking over medium heat. Add the bell pepper and garlic and cook, stirring, until well coated, about 1 minute. Add ¼ cup of the clam juice and cook until the pepper is softened, about 3 minutes. Stir in the remaining ½ cup clam juice, the tomato, olives, oregano, ginger, rosemary, red pepper flakes, and salt and cook for 3 minutes to reduce slightly.

2. Add the shrimp to the pan and cook until the shrimp are just opaque, about 2 minutes. Bring to a boil, stir in the cornstarch mixture, and cook, stirring, until slightly thickened, about 1 minute. Divide the shrimp mixture among 4 plates and serve.

Helpful hint: Clam juice is ideal for seafood sauces, but you can substitute chicken broth if necessary.

FAT: 4G/26%
CALORIES: 139
SATURATED FAT: .6G
CARBOHYDRATE: 5G
PROTEIN: 19G
CHOLESTEROL: 140MG
SODIUM: 448MG

WELSH RAREBIT WITH BROCCOLI

SERVES: 4
WORKING TIME: 10 MINUTES
TOTAL TIME: 20 MINUTES

*W*hether you call it "rarebit" or "rabbit," this cozy supper dish is an all-around favorite. Traditionally, rarebit is made by simply melting cheese with beer or ale, which adds up to a delicious but terribly rich dish. We've based our rarebit on a low-fat white sauce instead, with enough Cheddar for full flavor. Broccoli florets stirred into the rarebit make it a more well-rounded meal.

2 cups low-fat (1%) milk
¼ cup flour
½ teaspoon dried oregano
½ teaspoon salt
¼ teaspoon cayenne pepper
¼ teaspoon freshly ground black pepper
1 red bell pepper, diced
2 cups frozen broccoli florets
¾ cup shredded Cheddar cheese (3 ounces)
2 teaspoons yellow mustard
8 slices (1 ounce each) white sandwich bread, toasted

1. In a large saucepan, whisk the milk into the flour. Bring to a boil over medium heat and stir in the oregano, salt, cayenne, and black pepper. Reduce the heat to a simmer and cook until slightly thickened and smooth, about 4 minutes.

2. Stir in the bell pepper and broccoli and simmer until the bell pepper is tender, about 4 minutes. Add the Cheddar and mustard and stir just until the cheese is melted, about 1 minute. Place 2 slices of toast on each of 4 plates, spoon the vegetable and cheese mixture over the toast, and serve.

Helpful hint: If the broccoli florets are frozen into a clump, place them in a colander and run tap water over them until the florets can be separated.

FAT: 11G/29%
CALORIES: 345
SATURATED FAT: 5.8G
CARBOHYDRATE: 45G
PROTEIN: 17G
CHOLESTEROL: 28MG
SODIUM: 820MG

For classic veal Milanese, veal scallopini are dipped in whole beaten eggs, coated with bread crumbs and Parmesan, and fried in butter. For this trimmed-down version, chicken breasts are dipped in Parmesan, egg whites, and bread crumbs, then baked in the oven with a mere drizzling of olive oil. Round out the meal with roasted new potatoes and Italian green beans.

CHICKEN MILANESE

SERVES: 4
WORKING TIME: 15 MINUTES
TOTAL TIME: 25 MINUTES

½ cup plain dried bread crumbs

¼ cup grated Parmesan cheese

1 egg white beaten with
1 tablespoon water

4 skinless, boneless chicken breast
halves (about 1 pound total)

2 teaspoons olive oil

⅔ cup dry white wine

½ cup reduced-sodium chicken
broth, defatted

2 tablespoons balsamic vinegar

3 cloves garlic, minced

2 teaspoons anchovy paste

½ teaspoon dried rosemary

1 teaspoon cornstarch mixed
with 1 tablespoon water

2 tablespoons chopped fresh
parsley

1. Preheat the oven to 400°. Line a large baking sheet with foil.

2. Place the bread crumbs, Parmesan, and egg white mixture in 3 shallow bowls. Dip the chicken into the Parmesan (see tip, top photo), then into the egg white (middle photo), and finally into the bread crumbs (bottom photo). Place the chicken on the prepared baking sheet and drizzle with the oil. Bake for 10 minutes, or until the chicken is cooked through and golden brown.

3. Meanwhile, in a large skillet, combine the wine, broth, vinegar, garlic, anchovy paste, and rosemary and bring to a boil over medium heat. Boil, stirring occasionally, until the garlic is tender and the sauce is slightly reduced, about 4 minutes. Stir in the cornstarch mixture and cook, stirring, until slightly thickened, about 1 minute. Add the parsley, stirring to combine. Add the chicken and turn to coat with the sauce. Place the chicken on 4 plates and serve.

Helpful hint: Anchovy paste comes in tubes, making it a convenient way to keep anchovies on hand. Keep the tube tightly capped and store it in the refrigerator. Anchovy paste will keep for 6 months or longer.

FAT: 6G/20%
CALORIES: 268
SATURATED FAT: 1.9G
CARBOHYDRATE: 12G
PROTEIN: 32G
CHOLESTEROL: 71MG
SODIUM: 491MG

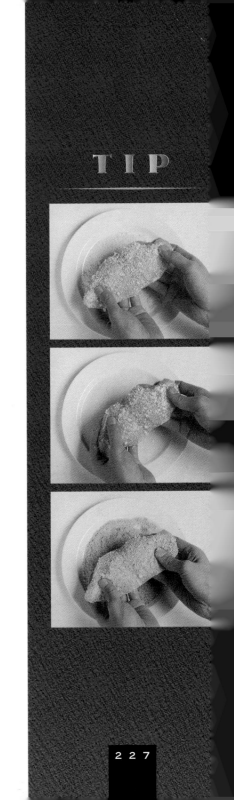

TIP

SWEET AND SOUR BRAISED PORK PATTIES

SERVES: 4
WORKING TIME: 20 MINUTES
TOTAL TIME: 30 MINUTES

T his meal of piquantly sauced pork patties and vegetables served over hot, fluffy rice may seem like a lot of work—you chop the pork yourself and the tricolor medley of vegetables is fresh, not frozen or canned—but it's not. The method is streamlined and the intriguing flavors are created with pantry-shelf ingredients, including mustard, ketchup, wine vinegar, and soy sauce.

1 cup long-grain rice

½ teaspoon salt

10 ounces well-trimmed pork tenderloin, cut into chunks

2 slices (2 ounces total) firm-textured white bread, crumbled

3 scallions, thinly sliced

3 tablespoons ketchup

1 tablespoon reduced-sodium soy sauce

1 teaspoon Dijon mustard

2 teaspoons olive oil

2 tablespoons flour

1 red bell pepper, cut into ½-inch squares

¼ pound green beans, cut into 1-inch lengths

1 yellow summer squash, cut into ½-inch cubes

1¼ cups reduced-sodium chicken broth, defatted

2 tablespoons red wine vinegar

2 teaspoons sugar

¼ teaspoon red pepper flakes

1½ teaspoons cornstarch mixed with 1 tablespoon water

1. In a medium saucepan, bring 2¼ cups of water to a boil. Add the rice and ¼ teaspoon of the salt, reduce to a simmer, cover, and cook until the rice is tender, about 17 minutes.

2. Meanwhile, in a food processor, process the pork until finely ground, about 1 minute. Transfer the pork to a large bowl and stir in the bread, scallions, 1 tablespoon of the ketchup, the soy sauce, mustard, and the remaining ¼ teaspoon salt. Mix well and shape into 4 oval patties.

3. In a large nonstick skillet, heat the oil until hot but not smoking over medium heat. Dredge the patties in the flour, shaking off the excess. Cook the patties until lightly browned, about 2 minutes per side. Transfer the patties to a plate.

4. Add the bell pepper, green beans, and squash to the skillet and cook, stirring, until the vegetables are lightly browned, about 4 minutes. Add the broth, vinegar, sugar, red pepper flakes, and the remaining 2 tablespoons ketchup. Bring to a boil and reduce to a simmer. Return the pork to the pan, cover, and cook until the patties are cooked through and the vegetables are tender, about 10 minutes. Add the cornstarch mixture and cook, stirring, until slightly thickened, about 1 minute. Divide the rice among 4 plates, spoon the patties and vegetable mixture over, and serve.

FAT: 6G/14%
CALORIES: 385
SATURATED FAT: 1.3G
CARBOHYDRATE: 60G
PROTEIN: 22G
CHOLESTEROL: 46MG
SODIUM: 881MG

PIZZA FRITTATA

SERVES: 4
WORKING TIME: 20 MINUTES
TOTAL TIME: 30 MINUTES

2 teaspoons olive oil
1 onion, coarsely chopped
2 cloves garlic, minced
1 red bell pepper, diced
1 green bell pepper, diced
1 whole egg
6 egg whites
2 tablespoons plus 2 teaspoons grated Parmesan cheese
½ teaspoon salt
¼ teaspoon freshly ground black pepper
1 cup canned white kidney beans (cannellini), rinsed and drained
½ cup no-salt-added tomato sauce
¼ cup shredded part-skim mozzarella cheese

1. In a large nonstick skillet, heat the oil until hot but not smoking over medium heat. Add the onion and garlic and cook, stirring frequently, until the onion is softened, about 5 minutes. Stir in the bell peppers and cook until crisp-tender, about 4 minutes.

2. Meanwhile, in a small bowl, combine the whole egg, egg whites, Parmesan, salt, and black pepper.

3. Add the beans to the skillet and mash with a wooden spoon. Stir to distribute the beans and vegetables evenly. Reduce the heat to low and pour the egg mixture over the vegetables and beans and cook, without stirring, until set around the edges, about 4 minutes. Cover and cook until the frittata is just set in the center, about 5 minutes.

4. Meanwhile, in a small saucepan, bring the tomato sauce to a boil over medium heat. Spoon the tomato sauce over the frittata, sprinkle with the mozzarella, cover, and cook until melted, about 1 minute.

Helpful hint: Sometimes a frittata is browned under the broiler for a moment after the stovetop cooking is done; you can do this if you use a broilerproof pan or wrap the handle of your skillet in foil.

FAT: 6G/29%
CALORIES: 181
SATURATED FAT: 1.8G
CARBOHYDRATE: 17G
PROTEIN: 15G
CHOLESTEROL: 58MG
SODIUM: 566MG

Y*ou might not recognize this as an omelet at first glance, but a frittata is the open-face Italian version of that versatile egg dish. There's no fussy folding to do—just choose your filling and cook it in the pan, then pour the eggs over it. To keep the fat content low, we've used just one whole egg and six egg whites (virtually all the fat in eggs is in the yolks).*

HERBED STUFFED SWORDFISH

SERVES: 4
WORKING TIME: 25 MINUTES
TOTAL TIME: 30 MINUTES

The dense flesh of swordfish (pesce spada in Italian) can actually be pounded like veal scallopini. And the flavor of swordfish is robust enough to be partnered with a tangy, aromatic mixture of marmalade, rosemary, oregano, and red wine vinegar. A salad made with arugula, which has a uniquely assertive flavor of its own, rounds out the meal.

½ cup chopped fresh parsley
¼ cup plain dried bread crumbs
½ teaspoon grated orange zest
½ teaspoon dried oregano
½ teaspoon dried rosemary
¾ teaspoon salt
4 swordfish steaks, cut ½ inch thick (about 1¼ pounds total)
½ cup orange juice
2 tablespoons orange marmalade
2 tablespoons red wine vinegar
2 teaspoons extra-virgin olive oil
½ cup finely diced jarred roasted red pepper
1 small red onion, finely diced
1 rib celery, finely diced

1. Preheat the oven to 400°. Spray a 9-inch square baking dish with nonstick cooking spray.

2. In a small bowl, combine ¼ cup of the parsley, the bread crumbs, orange zest, oregano, rosemary, and ½ teaspoon of the salt.

3. Place the swordfish steaks between 2 sheets of waxed paper and, with the flat side of a small skillet or meat pounder, pound the swordfish to a ¼-inch thickness. Lay the swordfish flat and sprinkle with ¼ cup of the orange juice. Spoon the parsley mixture over the fish and, starting from a short side, neatly roll up each piece. Place the fish, seam-side down, in the prepared baking dish, cover with foil, and bake for 7 minutes, or until the rolls are just opaque in the center.

4. Meanwhile, in a medium bowl, combine the remaining ¼ cup orange juice, the marmalade, vinegar, oil, red pepper, onion, celery, the remaining ¼ cup parsley, and the remaining ¼ teaspoon salt. Place the fish rolls on 4 plates, spoon the sauce on top, and serve.

Helpful hint: Although meat pounders come in various shapes—some look like mallets, others like long-stemmed mushrooms—their one essential quality is weight.

FAT: 8G/27%
CALORIES: 263
SATURATED FAT: 1.8G
CARBOHYDRATE: 20G
PROTEIN: 27G
CHOLESTEROL: 49MG
SODIUM: 640MG

MEDITERRANEAN VEGETABLES WITH COUSCOUS

SERVES: 4
WORKING TIME: 30 MINUTES
TOTAL TIME: 30 MINUTES

There are three marvelous layers of texture and flavor in this unusual pasta dish. A bed of couscous—a pasta in the form of fine granules—cradles crisp-tender vegetables and black olives, which are in turn graced with a topping of feta, Parmesan, fresh basil, and toasted pine nuts. Greek Calamata olives make a tastier, more authentic dish than canned black olives.

¼ cup crumbled feta cheese

1 tablespoon grated Parmesan cheese

1 teaspoon olive oil

2 red bell peppers, cut into ¼-inch dice

1 onion, finely chopped

½ pound green beans, cut into ½-inch pieces

1 cup couscous

1¼ cups boiling water

¾ teaspoon salt

1 pound tomatoes, seeded and cut into ½-inch chunks

2 tablespoons chopped Calamata or other brine-cured black olives

1 teaspoon dried oregano

¼ teaspoon freshly ground black pepper

⅓ cup chopped fresh basil

2 tablespoons pine nuts, toasted

1. In a small bowl, combine the feta and Parmesan.

2. In a large nonstick skillet, heat the oil until hot but not smoking over medium heat. Add the bell peppers, onion, and green beans; cover and cook, stirring occasionally, until the green beans are crisp-tender, about 10 minutes.

3. Meanwhile, in a medium bowl, combine the couscous, boiling water, and ¼ teaspoon of the salt. Stir well, cover, and let stand until the couscous has softened, about 5 minutes.

4. Stir the tomatoes, olives, oregano, black pepper, and the remaining ½ teaspoon salt into the skillet and cook until the tomatoes are softened, about 3 minutes. Fluff the couscous with a fork and spread onto 4 plates. Spoon the vegetables over, top with the cheese mixture, sprinkle the basil and pine nuts over, and serve.

Helpful hint: To toast the pine nuts, place them in a small, dry skillet and cook over medium heat, stirring and shaking the pan, for 3 to 4 minutes, or until golden.

FAT: 8G/23%
CALORIES: 319
SATURATED FAT: 2.3G
CARBOHYDRATE: 54G
PROTEIN: 12G
CHOLESTEROL: 9MG
SODIUM: 626MG

BRAISED PORK WITH SUN-DRIED TOMATOES

SERVES: 4
WORKING TIME: 30 MINUTES
TOTAL TIME: 30 MINUTES

12 sun-dried (not oil-packed) tomato halves

¾ pound well-trimmed pork tenderloin, cut into 1-inch-wide strips

1½ teaspoons balsamic vinegar

1 teaspoon olive oil

4 cups small broccoli florets

1 red onion, diced

1 cup reduced-sodium chicken broth, defatted

1 cup dry white wine

1 clove garlic, minced

¼ teaspoon salt

⅔ cup pastina or other tiny pasta

2 teaspoons capers, rinsed and drained

1. With kitchen scissors or a small sharp knife, cut the sun-dried tomatoes into thin strips. Set aside. In a medium bowl, toss the pork with the vinegar. Set aside.

2. In a large nonstick saucepan, heat the oil until hot but not smoking over medium heat. Add the broccoli and onion and cook, stirring occasionally, until the onion is softened, about 5 minutes. Add the broth, wine, ½ cup of water, the sun-dried tomatoes, garlic, and salt. Bring to a simmer, cover, and cook for 3 minutes to reduce slightly and blend the flavors.

3. Add the pastina, capers, and reserved pork mixture. Cover and cook until the pasta is just tender and the pork is cooked through, about 5 minutes. Divide the mixture among 4 plates and serve.

Helpful hint: It's usually necessary to soak sun-dried tomatoes to soften them, but when they cook in liquid (as in step 2 of this recipe), you can eliminate the soaking.

FAT: 5G/13%
CALORIES: 337
SATURATED FAT: 1.2G
CARBOHYDRATE: 37G
PROTEIN: 29G
CHOLESTEROL: 55MG
SODIUM: 423MG

Sun-dried tomatoes have a powerful essence-of-tomato flavor, with a concentrated fruitiness akin to the flavor of raisins or figs. Oil-packed tomatoes are plumper and softer, but they're swimming in fat, so we prefer to use the dry-packed variety. The pastina (tiny pasta shapes) cooked with the pork are commonly served in broth; here, they serve as a built-in starchy "side dish."

MAIN-DISH SALADS

Left, Spiced Beef with Creamy Mango Dressing
Above, Fresh Corn Confetti Salad with Jack Cheese

Hot Spinach Salad

SERVES: 4
WORKING TIME: 30 MINUTES
TOTAL TIME: 30 MINUTES

4 ounces crusty Italian or French bread, sliced ½ inch thick

2 cloves garlic, peeled and halved

1 tablespoon olive oil

3 tablespoons slivered Canadian bacon (1 ounce)

1 red onion, cut into ½-inch chunks

½ pound button mushrooms, thickly sliced

¼ pound fresh shiitake mushrooms, thickly sliced

2½ cups frozen corn kernels

1¼ pounds fresh spinach

1 cup reduced-sodium chicken broth, defatted

2 tablespoons balsamic or red wine vinegar

1 tablespoon Dijon mustard

2 teaspoons cornstarch mixed with 1 tablespoon water

1 tablespoon sesame seeds

1. Preheat the oven to 400°. Rub the bread slices with the garlic. Cut the bread into ½-inch cubes, place on a baking sheet, and bake until crisp, turning the croutons over once during baking, about 7 minutes.

2. Meanwhile, in a large nonstick skillet or wok, heat the oil until hot but not smoking over medium heat. Add the Canadian bacon and onion and stir-fry until the onion is crisp-tender, about 4 minutes. Add the button and shiitake mushrooms and stir-fry until the mushrooms begin to soften, about 4 minutes. Add the corn and stir-fry until heated through, about 2 minutes. Transfer the vegetables to a large salad bowl along with the croutons and spinach.

3. In a small bowl, whisk together the broth, vinegar, and mustard. Pour the mixture into the skillet and bring to a boil. Stir in the cornstarch mixture and cook, stirring, until slightly thickened, about 1 minute. Pour the hot dressing over the spinach and vegetables, tossing to combine. Sprinkle the sesame seeds on top and serve.

Helpful hint: Shiitake mushrooms are much more flavorful than button mushrooms, but if you can't find shiitakes, you can substitute another ¼ pound of button mushrooms.

This update of spinach and bacon salad has much to recommend it. The main ingredient, nutrient-packed fresh spinach, keeps company with two kinds of sautéed mushrooms, golden corn kernels, and garlicky croutons. For a healthier salad, leaner Canadian bacon takes the place of regular sliced bacon, and the aromatic warm vinaigrette is fat-free.

FAT: 8G/24%
CALORIES: 307
SATURATED FAT: 1.2G
CARBOHYDRATE: 51G
PROTEIN: 15G
CHOLESTEROL: 4MG
SODIUM: 641MG

S*hrimp* *are always a treat, and they cook in a flash. So they're just the thing for this quick meal that's sure to please everyone. To enhance their flavor, the shrimp are cooked in a garlic-flavored broth; using the broth in the dressing saves its goodness. The salad is seasoned with tarragon, an herb that is particularly effective with seafood.*

ALL-AMERICAN SHRIMP SALAD

SERVES: 4
WORKING TIME: 20 MINUTES
TOTAL TIME: 25 MINUTES

1¼ pounds all-purpose potatoes, peeled and cut into ½-inch cubes

1 cup reduced-sodium chicken broth, defatted

2 cloves garlic, minced

1 pound medium shrimp, shelled and deveined (see tip)

¾ cup plain nonfat yogurt

3 tablespoons reduced-fat mayonnaise

2 tablespoons fresh lemon juice

½ teaspoon dried tarragon

½ teaspoon salt

¼ teaspoon freshly ground black pepper

3 scallions, thinly sliced

1 red bell pepper, cut into ½-inch squares

12 Boston lettuce leaves

12 green leaf lettuce leaves

1. In a large pot of boiling water, cook the potatoes until firm-tender, about 7 minutes. Drain.

2. Meanwhile, in a large skillet, bring the broth and garlic to a boil. Reduce to a simmer, add the shrimp, and cook until the shrimp are just opaque, about 4 minutes. Drain, reserving ⅓ cup of the cooking liquid. When cool enough to handle, halve the shrimp crosswise.

3. In a large bowl, combine the reserved cooking liquid, the yogurt, mayonnaise, lemon juice, tarragon, salt, and black pepper. Add the potatoes, shrimp, scallions, and bell pepper, stirring to coat. Divide the Boston and green leaf lettuce among 4 plates, spoon the shrimp mixture over, and serve warm, at room temperature, or chilled.

Helpful hints: The salad can be made up to 8 hours ahead; don't spoon it over the lettuce until just before serving. Feel free to use other lettuces for the Boston and green leaf: Bibb, romaine, iceberg, and red leaf would all work well.

FAT: 4G/14%
CALORIES: 260
SATURATED FAT: 0.8G
CARBOHYDRATE: 31G
PROTEIN: 25G
CHOLESTEROL: 141MG
SODIUM: 615MG

TIP

To shell fresh shrimp, pull apart the shell at the belly of the shrimp with your fingers, splitting the shell, and remove. To devein, with the point of a sharp knife, score the shrimp along the back, and remove the dark vein.

BEEF AND BROCCOLI WITH MUSTARD VINAIGRETTE

SERVES: 4
WORKING TIME: 20 MINUTES
TOTAL TIME: 30 MINUTES

Although the resemblance is not immediately apparent, broccoli and mustard come from the same plant family. Perhaps that's why broccoli is so tasty with a mustard vinaigrette. Even with no botanical kinship, however, the salad's other ingredients—potatoes, carrots, bell pepper, and juicy squares of sirloin steak—take equally well to the Dijon dressing.

⅓ cup red wine vinegar

⅓ cup reduced-sodium chicken broth, defatted

2 tablespoons Dijon mustard

1 tablespoon plus 2 teaspoons olive oil

½ teaspoon dried tarragon

¼ teaspoon salt

4 teaspoons capers, rinsed and drained

3 cups broccoli florets

1½ pounds all-purpose potatoes, peeled and cut into ½-inch cubes

1 cup peeled baby carrots

1 red bell pepper, cut into ½-inch squares

¾ pound well-trimmed sirloin

1. In a large bowl, combine the vinegar, broth, 1 tablespoon of the mustard, the oil, tarragon, and salt. Add the capers, stirring to combine.

2. In a large pot of boiling water, cook the broccoli for 1 minute to blanch. With a slotted spoon, remove the broccoli and set aside. Add the potatoes and carrots to the water, return to a boil, and cook until the potatoes are tender, about 7 minutes. Drain well. Add the potatoes, carrots, and bell pepper to the bowl with the vinegar mixture, tossing to combine.

3. Meanwhile, preheat the broiler. Brush the beef with the remaining 1 tablespoon mustard and broil 6 inches from the heat for about 4 minutes per side, or until medium-rare. Place the beef on a plate and let it stand for 10 minutes. Thinly slice the beef on the diagonal, then cut it into 1-inch squares, reserving any juices on the plate. Add the beef, beef juices, and broccoli to the bowl with the vegetables. Serve warm, at room temperature, or chilled.

Helpful hint: The salad can be made up to 8 hours in advance; don't add the blanched broccoli until just before serving.

FAT: 11G/29%
CALORIES: 342
SATURATED FAT: 2.7G
CARBOHYDRATE: 34G
PROTEIN: 26G
CHOLESTEROL: 57MG
SODIUM: 548MG

CHICKEN AND WHITE BEAN SALAD

SERVES: 4
WORKING TIME: 20 MINUTES
TOTAL TIME: 25 MINUTES

*S*erve this picture-perfect salad for a lovely lunch or light summer supper. Soaking the onion in ice water removes its bitterness.

½ cup chopped red onion

1 pound skinless, boneless chicken breasts, cut into ½-inch-thick strips

1 cup reduced-sodium chicken broth, defatted

1 cup plain nonfat yogurt

2 tablespoons reduced-fat mayonnaise

½ teaspoon salt

¼ teaspoon freshly ground black pepper

16-ounce can white kidney beans, rinsed and drained

2 tomatoes, diced

2 cucumbers, peeled, halved lengthwise, seeded, and diced

⅓ cup chopped fresh dill

3 tablespoons fresh lemon juice

2 teaspoons olive oil

4 cups ¼-inch-wide shredded romaine lettuce

1. In a small bowl, combine the red onion with ice water to cover and let stand for 10 minutes.

2. Meanwhile, in a large skillet, combine the chicken and broth. Bring to a boil over high heat, reduce to a simmer, cover, and cook until the chicken is cooked through, about 5 minutes. With a slotted spoon, transfer the chicken to a plate and set aside. Return the broth to a boil and cook, uncovered, until reduced to ⅓ cup, about 5 minutes. Remove the broth from the heat and cool slightly. Skim the fat from the broth.

3. In a large bowl, combine the yogurt, mayonnaise, cooled broth, salt, and pepper. Add the chicken and toss well to coat. Drain the red onion, pat dry with paper towels, and add to the chicken mixture. Gently stir in the kidney beans, tomatoes, cucumbers, and half of the dill. Cover and refrigerate if not serving immediately.

4. In a medium bowl, whisk together the lemon juice, oil, and remaining dill. Add the lettuce and toss to coat. Spoon the lettuce mixture onto 4 plates, spoon the chicken salad on top, and serve.

Suggested accompaniments: Seven-grain bread, and thin slices of part-skim mozzarella cheese.

FAT: 8G/21%
CALORIES: 342
SATURATED FAT: 1.8G
CARBOHYDRATE: 30G
PROTEIN: 38G
CHOLESTEROL: 72MG
SODIUM: 752MG

Pasta Wheel Salad Mexicana

SERVES: 4
WORKING TIME: 15 MINUTES
TOTAL TIME: 20 MINUTES

1 cup frozen corn kernels

8 ounces ruote (wagon wheel) pasta

¼ cup fresh lime juice

1 tablespoon olive oil

1 teaspoon grated lime zest

1 teaspoon minced jalapeño pepper (use gloves)

½ teaspoon ground cumin

½ teaspoon salt

¾ pound plum tomatoes (about 3), diced

¾ cup diced mango

⅔ cup diced avocado

⅔ cup thinly sliced scallions

⅓ cup chopped fresh cilantro or parsley

1. Heat a large pot of water to boiling, and blanch the corn in the boiling water for 30 seconds. Reserve the water for the pasta and, with a slotted spoon, transfer the corn to a colander to drain. Cook the ruote in the reserved boiling water until just tender. Drain well.

2. Meanwhile, in a large serving bowl, whisk together the lime juice, oil, zest, jalapeño, cumin, and salt. Stir in the corn, tomatoes, mango, avocado, scallions, and cilantro. Add the ruote, toss gently to combine, and serve.

Suggested accompaniment: Chunks of cantaloupe and honeydew melon tossed with lime juice and brown sugar for dessert.

FAT: 9G/22%
CALORIES: 371
SATURATED FAT: 1.4G
CARBOHYDRATE: 65G
PROTEIN: 10G
CHOLESTEROL: 0MG
SODIUM: 293MG

T his refreshing pasta salad, sharpened with tangy lime juice and accented with avocado, is a snap to prepare.

MUSHROOM BARLEY SALAD

SERVES: 4
WORKING TIME: 20 MINUTES
TOTAL TIME: 25 MINUTES

One of the lesser-used grains, barley has a rich, nutlike flavor and, like all grains, it absorbs sauces and dressings beautifully. We've combined quick-cooking barley (just as nutritious as pearl barley, but ready in about one-quarter the time) with two kinds of mushrooms, corn, and bell peppers. The garlicky mushrooms are nicely balanced by the fresh flavors of lemon and mint.

1¼ cups reduced-sodium chicken broth, defatted
1 cup quick-cooking barley
½ teaspoon salt
½ teaspoon dried thyme
3 cloves garlic, minced
¼ cup fresh lemon juice
½ pound fresh shiitake mushrooms, trimmed and thinly sliced
½ pound button mushrooms, thinly sliced
1 tablespoon olive oil
½ teaspoon freshly ground black pepper
6 scallions, thinly sliced
2 red bell peppers, cut into ½-inch squares
2 cups thawed frozen or no-salt-added canned corn kernels
½ cup chopped fresh mint or basil
1¼ cups crumbled feta cheese (5 ounces)

1. In a medium saucepan, bring 1 cup of the broth and 1 cup of water to a boil over medium heat. Add the barley, ¼ teaspoon of the salt, and the thyme. Reduce to a simmer, cover, and cook until the barley is tender, about 12 minutes.

2. Meanwhile, in a large skillet, bring the remaining ¼ cup broth, the garlic, and 1 tablespoon of the lemon juice to a boil over medium heat. Add the shiitake and button mushrooms, cover, and cook until just tender, about 5 minutes.

3. In a large bowl, combine the oil, black pepper, the remaining 3 tablespoons lemon juice, and remaining ¼ teaspoon salt. Add the barley (and its cooking liquid, if any), the mushrooms (and their cooking liquid, if any), the scallions, bell peppers, corn, and mint. Fold to combine. Divide among 4 plates, sprinkle the feta over, and serve warm, at room temperature, or chilled.

Helpful hints: The salad can be made up to 8 hours in advance; don't add the feta until just before serving. If shiitake mushrooms are not available, you can use all button mushrooms.

FAT: 13G/29%
CALORIES: 384
SATURATED FAT: 5.9G
CARBOHYDRATE: 58G
PROTEIN: 16G
CHOLESTEROL: 32MG
SODIUM: 856MG

There's a summery seashore flavor to this pasta salad. The cod, shrimp, and scallops are cooked in a zesty broth of clam juice, lemon juice, and seasonings; and there's still more lemon (both juice and zest) in the peppery dressing. The vivid colors of asparagus, strips of yellow bell pepper, and slivers of red onion are laced throughout the linguine.

SEAFOOD SALAD WITH LEMON-PEPPER DRESSING

SERVES: 4
WORKING TIME: 25 MINUTES
TOTAL TIME: 30 MINUTES

8 ounces linguine

½ pound asparagus, trimmed and cut into 2-inch lengths

½ cup bottled clam juice, or reduced-sodium chicken broth, defatted

5 tablespoons fresh lemon juice

1 cup diced celery

1 tablespoon fennel seeds, crushed

2 cloves garlic, minced

½ teaspoon red pepper flakes

¼ pound medium shrimp, shelled, deveined, and halved lengthwise

¼ pound bay scallops (see tip)

½ pound cod fillet, cut into bite-size pieces

2 tablespoons olive oil

¾ teaspoon grated lemon zest

1 teaspoon salt

⅛ teaspoon freshly ground black pepper

1 yellow bell pepper, cut into thin strips

½ cup thinly sliced red onion

1. In a large pot of boiling water, cook the linguine until just tender. Add the asparagus during the last 2 minutes of cooking time. Drain well and set aside to cool.

2. Meanwhile, in a medium saucepan, combine the clam juice, 2 tablespoons of the lemon juice, the celery, fennel seeds, garlic, and ¼ teaspoon of the red pepper flakes. Bring to a boil over medium heat. Add the the shrimp, scallops, and cod; return to a boil, cover, and cook until the shrimp are just opaque, 3 to 4 minutes. Drain, reserving ⅓ cup of the cooking liquid.

3. In a large bowl, combine the reserved cooking liquid, the remaining 3 tablespoons lemon juice, the oil, lemon zest, salt, the remaining ¼ teaspoon red pepper flakes, and the black pepper. Add the linguine, asparagus, bell pepper, and onion, tossing to coat thoroughly. Gently fold in the shrimp, scallops, and cod. Divide among 4 plates and serve at room temperature or chilled.

Helpful hints: Use a mortar and pestle to crush whole fennel seeds. If you're fond of fresh fennel, substitute it for the celery; the fennel seeds will further accentuate its flavor.

FAT: 9G/20%
CALORIES: 408
SATURATED FAT: 1.2G
CARBOHYDRATE: 52G
PROTEIN: 30G
CHOLESTEROL: 70MG
SODIUM: 740MG

TIP

Tender, sweet bay scallops, no bigger across than a dime, may only be available seasonally. The larger sea scallops—about 1½ inches in diameter—are usually available year-round. If you can't find the smaller bay scallops, cut sea scallops into quarters to produce a reasonable facsimile.

2 5 1

O_n Chinese restaurant menus, an all-vegetable stir-fry is sometimes called "Buddhist's Delight." We've come up with a salad-bowl version of the dish, replete with Chinese vegetables—Napa cabbage, snow peas, baby corn, and bamboo shoots—as well as tofu. The dressing is much like a tangy stir-fry sauce.

ORIENTAL VEGETABLE SALAD

SERVES: 4
WORKING TIME: 20 MINUTES
TOTAL TIME: 25 MINUTES PLUS CHILLING TIME

¼ cup rice vinegar

3 tablespoons reduced-sodium soy sauce

2 tablespoons ketchup

1 tablespoon dark Oriental sesame oil

1 tablespoon firmly packed dark brown sugar

¼ teaspoon salt

3 cups broccoli florets

6 ounces snow peas, strings removed

3 cups shredded Napa cabbage (see tip)

¼ pound mushrooms, thinly sliced

1 red bell pepper, cut into ½-inch-wide strips

2 cups canned baby corn, rinsed and drained

8-ounce can sliced bamboo shoots, drained

4 ounces firm low-fat tofu, cut into ¼-inch dice

1. In a large bowl, whisk together the vinegar, soy sauce, ketchup, sesame oil, brown sugar, and salt until well combined.

2. In a medium pot of boiling water, cook the broccoli for 2 minutes to blanch, adding the snow peas during the last 30 seconds of cooking time. Drain well, run under cold water to stop the cooking, and drain again.

3. Add the broccoli and snow peas to the bowl with the dressing, along with the cabbage, mushrooms, bell pepper, corn, and bamboo shoots. Toss well to combine, add the tofu, and toss gently. Refrigerate for at least 1 hour or up to 4 hours before dividing among 4 bowls and serving.

Helpful hint: If you have a hinged egg slicer, you can use it to slice mushrooms quickly. Buy large mushrooms and place them stemmed-side up in the slicer.

FAT: 6G/29%
CALORIES: 187
SATURATED FAT: 0.6G
CARBOHYDRATE: 27G
PROTEIN: 12G
CHOLESTEROL: 0MG
SODIUM: 760MG

TIP

To shred Napa cabbage, first remove each leaf individually. Stack 3 to 4 leaves at a time and, with a large chef's knife, trim off and discard the tough ends. Then cut the stacked leaves crosswise into thin shreds about ¼ inch wide.

MEDITERRANEAN WHITE BEAN SALAD

SERVES: 4
WORKING TIME: 20 MINUTES
TOTAL TIME: 25 MINUTES

*E*ggplant cooked with tomato paste and herbs takes on a robust, meaty flavor here that makes a pleasing contrast to the cannellini.

Two 19-ounce cans white kidney beans (cannellini), rinsed and drained

¾ cup chopped fresh basil

3 tablespoons balsamic vinegar

2 tablespoons olive oil

1 eggplant, cut into ½-inch cubes

1 cup reduced-sodium vegetable broth

3 tablespoons no-salt-added tomato paste

¾ teaspoon dried tarragon

½ teaspoon salt

1 green bell pepper, cut into ½-inch squares

1 yellow summer squash, halved lengthwise and cut into ½-inch slices

2 ribs celery, cut into ½-inch slices

2 cups cherry tomatoes, halved

4 ounces bread sticks

1. In a large bowl, gently stir together the beans, ¼ cup of the basil, the vinegar, and 4 teaspoons of the olive oil.

2. In a large nonstick skillet, heat the remaining 2 teaspoons oil until hot but not smoking over medium heat. Add the eggplant, stirring to coat. Cook, stirring frequently, until lightly golden, about 4 minutes. Add the broth, tomato paste, tarragon, and ¼ teaspoon of the salt and bring to a boil. Reduce to a simmer, cover, and cook until the eggplant is tender, about 5 minutes.

3. Transfer the eggplant mixture to the bowl with the beans, add the bell pepper, squash, and celery, tossing to combine. Add the tomatoes, the remaining ½ cup basil, and remaining ¼ teaspoon salt. Serve at room temperature or chill for up to 8 hours. Divide among 4 plates and serve with the bread sticks.

Helpful hint: Green or golden zucchini can be substituted for the yellow squash.

FAT: 12G/24%
CALORIES: 452
SATURATED FAT: 1.5G
CARBOHYDRATE: 69G
PROTEIN: 21G
CHOLESTEROL: 0MG
SODIUM: 891MG

FESTIVE RICE SALAD

SERVES: 4
WORKING TIME: 15 MINUTES
TOTAL TIME: 25 MINUTES

1¼ cups long-grain rice

½ teaspoon salt

½ cup frozen apple juice concentrate

⅓ cup snipped fresh dill

2 tablespoons Dijon mustard

2 tablespoons cider vinegar

2 teaspoons olive oil

½ teaspoon freshly ground black pepper

2 Granny Smith apples, cored and cut into 1-inch cubes

2 Belgian endives, cut into 1-inch pieces, or 2 cups torn Boston lettuce

16-ounce can sliced beets, drained, slices cut in half

1 cup crumbled goat cheese or feta cheese (4 ounces)

2 tablespoons coarsely chopped pecans (1 ounce)

1. In a medium saucepan, bring 2¾ cups of water to a boil. Add the rice and ¼ teaspoon of the salt, reduce to a simmer, cover, and cook until the rice is tender, about 17 minutes.

2. Meanwhile, in a large bowl, combine the apple juice concentrate, dill, mustard, vinegar, oil, pepper, and the remaining ¼ teaspoon salt. Add the apples, endives, and beets, tossing to coat with the dressing.

3. Add the rice, toss again, and spoon onto 4 plates. Sprinkle with the goat cheese and pecans and serve.

Helpful hint: If you make the salad in advance, add the beets just before serving so their juice doesn't color the rice and apples too much.

FAT: 16G/28%
CALORIES: 516
SATURATED FAT: 6.7G
CARBOHYDRATE: 81G
PROTEIN: 12G
CHOLESTEROL: 22MG
SODIUM: 790MG

Delicious warm or cold, this main-dish salad features the snap of apples and the savor of goat cheese.

In considerably less time than it takes to cook a pot of rice, you can have a steaming bowl of spiced couscous, laced with lemon and tossed with chopped apricots and pecans, ready to serve. More the consistency of a pasta than a grain, quick-cooking couscous is the ideal companion for quickly broiled meat, such as this juicy medium-rare beef.

SPICY BEEF SALAD WITH APRICOT-PECAN COUSCOUS

SERVES: 4
WORKING TIME: 15 MINUTES
TOTAL TIME: 30 MINUTES

1 teaspoon paprika

¾ teaspoon ground cumin

¾ teaspoon ground coriander

¾ teaspoon salt

½ teaspoon ground ginger

½ teaspoon freshly ground black pepper

10 ounces well-trimmed top round of beef

¾ teaspoon grated lemon zest

3 tablespoons fresh lemon juice

1 tablespoon olive oil

1½ cups couscous (see tip)

2½ cups reduced-sodium chicken broth, defatted

½ cup dried apricots, cut into ¼-inch dice

¼ cup coarsely chopped pecans

4 scallions, thinly sliced

4 cups mixed torn greens

1. Preheat the broiler. In a large heatproof bowl, combine the paprika, cumin, coriander, salt, ginger, and pepper. Remove 1½ teaspoons of the spice mixture and rub it into the meat. Broil the meat 6 inches from the heat for about 3½ minutes per side, or until medium-rare. Place the beef on a plate and let it stand for 10 minutes. Thinly slice the beef on the diagonal, reserving any juices on the plate.

2. Meanwhile, add the lemon zest, lemon juice, and oil to the spice mixture remaining in the bowl. Add the couscous, stirring to combine. In a small saucepan, bring the broth, apricots, and 1 cup of water to a boil over medium heat. Pour over the couscous, cover, and let stand until most of the liquid has been absorbed and the couscous is tender, about 5 minutes.

3. Stir the beef juices, pecans, and scallions into the couscous. Line 4 plates with the greens, top with the couscous, arrange the sliced beef alongside, and serve warm or at room temperature.

Helpful hint: Store pecans and other nuts in airtight containers in the freezer. Rich in oils, nuts spoil easily.

TIP

Traditional North African couscous takes a long time and quite a bit of work to prepare. But couscous found in supermarkets is precooked and requires only steeping. Fluff the softened couscous with a fork, which will separate the grains without crushing them.

FAT: 11G/20%
CALORIES: 501
SATURATED FAT: 1.8G
CARBOHYDRATE: 69G
PROTEIN: 30G
CHOLESTEROL: 45MG
SODIUM: 822MG

SPRING LAMB AND ASPARAGUS SALAD

SERVES: 4
WORKING TIME: 20 MINUTES
TOTAL TIME: 30 MINUTES

1¼ pounds sweet potatoes, peeled and cut into ½-inch cubes

1 pound asparagus, tough ends trimmed, cut into 2-inch lengths

¼ cup frozen apple juice concentrate

¼ cup reduced-sodium chicken broth, defatted

1 tablespoon rice vinegar

1 tablespoon Dijon mustard

2 teaspoons olive oil

½ teaspoon ground ginger

¾ teaspoon salt

1 red bell pepper, cut into 1-inch squares

1 yellow bell pepper, cut into 1-inch squares

¾ pound well-trimmed boneless lamb shoulder

4 cups arugula or watercress, tough stems removed

1. In a large pot of boiling water, cook the sweet potatoes until almost tender, about 8 minutes. Add the asparagus and cook until the asparagus are crisp-tender and the sweet potatoes are tender, about 2 minutes. Drain well.

2. Meanwhile, in a large bowl, combine the apple juice concentrate, broth, vinegar, mustard, oil, ginger, and ½ teaspoon of the salt. Add the sweet potatoes, asparagus, and bell peppers, tossing to coat.

3. Preheat the broiler. Sprinkle the lamb with the remaining ¼ teaspoon salt and broil 6 inches from the heat for about 4 minutes per side, or until medium. Place the lamb on a plate and let it stand for 10 minutes. Cut the lamb into 1 x ¼-inch strips, reserving any juices on the plate. Add the lamb and juices to the bowl along with the arugula and toss well. Divide among 4 plates and serve warm, at room temperature, or chilled.

Helpful hints: The salad may be prepared up to 1 day in advance; do not add the arugula until just before serving. Chicory or escarole, torn into bite-size pieces, may be substituted for the arugula or watercress.

FAT: 10G/27%
CALORIES: 331
SATURATED FAT: 3G
CARBOHYDRATE: 38G
PROTEIN: 22G
CHOLESTEROL: 58MG
SODIUM: 627MG

Among the tastiest signs of spring is plump asparagus. California asparagus may appear on the market as early as February, and happily for those who love this vegetable, its growing season extends well into the summer. The lush taste of lamb is a perfect match for asparagus. In this salad, sweet potatoes add substance and arugula provides a tart counterpoint to the rich flavors.

TOMATO-MOZZARELLA SALAD WITH PESTO DRESSING

SERVES: 4
WORKING TIME: 15 MINUTES
TOTAL TIME: 25 MINUTES

The time to make this salad is when tasty vine-ripened tomatoes are available. Luckily, that's high season for fresh basil, too.

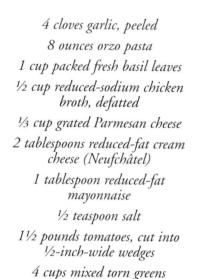

4 cloves garlic, peeled

8 ounces orzo pasta

1 cup packed fresh basil leaves

½ cup reduced-sodium chicken broth, defatted

⅓ cup grated Parmesan cheese

2 tablespoons reduced-fat cream cheese (Neufchâtel)

1 tablespoon reduced-fat mayonnaise

½ teaspoon salt

1½ pounds tomatoes, cut into ½-inch-wide wedges

4 cups mixed torn greens

1 cup shredded part-skim mozzarella cheese (4 ounces)

1. In a large pot of boiling water, cook the garlic for 2 minutes to blanch. With a slotted spoon, remove the garlic and set aside. Add the pasta to the boiling water and cook until just tender. Drain well.

2. In a food processor, combine the blanched garlic, basil, broth, Parmesan, cream cheese, mayonnaise, and salt and process to a smooth purée. Transfer the purée to a large bowl along with the pasta and tomatoes, tossing well to combine.

3. Divide the greens evenly among 4 plates, top with the pasta mixture, sprinkle the mozzarella over, and serve at room temperature or chilled.

Helpful hint: The salad can be made up to 1 hour in advance; don't place it on the greens or add the cheese until just before serving.

FAT: 11G/24%
CALORIES: 415
SATURATED FAT: 5.3G
CARBOHYDRATE: 61G
PROTEIN: 22G
CHOLESTEROL: 25MG
SODIUM: 694MG

PO' BOY SALAD WITH CAJUN SEASONING

SERVES: 4
WORKING TIME: 15 MINUTES
TOTAL TIME: 25 MINUTES

1 teaspoon dried oregano

¼ teaspoon salt

½ teaspoon dried thyme

¼ teaspoon cayenne pepper

¼ teaspoon freshly ground black pepper

10 ounces well-trimmed flank steak

¼ cup fresh lime juice

½ cup reduced-sodium chicken broth, defatted

1 tablespoon chili sauce

2 teaspoons Dijon mustard

19-ounce can chick-peas, rinsed and drained

1 cup cherry tomatoes, halved

1 red onion, halved and thinly sliced

Four 6-inch pita breads, each cut into 6 wedges

4 cups mixed torn greens

1. Preheat the broiler. In a small bowl, combine the oregano, salt, thyme, cayenne, and black pepper. Sprinkle the steak with 2 tablespoons of the lime juice. Sprinkle with the herb mixture, rubbing it in. Broil the steak 6 inches from the heat for about 3½ minutes per side, or until medium-rare. Place the beef on a plate and let it stand for 10 minutes. Thinly slice the beef on the diagonal, reserving any juices on the plate.

2. Meanwhile, in a medium bowl, combine the broth, chili sauce, mustard, and the remaining 2 tablespoons lime juice. Stir in the beef juices. Add the sliced beef, the chick-peas, tomatoes, onion, pita bread, and greens, tossing to combine. Divide among 4 plates and serve warm, at room temperature, or chilled.

Helpful hints: Crisp yet tender greens work well in this salad—baby romaine, or green or red leaf lettuce, are good choices. If you're serving this salad chilled, don't add the greens or pita bread to the other ingredients until just before serving.

FAT: 9G/20%
CALORIES: 415
SATURATED FAT: 2.5G
CARBOHYDRATE: 57G
PROTEIN: 27G
CHOLESTEROL: 36MG
SODIUM: 859MG

A po' boy is the New Orleans version of a hero sandwich. This po' boy salad is packed with flavor.

SALMON AND SUGAR SNAPS WITH DILL DRESSING

SERVES: 4
WORKING TIME: 20 MINUTES
TOTAL TIME: 30 MINUTES

Sugar snap peas—a cross between snow peas and regular green peas—have only been around since the 1970s, but they've certainly caught on. Plump and sweet, with a completely edible pod, sugar snaps are tasty raw, blanched, steamed, or stir-fried. You'll love them in this potato-and-salmon salad with a dilled mustard-lemon dressing; be sure to buy extra to munch while you're cooking.

1 pound red potatoes, cut into bite-size chunks

2 cups sugar snap peas, strings removed

10-ounce package frozen corn kernels

½ cup bottled clam juice, or reduced-sodium chicken broth, defatted

¾ pound salmon fillet

2 tablespoons reduced-fat mayonnaise

1 teaspoon grated lemon zest

2 tablespoons fresh lemon juice

1 tablespoon olive oil

1 tablespoon Dijon mustard

½ teaspoon salt

¼ teaspoon freshly ground black pepper

¼ cup snipped fresh dill

6 cups mixed torn greens

1. In a large pot of boiling water, cook the potatoes until just tender, about 12 minutes. Add the sugar snap peas and corn for the last 2 minutes of cooking time. Drain well.

2. Meanwhile, in a small skillet, bring the clam juice to a boil over medium heat. Add the salmon, return to a boil, cover, and cook until just opaque, 8 to 10 minutes. With a slotted spatula, transfer the salmon to a plate and set aside to cool. Reserve ⅓ cup of the cooking liquid. When cool enough to handle, discard the skin and cut the salmon into bite-size chunks.

3. In a large bowl, combine the reserved cooking liquid, the mayonnaise, lemon zest, lemon juice, oil, mustard, salt, and pepper, whisking to blend. Stir in the dill. Add the potatoes, sugar snap peas, and corn, tossing to coat with the dressing. Gently fold in the salmon. Divide the greens among 4 plates, spoon the salmon mixture over, and serve warm, at room temperature, or chilled.

Helpful hint: Mild-flavored green and red leaf lettuces would work well in this salad, as would a mix of escarole, endive, and radicchio.

FAT: 11G/26%
CALORIES: 386
SATURATED FAT: 1.7G
CARBOHYDRATE: 48G
PROTEIN: 25G
CHOLESTEROL: 47MG
SODIUM: 564MG

Marinated Bean Salad

SERVES: 4
WORKING TIME: 15 MINUTES
TOTAL TIME: 25 MINUTES

Get out the picnic basket and put this summery favorite at the top of the menu. Promoted from side-dish to main-dish status, this salad offers the luxurious accent of artichoke hearts, plus cherry tomatoes and Cheddar cheese. Try it as a sandwich filling, in sturdy French or Italian rolls lined with lettuce leaves—or simply serve the salad with good crusty bread.

½ cup red wine or balsamic vinegar

2 tablespoons fresh lemon juice

2½ teaspoons extra-virgin olive oil

2 teaspoons Dijon mustard

2 cloves garlic, minced

¼ teaspoon salt

19-ounce can chick-peas, rinsed and drained

19-ounce can red kidney beans, rinsed and drained

1 green bell pepper, cut into ½-inch squares

9-ounce package frozen artichoke hearts

½ pound green beans, cut into 1-inch lengths

2 cups cherry tomatoes, halved

2 ounces Cheddar cheese, cut into ¼-inch dice

1. In a medium bowl, combine the vinegar, lemon juice, oil, mustard, garlic, and salt. Add the chick-peas, kidney beans, and bell pepper. Let stand at room temperature while you prepare the remainder of the salad, or cover and refrigerate for several hours or up to 2 days before finishing the salad.

2. In a medium pot of boiling water, cook the artichoke hearts for 7 minutes. Add the green beans and cook until the green beans and artichokes are tender, about 4 minutes. Add to the bowl with the kidney beans, stir in the tomatoes and Cheddar, and serve at room temperature or chilled.

Helpful hint: Artichoke hearts canned in brine can be used instead of frozen artichokes; rinse and drain them before using (they don't need to be cooked). Don't substitute marinated artichoke hearts sold in jars, because they're packed in oil.

FAT: 11G/29%
CALORIES: 337
SATURATED FAT: 3.6G
CARBOHYDRATE: 43G
PROTEIN: 19G
CHOLESTEROL: 15MG
SODIUM: 638MG

Indonesian Vegetable Salad

Serves: 4
Working time: 20 minutes
Total time: 20 minutes

One of Indonesia's best known dishes is "gado-gado," a salad of blanched and raw vegetables attractively arranged on a big platter. What makes it extra-special is the chilied peanut sauce that's spooned over the vegetables. We've subtracted the oil and coconut milk from the sauce. Still nutty and tangy, with the bite of red pepper, it's now a far healthier dressing.

1 pound all-purpose potatoes, peeled and cut into ½-inch cubes

¾ pound green beans

¼ cup reduced-sodium soy sauce

3 tablespoons fresh lime juice

3 tablespoons smooth peanut butter

2 teaspoons firmly packed dark brown sugar

2 cloves garlic, peeled

¼ teaspoon red pepper flakes

16 Boston lettuce leaves

2 cups bean sprouts

2 tomatoes, cut into 8 wedges each

1 cucumber, peeled, halved lengthwise, seeded, and thinly sliced

2 cups juice-packed canned pineapple chunks, drained

1. In a large pot of boiling water, cook the potatoes until tender, about 7 minutes. With a slotted spoon, remove the potatoes. Add the green beans to the boiling water and cook until crisp-tender, about 4 minutes. Drain.

2. Meanwhile, in a food processor, combine the soy sauce, lime juice, peanut butter, brown sugar, garlic, red pepper flakes, and ¼ cup of water. Process to a smooth purée.

3. Line 4 plates with the lettuce leaves. Top with the bean sprouts, tomatoes, cucumber, and pineapple. Spoon the potatoes and green beans on top, drizzle the peanut sauce over, and serve.

Helpful hint: To seed a cucumber, cut it in half lengthwise and use the tip of a spoon to scrape out the seeds.

Fat: 7g/20%
Calories: 311
Saturated Fat: 1.1g
Carbohydrate: 58g
Protein: 11g
Cholesterol: 0mg
Sodium: 686mg

HAM AND SWEET POTATO SALAD

SERVES: 4
WORKING TIME: 15 MINUTES
TOTAL TIME: 25 MINUTES

1 pound sweet potatoes, peeled and cut into ½-inch cubes

½ pound all-purpose potatoes, peeled and cut into ½-inch cubes

½ cup reduced-sodium chicken broth, defatted

¼ cup frozen apple juice concentrate, thawed

2 tablespoons balsamic vinegar

2½ teaspoons Dijon mustard

¾ teaspoon ground ginger

2 ripe pears, peeled, cored, and cut into ½-inch cubes

2 ribs celery, thinly sliced

1½ cups frozen peas, thawed

½ pound thinly sliced baked ham, slivered

1. In a large pot of boiling water, cook the sweet potatoes and all-purpose potatoes until firm-tender, about 10 minutes. Drain.

2. Meanwhile, in a large bowl, combine the broth, apple juice concentrate, vinegar, mustard, and ginger. Add the cooked potatoes, tossing gently to coat. Add the pears, celery, peas, and ham, tossing to combine. Divide among 4 plates and serve warm, at room temperature, or chilled.

Helpful hint: You have lots of options for varying this salad: Try apples instead of pears, fennel in place of celery, or asparagus tips instead of peas.

Ribbons of baked ham mingle with sweet and white potatoes, pears, celery, and peas for a colorful, confetti-like salad. The tangy dressing features the warming flavors of mustard and ginger. Delicious warm, at room temperature, or chilled, this salad makes a great second-day lunch if you have some left over. Serve the salad with whole-grain rolls or crunchy bread sticks.

FAT: 4G/11%
CALORIES: 332
SATURATED FAT: 1.1G
CARBOHYDRATE: 57G
PROTEIN: 18G
CHOLESTEROL: 30MG
SODIUM: 924MG

BLACK BEAN SALAD WITH SMOKED MOZZARELLA

SERVES: 4
WORKING TIME: 15 MINUTES
TOTAL TIME: 30 MINUTES

In this festive Southwestern-style salad, we've baked the corn tortilla chips so there's no hidden fat. The black beans get a deep, robust flavor from just a little smoked mozzarella and lean Canadian bacon (omit the bacon if you want a meatless meal).

Four 6-inch corn tortillas, each cut into 6 wedges

⅓ cup reduced-sodium chicken broth, defatted, or reduced-sodium vegetable broth

3 tablespoons fresh lemon juice

1 tablespoon tomato paste

¾ teaspoon dried tarragon

½ teaspoon salt

¼ teaspoon hot pepper sauce

Two 16-ounce cans black beans, rinsed and drained

6 scallions, thinly sliced

1½ cups cherry tomatoes

⅓ cup chopped fresh parsley

3 ounces smoked mozzarella, diced

1 large onion, diced

3 cloves garlic, minced

1 ounce Canadian bacon, diced

1. Preheat the oven to 400°. Place the tortilla wedges on a baking sheet and bake for 5 minutes, or until lightly crisp. Set aside.

2. Meanwhile, in a large bowl, whisk together the broth, lemon juice, tomato paste, tarragon, salt, and pepper sauce. Add the black beans, scallions, tomatoes, parsley, and mozzarella and toss to combine.

3. In a large skillet, combine the onion, garlic, ⅓ cup of water, and the bacon and cook over medium heat, stirring occasionally, until the onion is softened and the liquid has evaporated, about 5 minutes. Add the onion mixture to the black bean mixture and toss to combine.

4. Spoon the black bean mixture onto a serving platter, place the tortilla wedges around the salad, and serve.

Helpful hints: The black bean mixture can be tossed together 1 day ahead and refrigerated. Try using other cheeses in this salad, such as feta, goat cheese, or even regular mozzarella.

FAT: 7G/21%
CALORIES: 302
SATURATED FAT: 3.1G
CARBOHYDRATE: 44G
PROTEIN: 17G
CHOLESTEROL: 20MG
SODIUM: 964MG

Beef-Barley Salad

Serves: 4
Working time: 20 minutes
Total time: 30 minutes

*W*hether in a salad or a soup, beef and barley are a winning combination. Here, the two are tossed with crisp fresh vegetables and pecans.

10 ounces well-trimmed flank steak

½ teaspoon salt

¼ cup fresh lemon juice

2½ cups reduced-sodium chicken broth, defatted

3 cloves garlic, minced

1 teaspoon grated lemon zest

½ teaspoon ground ginger

1½ cups quick-cooking barley

6 ounces green beans, cut into 1-inch lengths

2 teaspoons olive oil

2 carrots, shredded

2 tomatoes, cut into 8 wedges each

2 tablespoons coarsely chopped pecans (½ ounce)

4 cups torn romaine lettuce leaves

1. Preheat the broiler. Rub the steak with the salt and 1 tablespoon of the lemon juice. Broil 6 inches from the heat for about 3½ minutes per side, or until medium-rare. Place the steak on a plate and let it stand for 10 minutes. Cut the steak into bite-size pieces, reserving any juices on the plate.

2. Meanwhile, in a medium saucepan, combine 2 cups of the broth, ½ cup of water, the garlic, lemon zest, and ginger and bring to a boil over medium heat. Add the barley, reduce to a simmer, cover, and cook until the barley is almost tender, about 8 minutes. Add the green beans and cook until the beans are crisp-tender and the barley is tender, about 3 minutes. Remove from the heat; do not drain any remaining liquid.

3. In a large bowl, combine the remaining ½ cup broth, the remaining 3 tablespoons lemon juice, the steak juices, and the oil. Add the beef, the barley mixture, carrots, tomatoes, and pecans to the bowl with the dressing, tossing well to combine.

4. Line 4 plates with the lettuce leaves and top with the beef and barley mixture. Serve warm, at room temperature, or chilled.

Helpful hint: If you're serving this salad chilled, don't spoon the beef and barley mixture onto the lettuce until just before serving.

Fat: 11g/24%
Calories: 415
Saturated Fat: 2.9g
Carbohydrate: 55g
Protein: 26g
Cholesterol: 36mg
Sodium: 694mg

PASTA SALAD WITH SUN-DRIED TOMATO VINAIGRETTE

SERVES: 4
WORKING TIME: 20 MINUTES
TOTAL TIME: 30 MINUTES

½ cup sun-dried (not oil-packed) tomatoes

1 cup boiling water

½ cup reduced-sodium vegetable broth

½ cup packed fresh basil leaves

¼ cup balsamic or red wine vinegar

2 tablespoons extra-virgin olive oil

¼ teaspoon salt

10-ounce package frozen Italian flat green beans

10 ounces medium pasta shells

4 cups cherry tomatoes, halved

19-ounce can chick-peas, rinsed and drained

1 red onion, cut into ¼-inch dice

1. In a small bowl, combine the sun-dried tomatoes and boiling water. Let stand at room temperature until softened, about 15 minutes. When softened, transfer the tomatoes and their soaking liquid to a food processor and process to a smooth purée, about 1 minute. Add the broth, basil, vinegar, oil, and salt and process until well combined. Transfer to a large bowl.

2. Meanwhile, in a large pot of boiling water, cook the green beans until crisp-tender, about 2 minutes. With a slotted spoon, transfer the beans to the bowl with the dressing; set aside. Add the pasta to the boiling water and cook until tender. Drain well and add to the bowl along with the cherry tomatoes, chick-peas, and onion, tossing to combine. Serve at room temperature or chill for up to 4 hours.

Helpful hint: If you can get fresh Italian flat green beans, use them in place of the frozen. The cooking time will be approximately the same, depending on the size of the fresh beans. Test them after 2 minutes and if they are still too raw, continue cooking them.

FAT: 11G/18%
CALORIES: 544
SATURATED FAT: 1.3G
CARBOHYDRATE: 94G
PROTEIN: 21G
CHOLESTEROL: 0MG
SODIUM: 352MG

R*ed, white, and green—the colors of the Italian flag—are fitting colors for this sensational Italian salad.*

Crab Louis originated on the West Coast. However opinions differ as to whether its birthplace was Seattle or San Francisco. At any rate, it's a wonderful way to showcase the luxury of lump crabmeat. We've lightened up the standard recipe, substituting nonfat yogurt for heavy cream and grapefruit sections for the traditional garnish of hard-cooked eggs.

CRAB LOUIS

SERVES: 4
WORKING TIME: 15 MINUTES
TOTAL TIME: 15 MINUTES

½ pound sugar snap peas, strings removed

½ cup plain nonfat yogurt

3 tablespoons chili sauce

1 tablespoon reduced-fat mayonnaise

1 tablespoon fresh lemon juice

½ teaspoon dried tarragon

¼ teaspoon salt

⅛ teaspoon cayenne pepper

1 pound lump crabmeat, picked over to remove any cartilage (see tip)

5 plum tomatoes, cut into 1-inch wedges

½ cup diced avocado

4 cups watercress, tough stems removed

3 grapefruits, peeled and sectioned

1. In a small pot of boiling water, cook the sugar snap peas for 30 seconds to blanch. Drain well.

2. In a large bowl, combine the yogurt, chili sauce, mayonnaise, lemon juice, tarragon, salt, and cayenne. Add the crabmeat, tomatoes, avocado, and sugar snap peas, tossing gently to combine.

3. Divide the watercress evenly among 4 plates. Arrange the grapefruit sections on top of the watercress, spoon the crab mixture over, and serve at room temperature or chilled.

Helpful hint: If fresh sugar snap peas are out of season, use frozen ones, if available. Or, substitute fresh or frozen snow peas.

TIP

Lump crabmeat consists of large chunks of meat from the body (rather than the claws) of the crab. Before using lump crabmeat, whether fresh or canned, look it over carefully and remove any bits of cartilage or shell that may have remained in the meat. Don't over-handle the crabmeat or the "lumps" will fall apart.

Mexican Salad with Salsa Vinaigrette

SERVES: 4
WORKING TIME: 15 MINUTES
TOTAL TIME: 25 MINUTES

1 pound small red potatoes, halved

1½ cups peeled baby carrots

1 cup frozen corn kernels

⅔ cup mild to medium-hot prepared salsa

½ cup low-sodium tomato-vegetable juice

3 tablespoons fresh lime juice

1 tablespoon olive oil

1 yellow or red bell pepper, cut into ½-inch-wide strips

1 cup radishes, thinly sliced

19-ounce can black beans, rinsed and drained

½ cup chopped fresh cilantro or basil

¾ cup diced avocado (6 ounces)

1. In a large pot of boiling water, cook the potatoes until firm-tender, about 10 minutes. Add the carrots and cook until the potatoes and carrots are tender, about 4 minutes. Add the corn and drain well.

2. Meanwhile, in a large bowl, combine the salsa, tomato-vegetable juice, lime juice, and oil. Add the potatoes, carrots, corn, bell pepper, radishes, black beans, and cilantro, tossing well to combine. Serve at room temperature or chill for up to 8 hours. To serve, divide the salad among 4 plates and sprinkle with the avocado.

Helpful hint: Prewashed peeled baby carrots, a wonderful convenience item, are sold in bags in most supermarkets. You can substitute thin regular carrots cut into 2-inch lengths, if you like.

FAT: 11G/28%
CALORIES: 354
SATURATED FAT: 1.6G
CARBOHYDRATE: 56G
PROTEIN: 10G
CHOLESTEROL: 0MG
SODIUM: 464MG

Even with salsa's huge popularity, the idea of using it as a salad dressing may not have occurred to you. We've transformed the chunky tomato-chili sauce into a pourable dressing by adding tomato-vegetable juice, lime juice, and a little olive oil. The salad features some Mexican favorites, including avocado, black beans, corn, and cilantro.

GRILLED SHRIMP AND SPRING VEGETABLE SALAD

SERVES: 4
WORKING TIME: 30 MINUTES
TOTAL TIME: 30 MINUTES

Chopped vegetables—bell peppers, scallion, and cucumber—make a colorful bed for a bounty of grilled shrimp. The shrimp are coated with an assertive spice rub before they go on the fire, and the same mixture of cumin, coriander, oregano, salt, and pepper seasons the dressing for the vegetable mixture. The salad is served over "Texas toast"—slices of grilled bread.

1 teaspoon ground cumin

1 teaspoon ground coriander

1 teaspoon dried oregano

¼ teaspoon salt

¼ teaspoon freshly ground black pepper

1 pound medium shrimp, shelled and deveined

1 red bell pepper, cut into 1-inch pieces

1 green bell pepper, cut into 1-inch pieces

1 scallion, cut into 1-inch lengths

½ cucumber, peeled, halved lengthwise, seeded, and cut into 1-inch pieces

⅔ cup low-sodium tomato-vegetable juice

1 tablespoon no-salt-added tomato paste

1 tablespoon white wine vinegar

1 tablespoon olive oil

4 ounces French bread, cut into ½-inch slices

1. In a medium bowl, combine the cumin, coriander, oregano, salt, and black pepper. Measure ¾ teaspoon of the spice mixture and set aside. Add the shrimp to the spices remaining in the bowl, tossing to combine. Let stand at room temperature for 10 minutes.

2. Meanwhile, in a food processor, combine the reserved ¾ teaspoon spice mixture, the bell peppers, scallion, cucumber, tomato-vegetable juice, tomato paste, vinegar, and oil. Process with on/off pulses until the vegetables are coarsely chopped. (Do this in batches if necessary.)

3. Preheat the grill. Thread the shrimp on skewers. Spray the rack—off the grill—with nonstick cooking spray. Place the skewers on the rack, cover, and grill at medium, or 6 inches from the heat, turning once, for 6 minutes, or until the shrimp are just opaque. Meanwhile, grill the bread, turning several times, for 4 minutes, or until lightly toasted.

4. Arrange the bread slices on 4 plates. Top with the shrimp, spoon the vegetable mixture over, and serve warm or at room temperature.

Helpful hints: You can cut up the vegetables by hand up to 4 hours in advance; to keep them from becoming soft, don't chop them in the food processor until close to serving time. You can measure out the spice mixture ahead of time as well.

FAT: 6G/23%
CALORIES: 237
SATURATED FAT: 0.9G
CARBOHYDRATE: 22G
PROTEIN: 22G
CHOLESTEROL: 140MG
SODIUM: 479MG

THREE-BEAN SALAD WITH WALNUTS

SERVES: 4
WORKING TIME: 15 MINUTES
TOTAL TIME: 20 MINUTES

2 cloves garlic, peeled

¾ pound green beans, cut into 2-inch pieces

¾ pound yellow wax beans, cut into 2-inch pieces

¾ cup plain nonfat yogurt

⅓ cup chopped fresh mint

2 tablespoons reduced-fat mayonnaise

¾ teaspoon salt

Two 16-ounce cans red kidney beans, rinsed and drained

1 cucumber, peeled, halved lengthwise, seeded, and cut into ¼-inch dice

¼ cup chopped walnuts

16 leaves Boston, Bibb, or iceberg lettuce

1. In a large pot of boiling water, cook the garlic for 2 minutes to blanch. With a slotted spoon, remove the garlic and when cool enough to handle, finely chop.

2. Add the green beans and wax beans to the boiling water and cook until crisp-tender, about 5 minutes. Drain, rinse under cold water, and drain again.

3. In a large bowl, combine the chopped garlic, yogurt, mint, mayonnaise, and salt. Fold in the green beans, wax beans, kidney beans, cucumber, and walnuts. Divide the lettuce among 4 plates, top with the bean mixture, and serve at room temperature or chilled.

Helpful hints: The salad can be made up to 8 hours in advance; don't spoon it over the lettuce or add the walnuts until just before serving. If yellow wax beans are not available, you can substitute additional fresh green beans or frozen Italian green beans, if you like.

FAT: 8G/22%
CALORIES: 321
SATURATED FAT: 0.8G
CARBOHYDRATE: 47G
PROTEIN: 19G
CHOLESTEROL: 1MG
SODIUM: 803MG

This salad is usually served as a side dish, but since its main component is kidney beans (which are high in protein), it can make a substantial main dish, too. For variety's sake, you can mix and match the canned beans you use: One can of kidney beans and one of chick-peas, for instance, would work well also. Accompany the salad with crusty rolls for a satisfying meal.

We've expanded the concept of a French potato salad to create this appealing mixture of beef and vegetables. Red potatoes, cauliflower, green beans, and cherry tomatoes are combined with herbed broiled beef for a substantial dinner dish. Snippets of sun-dried tomato add sunny flavor. A warm baguette is a lovely accompaniment for this salad.

Marinated Vegetable and Beef Salad

SERVES: 4
WORKING TIME: 20 MINUTES
TOTAL TIME: 30 MINUTES

10 ounces well-trimmed top round of beef

½ teaspoon salt

½ teaspoon dried oregano

1 pound red potatoes, cut into ½-inch chunks

3 cups small cauliflower florets

½ pound green beans, cut into 1-inch lengths

½ cup sun-dried (not oil-packed) tomatoes, snipped into ½-inch pieces (see tip)

½ cup reduced-sodium chicken broth, defatted

2 tablespoons red wine vinegar

1 tablespoon olive oil

2 teaspoons Dijon mustard

½ teaspoon freshly ground black pepper

2 cups cherry tomatoes, halved

1. Preheat the broiler. Rub the beef with ¼ teaspoon of the salt and ¼ teaspoon of the oregano. Broil the beef 6 inches from the heat for about 3½ minutes per side, or until medium-rare. Place the beef on a plate and let it stand for 10 minutes. Thinly slice the beef on the diagonal, then cut it into bite-size pieces, reserving any juices on the plate.

2. Meanwhile, in a large pot of boiling water, cook the potatoes until firm-tender, about 10 minutes. Add the cauliflower, green beans, and sun-dried tomatoes during the last 4 minutes of cooking time. Drain well.

3. In a large bowl, combine the broth, vinegar, oil, mustard, pepper, the remaining ¼ teaspoon salt, and remaining ¼ teaspoon oregano. Add the cherry tomatoes, tossing to combine. Add the cooked potatoes, cauliflower, green beans, and sun-dried tomatoes, tossing to combine.

4. Add the meat and juices to the bowl with the vegetables, tossing well to combine. Serve warm, at room temperature, or chilled.

Helpful hint: If you have a cutting board with a well or channel to collect the juices, you can transfer the beef to the cutting board, rather than to a plate, to let it stand before slicing.

TIP

Sun-dried tomatoes are somewhat tough and leathery before they've been soaked, but it's easy to snip them into small pieces if you use kitchen scissors rather than a knife.

FAT: 6G/18%
CALORIES: 294
SATURATED FAT: 1.3G
CARBOHYDRATE: 37G
PROTEIN: 24G
CHOLESTEROL: 40MG
SODIUM: 479MG

With its intriguing, faintly citrusy fragrance, coriander works well in both sweet and savory dishes. Moroccan recipes often embody a bit of both; as in this potato and egg salad tossed with a sweet-and-savory dressing flavored with marmalade as well as coriander and cumin.

MOROCCAN POTATO SALAD

SERVES: 4
WORKING TIME: 15 MINUTES
TOTAL TIME: 30 MINUTES

1½ pounds small red potatoes, quartered

¾ teaspoon salt

3 carrots, thinly sliced

2 eggs

⅓ cup fresh lemon juice

1 tablespoon orange marmalade

2 teaspoons extra-virgin olive oil

1½ teaspoons paprika

1 teaspoon ground coriander

1 teaspoon ground cumin

1 cup jarred roasted red peppers, rinsed, drained, and cut into wide strips

2 scallions, thinly sliced

1. In a large pot of boiling water, cook the potatoes with ¼ teaspoon of the salt until the potatoes are almost tender, about 10 minutes. Add the carrots and cook until the potatoes and carrots are tender, about 2 minutes. Drain well.

2. Place the eggs in a small saucepan, add cold water to cover by 1 inch, and bring to a boil over medium-high heat. As soon as the water comes to a boil, cover the pan, remove from the heat, and let stand for exactly 17 minutes. Peel (see tip) and coarsely chop the eggs.

3. Meanwhile, in a large bowl, combine the lemon juice, marmalade, oil, paprika, coriander, cumin, and the remaining ½ teaspoon salt. Add the potatoes and carrots, the roasted red peppers, eggs, and scallions, tossing to coat with the dressing. Divide among 4 plates and serve warm, at room temperature, or chilled.

Helpful hint: If you're serving the salad chilled, you can make it up to 8 hours in advance and keep it covered in the refrigerator until you are ready to serve it.

FAT: 6G/21%
CALORIES: 254
SATURATED FAT: 1.1G
CARBOHYDRATE: 45G
PROTEIN: 7G
CHOLESTEROL: 106MG
SODIUM: 553MG

T I P

Here's a quick and easy way to peel hard-cooked eggs: As soon as the eggs are cooked, drain them, return them to the pan, and cover it. Shake the pan until the shells are cracked all over. Then fill the pan with cold water; in addition to cooling the eggs, this will loosen the shells so that they slip off in one piece.

Winter Squash and Broccoli Salad

Serves: 4
Working time: 20 minutes
Total time: 30 minutes

4 cups peeled, cut butternut squash (2 x 1-inch strips)

4 cups broccoli florets

2 cups cherry tomatoes, halved

19-ounce can pinto beans, rinsed and drained

6 tablespoons shredded Monterey jack cheese

4-ounce can chopped mild green chilies

⅓ cup chopped fresh cilantro

¼ cup fresh lime juice

2 teaspoons olive oil

½ teaspoon honey

¼ teaspoon salt

3 scallions, thinly sliced

1. In a large pot of boiling water, cook the squash for 2 minutes. Add the broccoli and cook until the squash and broccoli are crisp-tender, about 3 minutes longer. Drain, rinse under cold water, and drain again. Transfer to a large bowl along with the tomatoes, beans, and cheese.

2. In a food processor, combine the chilies, cilantro, lime juice, oil, honey, and salt and purée until smooth. Pour the dressing over the squash mixture, add the scallions, and toss to combine. Divide the salad among 4 plates and serve.

Helpful hints: Choose a butternut squash free of cracks and bruises that feels heavy for its size—a small squash weighing 2 pounds or so will be more than enough. The squash and broccoli can be prepared up to 1 day ahead and refrigerated, as can the dressing. Other beans, such as chick-peas or red kidney beans, would also be good in this recipe.

Fat: 7g/23%
Calories: 265
Saturated Fat: 2.3g
Carbohydrate: 43g
Protein: 14g
Cholesterol: 11mg
Sodium: 626mg

Vegetable salads don't get much chunkier than this, and the combination of green broccoli, red cherry tomatoes, and orange squash provides ample color appeal as well. Both the butternut squash and the pinto beans are distinctive enough to stand up to the big flavor of the dressing— a bouncy mix of chilies, cilantro, fresh lime juice, and honey. Serve the salad with sesame bread sticks.

In Italy, roast pork loin is often anointed with olive oil and sprinkled with rosemary or fennel. Here we've used both of these distinctive seasonings on grilled pork tenderloin. Tomatoes, mushrooms, and watercress are the other components of the salad, which is served with grilled "croutons" and Parmesan curls.

Italian Pork Parmesan Salad

Serves: 4
Working time: 20 minutes
Total time: 30 minutes

3 cloves garlic, minced

1½ teaspoons dried rosemary, crumbled

1 teaspoon fennel seeds, crushed

1 teaspoon salt

½ teaspoon freshly ground black pepper

¾ pound well-trimmed pork tenderloin, halved lengthwise

⅓ cup apple juice

2 tablespoons fresh lemon juice

2 teaspoons olive oil

6 ounces French bread, cut into 8 slices

2 tomatoes, cut into thin wedges

2 cups sliced mushrooms

2 cups packed watercress, tough stems removed, chopped

¼ cup shaved Parmesan cheese (see tip)

1. In a medium bowl, combine the garlic, rosemary, fennel, ¼ teaspoon of the salt, and the pepper. Use 2 teaspoons of the mixture to rub over the pork. Add the apple juice, lemon juice, oil, and the remaining ¾ teaspoon salt to the mixture remaining in the bowl; set the dressing aside.

2. Preheat the grill. Spray the rack—off the grill—with nonstick cooking spray. Place the pork on the rack, cover, and grill at medium, or 6 inches from the heat, turning once, for 10 minutes, or until the pork is cooked through but still juicy. Place the bread on the grill for the last 2 to 4 minutes of cooking time, or until toasted on both sides. Place the pork on a plate and let it stand for 10 minutes. Cut the pork into ½-inch-thick slices, reserving any juices on the plate.

3. Add the pork and juices, tomatoes, mushrooms, and watercress to the dressing, tossing to coat. Divide the pork salad and bread among 4 plates, top with the Parmesan, and serve warm or at room temperature.

Helpful hint: If you have a cutting board with a channel or lip to collect the juices, you can transfer the pork to your cutting board, rather than to a plate, to let it stand for 10 minutes before slicing.

TIP

A swivel-bladed vegetable peeler is the perfect tool for cutting broad shavings from a wedge of Parmesan.

Fat: 10g/27%
Calories: 328
Saturated Fat: 3.2g
Carbohydrate: 32g
Protein: 28g
Cholesterol: 65mg
Sodium: 987mg

POTATO, HAM, AND CHEESE SALAD

SERVES: 4
WORKING TIME: 20 MINUTES
TOTAL TIME: 30 MINUTES

Tender asparagus lifts this simple salad out of the ordinary. But there's no extra fuss because the asparagus is cooked right along with the potatoes. The dressing is a versatile mustard vinaigrette that suits all sorts of salads. In fact, you might want to mix up an extra batch of the dressing and store it in the refrigerator for spur-of-the-moment use.

2 pounds red potatoes, quartered (or cut into eighths if large)
¾ pound asparagus, cut into 2-inch lengths
¼ cup balsamic or red wine vinegar
¼ cup reduced-sodium chicken broth, defatted
1 tablespoon Dijon mustard
2 teaspoons olive oil
½ teaspoon salt
1 red onion, finely chopped
1½ cups thawed frozen or no-salt-added canned corn kernels
3 ounces Cheddar cheese, cut into 1 x ¼-inch strips
3 ounces baked ham, in one piece, cut into 1 x ¼-inch strips

1. In a large pot of boiling water, cook the potatoes until tender, about 10 minutes. Add the asparagus for the last 2 minutes of cooking time to blanch. Drain.

2. Meanwhile, in a large bowl, combine the vinegar, broth, mustard, oil, and salt. Add the onion, stirring to combine. Add the potatoes and asparagus, tossing to coat.

3. Fold in the corn, Cheddar, and ham and serve warm, at room temperature, or chilled.

Helpful hint: The salad can be made up to 8 hours in advance; don't add the blanched asparagus until just before serving, otherwise, the vinegar in the dressing will cause the green vegetable to change color.

FAT: 12G/26%
CALORIES: 424
SATURATED FAT: 5.6G
CARBOHYDRATE: 61G
PROTEIN: 20G
CHOLESTEROL: 35MG
SODIUM: 876MG

If the combination of leeks and potatoes sounds familiar, that's because those vegetables are the main ingredients of vichyssoise, the world-famous cream soup. In a lighter vein, this salad combines red potatoes with blanched leeks and asparagus in a dilled mustard vinaigrette. To make a low-fat vinaigrette, we substitute broth for some of the oil.

POTATO, LEEK, AND ASPARAGUS SALAD

SERVES: 4
WORKING TIME: 15 MINUTES
TOTAL TIME: 25 MINUTES

1½ pounds red potatoes, cut into 1-inch chunks

¾ teaspoon salt

1¼ pounds asparagus, trimmed and cut on the diagonal into 1-inch lengths

3 leeks, halved lengthwise and cut into 1-inch pieces (see tip)

⅔ cup reduced-sodium vegetable broth

2 tablespoons red wine vinegar

1 tablespoon Dijon mustard

1 tablespoon extra-virgin olive oil

¼ cup snipped fresh dill

½ pound mushrooms, thinly sliced

½ cup crumbled feta cheese (2 ounces)

1. In a large pot of boiling water, cook the potatoes with ¼ teaspoon of the salt until tender, about 10 minutes. Add the asparagus and leeks during the last 2 minutes of cooking time. Drain well.

2. In a large bowl, combine the broth, vinegar, mustard, oil, and the remaining ½ teaspoon salt. Stir in the dill. Add the potatoes, asparagus, leeks, and mushrooms, tossing gently to coat. Spoon onto 4 plates, sprinkle with the feta, and serve at room temperature.

Helpful hint: If you can't get leeks, you can make this salad with 12 scallions, blanched for just 30 seconds and cut into 1-inch lengths.

TIP

When a recipe calls for leeks to be sliced, first trim the root end and the dark green leaves, then cut the leeks as directed. Place the cut leeks in a bowl of tepid water, let them sit for 1 to 2 minutes, then lift the leeks out of the water, leaving any dirt and grit behind in the bowl. This is easier and faster than splitting and washing whole leeks before slicing them.

FAT: 8G/24%
CALORIES: 306
SATURATED FAT: 2.7G
CARBOHYDRATE: 51G
PROTEIN: 11G
CHOLESTEROL: 13MG
SODIUM: 672MG

BEEF AND ORZO SALAD

SERVES: 4
WORKING TIME: 15 MINUTES
TOTAL TIME: 30 MINUTES

Bring your heartiest appetite to the table, and this salad will satisfy it. While low in fat, the dish is no lightweight: Pasta and sirloin steak are its two main components, with broccoli, bell pepper, and greens adding textural variety as well as admirable nutritional value. The dressing is a balsamic vinaigrette seasoned with the same herbs that flavor the beef.

¼ teaspoon freshly ground black pepper

½ teaspoon salt

½ teaspoon dried rosemary, crumbled

½ teaspoon dried thyme

10 ounces well-trimmed beef sirloin

8 ounces orzo pasta

4 cups broccoli florets

¼ cup balsamic or red wine vinegar

4 teaspoons olive oil

2 scallions, thinly sliced

1 red bell pepper, cut into ½-inch squares

6 cups mixed torn greens

1. Preheat the broiler. In a small bowl, combine the black pepper, ¼ teaspoon of the salt, ¼ teaspoon of the rosemary, and ¼ teaspoon of the thyme. Rub the beef with the herb mixture and broil for about 3½ minutes per side, or until medium-rare. Place the beef on a plate and let it stand for 10 minutes. Thinly slice the beef on the diagonal, then cut it into bite-size pieces, reserving any juices on the plate.

2. Meanwhile, in a large pot of boiling water, cook the orzo until just tender. Add the broccoli during the last 2 minutes of cooking time. Drain well.

3. In a large bowl, combine the beef juices, vinegar, oil, the remaining ¼ teaspoon salt, remaining ¼ teaspoon rosemary, and remaining ¼ teaspoon thyme. Stir in the beef, orzo, broccoli, scallions, bell pepper, and greens, tossing to combine. Serve warm, at room temperature, or chilled.

Helpful hints: This salad calls for sturdy greens, such as romaine, escarole, radicchio, or curly chicory. If you want to serve the salad chilled, do not add the greens until just before serving.

FAT: 10G/21%
CALORIES: 420
SATURATED FAT: 2.3G
CARBOHYDRATE: 54G
PROTEIN: 30G
CHOLESTEROL: 47MG
SODIUM: 392MG

Greek Salad with White Beans

Serves: 4
Working time: 30 minutes
Total time: 30 minutes

Crumbly, slightly salty feta cheese, white beans, bell peppers, and juicy tomatoes—these are the refreshing components of our Greek salad. The dressing is a lively blend of fresh lemon juice, olive oil, and dill, with a pinch of cayenne pepper for some heat.

¼ cup fresh lemon juice

3 tablespoons chopped fresh dill

2 teaspoons olive oil

½ teaspoon dried oregano

¼ teaspoon salt

⅛ teaspoon cayenne pepper

2 green bell peppers, cut into 1-inch squares

2 cucumbers, peeled, halved lengthwise, seeded, and cut into ½-inch-thick slices

1 pound tomatoes, diced

19-ounce can white kidney beans (cannellini), rinsed and drained

6 scallions, thinly sliced

6 cups torn romaine lettuce leaves

2½ ounces crumbled feta cheese

1. In a large bowl, whisk together the lemon juice, dill, oil, oregano, salt, and cayenne. Add the bell peppers, cucumbers, tomatoes, beans, and scallions and toss to combine.

2. Cover 4 serving plates with the lettuce. Spoon the vegetable mixture on top, sprinkle the cheese over, and serve.

Helpful hint: Escarole leaves or even iceberg lettuce leaves can stand in for the romaine.

Fat: 7g/29%
Calories: 232
Saturated Fat: 3.1g
Carbohydrate: 35g
Protein: 12g
Cholesterol: 16mg
Sodium: 580mg

SHRIMP CAESAR SALAD

SERVES: 4
WORKING TIME: 15 MINUTES
TOTAL TIME: 25 MINUTES

1 cup reduced-sodium chicken broth, defatted

1 pound medium shrimp, shelled and deveined

5 cloves garlic, peeled

3 tablespoons reduced-fat mayonnaise

¼ cup grated Parmesan cheese

½ teaspoon grated lemon zest

2 tablespoons fresh lemon juice

½ teaspoon salt

¼ teaspoon freshly ground black pepper

4 ounces Italian bread, halved horizontally

2 cups cherry tomatoes, halved

8 cups torn romaine or iceberg lettuce

1. In a large skillet, bring the broth to a boil over medium heat. Reduce to a simmer, add the shrimp, cover, and cook until the shrimp are just opaque, about 4 minutes. With a slotted spoon, transfer the shrimp to a plate. When cool enough to handle, halve the shrimp lengthwise.

2. Return the broth to a boil, add 4 of the garlic cloves, and cook for 2 minutes to blanch. Remove the garlic and reserve ¼ cup of the cooking liquid. In a food processor, combine the blanched garlic, the reserved cooking liquid, the mayonnaise, Parmesan, lemon zest, lemon juice, salt, and pepper and process to a smooth purée, about 1 minute. Transfer to a large bowl.

3. Preheat the broiler. Toast the bread 6 inches from the heat for about 1 minute per side, or until lightly browned. Rub the bread with the remaining clove of garlic, then cut the bread into ½-inch chunks. Add the bread to the dressing, along with the shrimp, tomatoes, and lettuce, tossing to combine. Divide the salad among 4 plates and serve at room temperature or chilled.

Helpful hint: We leave the tails on the shrimp for a prettier presentation, but if you prefer, you can remove the tails when shelling the shrimp.

FAT: 7G/24%
CALORIES: 264
SATURATED FAT: 1.9G
CARBOHYDRATE: 24G
PROTEIN: 26G
CHOLESTEROL: 144MG
SODIUM: 807MG

The basic Caesar salad, created in the 1920s, has enjoyed a recent renaissance. These days, it often moves up to main-dish status when grilled chicken is added. We think plump shrimp make it an even more appealing dish. Furthermore, our eggless dressing and toasted (not fried) croutons render it a healthier meal.

Bean and Potato Salad with Yogurt Dressing

SERVES: 4
WORKING TIME: 20 MINUTES
TOTAL TIME: 30 MINUTES

A great American side dish, potato salad, has the potential to be a solidly satisfying entrée as well. Two kinds of beans—pinto and lima—supply a hefty helping of protein, while celery and red onion add crunch. It would be a shame to drown these tasty ingredients in mayonnaise, so we've devised a yogurt vinaigrette, instead.

10-ounce package frozen baby lima beans

1 pound red potatoes, cut into ½-inch chunks

¾ teaspoon salt

1 cup plain nonfat yogurt

¼ cup cider vinegar

1 tablespoon Dijon mustard

½ teaspoon freshly ground black pepper

½ cup snipped fresh dill

16-ounce can pinto beans, rinsed and drained

1 red onion, cut into ¼-inch dice

3 ribs celery, thinly sliced

4 cups torn romaine lettuce

1. In a large pot of boiling water, cook the lima beans and potatoes with ¼ teaspoon of the salt until the potatoes are tender, about 10 minutes. Drain.

2. In a large bowl, combine the yogurt, vinegar, mustard, pepper, and the remaining ½ teaspoon salt. Stir in the dill. Add the lima beans, potatoes, pinto beans, onion, and celery, tossing gently to coat. Serve at room temperature or chill for up to 8 hours. To serve, divide the lettuce among 4 plates and top with the salad mixture.

Helpful hint: You can substitute another mustard (but preferably a fairly spicy one) for the Dijon, if you like. Creole mustard, which has a touch of horseradish added, would work well.

FAT: 1G/3%
CALORIES: 321
SATURATED FAT: 0.1G
CARBOHYDRATE: 61G
PROTEIN: 17G
CHOLESTEROL: 1MG
SODIUM: 746MG

MINESTRONE SALAD

SERVES: 4
WORKING TIME: 15 MINUTES
TOTAL TIME: 30 MINUTES

1 pound small red potatoes,
quartered

¾ teaspoon salt

¾ pound green beans

1 cup reduced-sodium tomato-
vegetable juice

2 tablespoons balsamic vinegar

1 tablespoon olive oil

¼ cup chopped fresh basil

2 yellow summer squash, halved
lengthwise and thinly sliced

2 cups cherry tomatoes

1 red onion, halved and thinly
sliced

16-ounce can chick-peas, rinsed
and drained

4 ounces part-skim mozzarella
cheese, cut into ½-inch dice

1. In a large pot of boiling water, cook the potatoes with ¼ teaspoon of the salt until almost tender, about 8 minutes. Add the green beans and cook until the potatoes are tender, about 2 minutes. Drain well.

2. Meanwhile, in a large bowl, combine the tomato-vegetable juice, vinegar, oil, basil, and the remaining ½ teaspoon salt. Add the potatoes, green beans, yellow squash, tomatoes, onion, chick-peas, and mozzarella, tossing to coat with the dressing.

Helpful hint: Quartered plum tomatoes can take the place of the cherry tomatoes.

FAT: 9G/24%
CALORIES: 344
SATURATED FAT: 2.5G
CARBOHYDRATE: 51G
PROTEIN: 17G
CHOLESTEROL: 10MG
SODIUM: 790MG

Many of the ingredients used in the classic Italian soup are found in this salad: As "minestrone" means "big soup," this salad could be called "insalatone." Warm potatoes and green beans—along with summer squash, tomatoes, chick-peas, basil, and mozzarella cubes—are dressed with a balsamic tomato vinaigrette. Like the soup, the salad goes well with Italian bread.

SPICED BEEF WITH CREAMY MANGO DRESSING

SERVES: 4
WORKING TIME: 20 MINUTES
TOTAL TIME: 30 MINUTES

The sweet-and-spicy seasonings that flavor the steak here are a Caribbean inspiration—a simplified version of the spice mixture rubbed on Jamaican jerk chicken. The spiced beef is just one attraction in this salad made with sweet sugar snap peas, cherry tomatoes, and crunchy water chestnuts. Mixed torn greens and warm pita wedges round out the dish.

¾ pound well-trimmed sirloin
½ teaspoon salt
¼ teaspoon sugar
¼ teaspoon freshly ground black pepper
⅛ teaspoon ground allspice
3 tablespoons fresh lime juice
Two 8-inch pita breads, cut into 6 wedges each
½ pound sugar snap peas or snow peas, strings removed
⅓ cup mango chutney, chopped if chunky
¼ cup reduced-fat sour cream
2 cups cherry tomatoes, halved
½ cup canned sliced water chestnuts, or ½ cup diced celery
3 scallions, thinly sliced
4 cups mixed torn greens

1. Preheat the broiler. Sprinkle the beef with ¼ teaspoon of the salt, the sugar, pepper, and allspice. Sprinkle 1 tablespoon of the lime juice over and broil 6 inches from the heat for about 4 minutes per side, or until medium-rare. Leave the broiler on. Place the beef on a plate and let it stand for 10 minutes. Thinly slice the beef on the diagonal, reserving any juices on the plate.

2. Meanwhile, broil the pitas wedges for about 1 minute per side, or until lightly crisped. In a medium saucepan of boiling water, cook the sugar snap peas for 1 minute to blanch. Drain well.

3. In a large bowl, combine the chutney, sour cream, the remaining 2 tablespoons lime juice, the beef juices, and 2 tablespoons of water. Add the beef, the sugar snap peas, tomatoes, water chestnuts, scallions, and the remaining ¼ teaspoon salt, tossing to combine. Divide the greens evenly among 4 plates. Top with the meat mixture, place the pita wedges alongside, and serve warm, at room temperature, or chilled.

Helpful hint: The beef-and-vegetable mixture can be made up to 8 hours in advance; do not warm the pita wedges or place the salad on the greens until just before serving.

FAT: 8G/17%
CALORIES: 432
SATURATED FAT: 2.9G
CARBOHYDRATE: 62G
PROTEIN: 29G
CHOLESTEROL: 62MG
SODIUM: 890MG

Corn

on the cob has an
ineffable sweetness that
is hard to duplicate.
Here we slice raw
kernels off the cob and
toss them with colorful
vegetables, cubes of
jack cheese, and a
tangy-sweet dressing
fired up with jalapeño
pepper. If you haven't
discovered it already,
you'll find the crunchy
sweetness of raw corn
to be one of the
delicious pleasures of
summertime.

FRESH CORN CONFETTI SALAD WITH JACK CHEESE

SERVES: 4
WORKING TIME: 20 MINUTES
TOTAL TIME: 20 MINUTES

⅓ cup balsamic vinegar

2 tablespoons honey

½ teaspoon salt

1 pickled jalapeño pepper, finely chopped

4 cups fresh corn kernels (see tip), or 4 cups no-salt-added canned corn kernels, drained

2 cups cherry tomatoes, halved

2 ribs celery, thinly sliced

1 red bell pepper, cut into ½-inch squares

1 green bell pepper, cut into ½-inch squares

1 red onion, finely chopped

¼ cup chopped fresh parsley

3 ounces Monterey jack cheese, cut into ¼-inch dice

1. In a large bowl, combine the vinegar, honey, salt, and jalapeño pepper.

2. Add the corn, tomatoes, celery, bell peppers, onion, parsley, and cheese. Toss to combine and serve at room temperature or chilled.

Helpful hints: Choose fresh ears of corn with moist green stalks and plump kernels. Refrigerate the corn as soon as you get it home: Warmth hastens the conversion of its natural sugars to starch. Time also robs fresh corn of its sweetness, so use corn within a day or two of purchase. If you use canned corn, be sure to get no-salt-added, which has a fresher taste and crunchier texture than regular canned corn.

FAT: 9G/28%
CALORIES: 290
SATURATED FAT: 4G
CARBOHYDRATE: 49G
PROTEIN: 12G
CHOLESTEROL: 23MG
SODIUM: 496MG

TIP

With a long, sharp knife, slice the corn kernels from the cob in strips. Then, with your fingers, break up the strips into individual kernels. You'll need about 4 medium ears of fresh corn to yield 4 cups of kernels.

ROAST BEEF, POTATO, AND BEET SALAD

SERVES: 4
WORKING TIME: 15 MINUTES
TOTAL TIME: 30 MINUTES

Every pantry should have at least one can of beets: Unlike many canned vegetables, beets retain their texture, flavor, and color beautifully, and are ready to brighten salads at any season. Here, red-skinned potatoes and strips of cooked roast beef are tossed with beets in a creamy dressing made with nonfat yogurt and reduced-fat mayonnaise.

1 pound red potatoes, cut into ¾-inch cubes

½ cup plain nonfat yogurt

2 tablespoons reduced-fat mayonnaise

3 tablespoons snipped fresh dill

2 tablespoons drained white horseradish

1 tablespoon cider vinegar

½ teaspoon salt

¼ teaspoon freshly ground black pepper

1 cucumber, peeled

6 ounces well-trimmed cooked roast beef, very thinly sliced and cut into thin strips

15-ounce can sliced beets, drained

8 leaves Boston lettuce

1. In a medium pot of boiling water, cook the potatoes until just tender, about 10 minutes. Drain and rinse under cold water. Set aside to cool slightly.

2. Meanwhile, in a large bowl, combine the yogurt, mayonnaise, dill, horseradish, vinegar, salt, and pepper. Halve the cucumber lengthwise, scoop out the seeds with a small spoon, and thinly slice. Stir the cucumber, beef, beets, and potatoes into the dressing, tossing to coat. Line 4 plates with the lettuce leaves, top with the beef mixture, and serve.

Helpful hint: For a change, you can make the salad with strips of cooked turkey breast.

FAT: 5G/19%
CALORIES: 243
SATURATED FAT: 1.3G
CARBOHYDRATE: 33G
PROTEIN: 17G
CHOLESTEROL: 35MG
SODIUM: 568MG

MARGARITA SCALLOP SALAD

SERVES: 4
WORKING TIME: 25 MINUTES
TOTAL TIME: 30 MINUTES

The margarita inspiration for this salad can be found in the dressing for the vegetables, which is made with orange juice, tequila, and lime juice. The plump sea scallops are also flavored with lime, as well as fresh herbs. Serve a basket of corn or flour tortillas with this Mexican-inspired meal: Heat the tortillas on the grill, then wrap them in a cloth napkin to keep them warm.

3 tablespoons fresh lime juice
2 tablespoons minced fresh parsley
1 teaspoon dried basil
1 pound sea scallops
¼ cup reduced-sodium chicken broth, defatted
2 tablespoons olive oil
¼ cup orange juice
1 tablespoon tequila
¼ teaspoon salt
¼ teaspoon freshly ground black pepper
1½ cups cherry tomatoes, halved
½ sweet onion, halved and thinly sliced
1 cup thinly sliced cucumber
1½ cups frozen corn kernels, thawed
2 cups mesclun or mixed torn greens

1. In a medium bowl, combine 2 tablespoons of the lime juice, the parsley, and basil. Add the scallops, tossing to coat. Let stand at room temperature for 10 minutes.

2. Meanwhile, in a large bowl, combine the broth, oil, orange juice, tequila, salt, pepper, and the remaining 1 tablespoon lime juice. Add the tomatoes, onion, cucumber, and corn, tossing to coat.

3. Preheat the grill. Thread the scallops on 8 skewers. Spray the rack—off the grill—with nonstick cooking spray. Place the skewers on the rack, cover, and grill at medium, or 6 inches from the heat, turning once, for 4 to 6 minutes, or until the scallops are just opaque throughout.

4. Place the mesclun on a platter and top with the tomato mixture and the scallops and serve warm or at room temperature.

Helpful hint: If you don't have any tequila on hand, try this with a white rum. Or, for an alcohol-free dish, simply leave out the tequila.

FAT: 8G/28%
CALORIES: 260
SATURATED FAT: 1.1G
CARBOHYDRATE: 24G
PROTEIN: 23G
CHOLESTEROL: 38MG
SODIUM: 366MG

PASTA DISHES

Left, Fettuccine with Chicken, Asparagus, and Peas
Above, Curried Vegetable Couscous

SUMMER SHRIMP AND TOMATO PASTA

SERVES: 4
WORKING TIME: 30 MINUTES
TOTAL TIME: 30 MINUTES

8 ounces rotelle pasta

1 tablespoon olive oil

2 yellow summer squash, thinly sliced

1 onion, coarsely chopped

1 clove garlic, minced

14-ounce can no-salt-added tomatoes

¼ cup ketchup

1 teaspoon dried tarragon

½ teaspoon salt

¼ teaspoon freshly ground black pepper

½ pound medium shrimp, shelled and deveined

1 cup frozen peas

1. In a large pot of boiling water, cook the pasta until just tender. Drain well.

2. Meanwhile, in a large nonstick skillet, heat the oil until hot but not smoking over medium heat. Add the squash, onion, and garlic, and cook, stirring, until the squash is crisp-tender, about 5 minutes.

3. Stir the tomatoes into the skillet, breaking them up with the back of a spoon. Add the ketchup, tarragon, salt, and pepper and bring to a boil. Reduce the heat to a simmer, cover, and cook for 3 minutes to blend the flavors. Add the shrimp and peas and cook until the shrimp are just opaque, about 2 minutes.

4. Transfer the mixture to a large bowl, add the pasta, and toss to combine. Divide the pasta mixture among 4 plates and serve.

Helpful hint: For a Tex-Mex twist, use salsa-style ketchup, substitute oregano for the tarragon, and sprinkle the pasta and sauce with minced fresh cilantro.

FAT: 6G/14%
CALORIES: 388
SATURATED FAT: 0.8G
CARBOHYDRATE: 64G
PROTEIN: 21G
CHOLESTEROL: 71MG
SODIUM: 581MG

Ketchup is a familiar component of "fast food." But for this quick dish, it is more than just a condiment. Here, ketchup plays a subtler role, adding sweetness and spice—as well as concentrated tomato taste—to the sauce. The shrimp cook right in the sauce, so they're absolutely drenched in flavor. Add a greens-and-tomato salad and the meal is ready.

CHICKEN AND BASIL-PEPPER CREAM SAUCE

SERVES: 4
WORKING TIME: 25 MINUTES
TOTAL TIME: 25 MINUTES

Roasted red peppers perk up any dish, and there's no reason to go without when you can buy them in jars, all ready to go. (Look for roasted red peppers in the Italian or gourmet foods section of your supermarket.) The peppers are puréed, along with evaporated milk and broth, to make a rosy, robust sauce for pasta, chicken, and green beans.

10 ounces shaped pasta, such as radiatore or rotini

½ pound green beans, cut into 2-inch lengths

1 tablespoon olive oil

¾ pound skinless, boneless chicken breasts, cut into ½-inch chunks

8-ounce jar roasted red peppers, drained

1 clove garlic, minced

¾ cup reduced-sodium chicken broth, defatted

¾ cup evaporated skimmed milk

¼ cup packed fresh basil leaves

¾ teaspoon salt

¼ teaspoon freshly ground black pepper

1 teaspoon cornstarch

¼ cup grated Parmesan cheese

1. In a large pot of boiling water, cook the pasta until just tender. Add the green beans for the last 2 minutes of cooking time. Drain well.

2. Meanwhile, in a large nonstick skillet, heat 2 teaspoons of the oil until hot but not smoking over medium heat. Add the chicken and cook, stirring, until browned, about 5 minutes. With a slotted spoon, transfer the chicken to a plate.

3. Add the remaining 1 teaspoon oil to the skillet. Add the roasted peppers and garlic and cook, stirring, until the garlic is fragrant, about 1 minute. Stir in the broth, ½ cup of the evaporated milk, the basil, salt, and black pepper and bring to a boil. Reduce to a simmer and cook until slightly thickened, about 3 minutes. Transfer the mixture to a food processor and process to a smooth purée.

4. In a small bowl, combine the remaining ¼ cup evaporated milk with the cornstarch. Return the basil-pepper purée to the skillet along with the chicken and the cornstarch mixture. Bring to a boil over medium heat and cook, stirring, until the sauce is slightly thickened, about 1 minute. Toss the sauce with the hot pasta and green beans. Divide among 4 plates, sprinkle the Parmesan over, and serve.

Helpful hint: You can substitute broccoli for the green beans, if you like.

FAT: 7G/13%
CALORIES: 497
SATURATED FAT: 1.9G
CARBOHYDRATE: 69G
PROTEIN: 36G
CHOLESTEROL: 55MG
SODIUM: 850MG

FETTUCCINE ALLA CARBONARA

SERVES: 4
WORKING TIME: 20 MINUTES
TOTAL TIME: 25 MINUTES

*W*e've retained the rich texture of the classic carbonara sauce, but have used a few tricks to create a scrumptious slimmed-down version with only one-fifth the fat. Instead of the usual pancetta bacon, we've used leaner Canadian bacon. And we've replaced the standard cream and egg yolks with low-fat cottage cheese and light sour cream.

⅔ cup low-fat (1%) cottage cheese

1 tablespoon olive oil

¼ pound Canadian bacon, diced

1 large onion, finely chopped

3 cloves garlic, minced

½ cup reduced-sodium beef broth, defatted

¼ teaspoon freshly ground black pepper

2 tablespoons light sour cream

2 tablespoons grated Parmesan cheese

12 ounces fettuccine

¼ cup chopped fresh parsley

1. Start heating a large pot of water to boiling for the pasta. In a blender or food processor, purée the cottage cheese until smooth, about 1 minute. Set aside. In a large nonstick skillet, heat the oil until hot but not smoking over medium heat. Add the bacon and cook until lightly crisped, about 5 minutes. With a slotted spoon, transfer the bacon to a plate.

2. Add the onion and garlic to the pan and cook, stirring frequently, until the onion has softened, about 7 minutes. Add the broth and pepper and cook until heated through, about 1 minute. Reduce the heat to low. Whisk in the cottage cheese purée until well combined. Whisk in the sour cream, Parmesan, and bacon and cook just until the mixture is heated through, about 1 minute longer.

3. Meanwhile, cook the fettuccine in the boiling water until just tender. Transfer the sauce to a large bowl, add the fettuccine and parsley, and toss to combine. Spoon the fettuccine mixture onto 4 plates and serve.

Suggested accompaniments: Mulled cider, and a red leaf lettuce salad with slivers of roasted red bell pepper. For dessert, chilled green and red seedless grapes.

FAT: 11G/21%
CALORIES: 478
SATURATED FAT: 3G
CARBOHYDRATE: 69G
PROTEIN: 25G
CHOLESTEROL: 101MG
SODIUM: 700MG

CHICKEN-FRIED PASTA

SERVES: 4
WORKING TIME: 20 MINUTES
TOTAL TIME: 30 MINUTES

Stir-frying the cooked bow-ties with the chicken and vegetables creates a slightly crisp pasta, which is then accented by a final sprinkle of vinegar and soy sauce in this exquisitely flavorful recipe. Store tightly wrapped fresh, unpeeled ginger in the refrigerator for up to a week or in the freezer for up to two months.

6 ounces bow-tie pasta

2 teaspoons peanut oil

1 pound skinless, boneless chicken thighs, cut into 2-inch chunks

4 cloves garlic, minced

2 teaspoons minced fresh ginger

½ teaspoon salt

2 leeks, cut into 2-inch julienne strips

2 carrots, cut into 2-inch julienne strips

½ cup frozen peas

2 tablespoons rice wine vinegar or cider vinegar

2 teaspoons reduced-sodium soy sauce

1. In a large pot of boiling water, cook the pasta until just tender. Drain, rinse under cold water, and drain again.

2. Meanwhile, in a large nonstick skillet, heat the oil until hot but not smoking over medium heat. Add the chicken and cook, stirring frequently, until lightly browned, about 5 minutes. Stir in the garlic, ginger, and salt and cook, stirring frequently, until fragrant, about 1 minute. Add the leeks and carrots and cook until the chicken is almost cooked through and the vegetables are tender, about 3 minutes.

3. Add the pasta and the peas and cook, stirring frequently, until the chicken is cooked through and the pasta is slightly crisp, about 3 minutes longer. Sprinkle with the vinegar and soy sauce. Spoon the chicken-pasta mixture onto 4 plates and serve.

Suggested accompaniments: Sesame bread sticks, and an orange and cucumber salad drizzled with a chive-flavored buttermilk dressing.

FAT: 8G/19%
CALORIES: 384
SATURATED FAT: 1.6G
CARBOHYDRATE: 48G
PROTEIN: 30G
CHOLESTEROL: 94MG
SODIUM: 520MG

*W*hat are fruit and nuts doing in a pasta sauce? The pear's delicate sweetness is a lovely complement to the Fontina, and the pistachios underscore the nutlike aspect of the cheese's flavor. Radiatore pasta is the perfect choice to catch and hold the creamy sauce; though cavatappi (hollow corkscrew pasta) or small shells would also work well.

322

RADIATORE WITH CREAMY FONTINA SAUCE

SERVES: 4
WORKING TIME: 20 MINUTES
TOTAL TIME: 30 MINUTES

10 ounces radiatore pasta

3 tablespoons flour

1 teaspoon salt

¼ teaspoon freshly ground black pepper

⅛ teaspoon cayenne pepper

2 cups low-fat (1%) milk

1 medium firm-ripe pear, peeled, cored, and diced

¾ cup (3 ounces) shredded Fontina cheese (see tip)

1 cup frozen peas, thawed

1 tablespoon coarsely chopped shelled pistachio nuts

¼ cup chopped fresh parsley

1. In a large pot of boiling water, cook the radiatore until just tender. Drain well.

2. Meanwhile, in a large saucepan, combine the flour, salt, black pepper, and cayenne, whisking well. Gradually whisk the milk into the flour mixture. Bring to a boil over medium heat, add the pear, and cook, stirring constantly, until the sauce is slightly thickened and the pear is softened, about 5 minutes. Stir in the Fontina and cook until just melted, about 2 minutes.

3. Add the peas, pistachios, and parsley and cook just until the peas are warmed through, about 2 minutes. Combine the penne with the sauce, divide among 4 bowls, and serve.

Helpful hints: You can substitute walnuts or pine nuts for the pistachios and a mild Monterey jack for the Fontina, if you like.

FAT: 10G/19%
CALORIES: 484
SATURATED FAT: 5.2G
CARBOHYDRATE: 76G
PROTEIN: 22G
CHOLESTEROL: 30MG
SODIUM: 828MG

TIP

Italian Fontina is a rich, buttery-tasting cheese with a thin brownish rind. The Danish, Swedish, and Argentine versions are sharper in flavor and come coated with red wax. All Fontinas have a mild nutty flavor and melt easily, which make them perfect for quick pasta sauces. While specialty stores may offer more variety, you can find at least one type of Fontina cheese in most supermarkets.

FUSILLI FLORENTINE

SERVES: 4
WORKING TIME: 20 MINUTES
TOTAL TIME: 20 MINUTES

Pasta with greens and garlic is a beloved Italian dish; bits of pancetta—an unsmoked Italian bacon—may be added for extra savory punch. For a similar flavor, we've used Canadian bacon, which is cut from the lean pork loin and has about one-eighth as much fat as regular bacon, and is readily available in supermarkets.

8 ounces fusilli pasta
1 tablespoon vegetable oil
2 ounces Canadian bacon, diced
1 yellow or red bell pepper, cut into strips
½ cup coarsely chopped scallions
1 clove garlic, minced
½ cup reduced-sodium chicken broth, defatted
¾ pound spinach leaves, torn into large pieces
¼ teaspoon freshly ground black pepper
1 tablespoon slivered Calamata or other brine-cured black olives
1 tablespoon chopped pine nuts

1. In a large pot of boiling water, cook the pasta until just tender. Drain well.

2. Meanwhile, in a large nonstick skillet, heat the oil until hot but not smoking over medium heat. Add the Canadian bacon, bell pepper, scallions, and garlic. Cook, stirring, until the bacon is lightly browned, about 5 minutes. Add the broth, spinach, and black pepper to the skillet and cook until the spinach is wilted, about 2 minutes. Stir in the olives and pine nuts.

3. Transfer the mixture to a large bowl, add the pasta, and toss to combine. Divide the pasta mixture among 4 bowls and serve.

Helpful hint: If you have a few moments to spare, toast the pine nuts to bring out their flavor. Cook them in a dry skillet over medium heat, shaking the pan frequently, for 3 to 4 minutes, or until golden.

FAT: 7G/20%
CALORIES: 312
SATURATED FAT: 1.2G
CARBOHYDRATE: 49G
PROTEIN: 14G
CHOLESTEROL: 7MG
SODIUM: 392MG

SHRIMP AND FRESH SALSA SAUCE

SERVES: 4
WORKING TIME: 20 MINUTES
TOTAL TIME: 20 MINUTES

10 ounces shaped pasta, such as orecchiette or farfalle (bow ties)

1 tablespoon olive oil

4 scallions, thinly sliced

3 cloves garlic, minced

1 teaspoon minced pickled jalapeño

¾ pound medium shrimp, shelled, deveined, and halved lengthwise

¾ pound tomatoes, coarsely chopped

½ cup chopped fresh cilantro or basil

2 tablespoons no-salt-added tomato paste

1 tablespoon red wine vinegar

½ teaspoon salt

¾ cup frozen corn kernels

1. In a large pot of boiling water, cook the pasta until just tender. Drain well.

2. Meanwhile, in a large nonstick skillet, heat the oil until hot but not smoking over medium heat. Add the scallions, garlic, and jalapeño and cook, stirring frequently, until the scallions are softened, about 2 minutes.

3. Add the shrimp to the pan, stirring to coat. Add the tomatoes, cilantro, tomato paste, vinegar, and salt and bring to a boil. Reduce to a simmer, stir in the corn, and cook, stirring occasionally, until the sauce is thickened and the shrimp are just opaque, about 3 minutes. Spoon the sauce over the hot pasta and serve.

Helpful hint: This dish is best when made with juicy vine-ripened tomatoes, but the fact is you can't always get them. If necessary, substitute 1½ cups canned no-salt-added tomatoes.

FAT: 6G/13%
CALORIES: 427
SATURATED FAT: 0.9G
CARBOHYDRATE: 68G
PROTEIN: 26G
CHOLESTEROL: 105MG
SODIUM: 409MG

Shrimp cook in so little time that they are a perfect starting point for quick and easy meals. Here, the shrimp cook right in the sauce, a tangy mixture of tomatoes and corn that's brightened with garlic, jalapeño, and red wine vinegar. Be sure not to overcook this—that would toughen the shrimp and lessen the textural "bite" of the corn and fresh tomatoes.

*T*hese days you can buy tomatoes in January and pumpkins in July, but it's still a pleasure to celebrate the seasons with locally grown produce. When asparagus is plentiful (in the spring or early summer, depending upon where you live), serve this delicate green-and-ivory pasta dish. Or, use tomato fettuccine for a pretty green-and-pink color scheme.

PASTA WITH SPRING VEGETABLES

Serves: 4
Working time: 30 minutes
Total time: 30 minutes

1 pound fresh plain or tomato fettuccine

14¾-ounce can vegetable broth

1½ teaspoons dried thyme

¾ pound asparagus, tough ends trimmed (see tip), cut into 1-inch pieces

4 scallions, sliced, white and green parts separated

10-ounce package frozen peas

¼ cup dry white wine

2 teaspoons cornstarch

2 teaspoons grated lemon zest

2 tablespoons fresh lemon juice

3 tablespoons grated Parmesan cheese

1. In a large pot of boiling water, cook the fettuccine until just tender. Drain well.

2. Meanwhile, in a large skillet, bring the broth and thyme to a boil over medium-high heat. Boil until reduced to 1¼ cups, about 3 minutes. Stir in the asparagus and the white parts of the scallions and cook until the asparagus is crisp-tender, about 5 minutes. Add the peas and reduce to a simmer.

3. In a jar with a tight-fitting lid, combine the wine and cornstarch and shake to blend. Add the cornstarch mixture to the skillet and cook, stirring, until the mixture is slightly thickened, about 2 minutes. Remove the pan from the heat and stir in the lemon zest, lemon juice, and the scallion greens.

4. Transfer the mixture to a large bowl, add the pasta, and toss to combine. Divide the pasta mixture among 4 bowls, sprinkle with the Parmesan, and serve.

Helpful hint: Vegetable pastas, which are colored and flavored with spinach, tomatoes, beets, carrots, and the like, have great eye appeal but are actually no more or less nutritious than regular pasta.

Fat: 7g/11%
Calories: 553
Saturated Fat: 1.8g
Carbohydrate: 98g
Protein: 24g
Cholesterol: 111mg
Sodium: 686mg

TIP

To prepare asparagus for cooking, hold each spear in your hands and bend it until the stem snaps off; it should break naturally where the woody base merges into the more tender part of the stalk.

SPAGHETTINI WITH GARLIC AND OIL

SERVES: 4
WORKING TIME: 15 MINUTES
TOTAL TIME: 25 MINUTES

Nothing could be simpler than this classic pasta throw-together, snappily accented with a drizzle of lemon juice and a scattering of grated lemon zest. The addition of bread crumbs gives a little extra body and stretches the Parmesan, keeping the fat low. If fresh chives are unavailable, you may substitute the chopped green tops of scallions.

12 ounces spaghettini
3 tablespoons olive oil
6 cloves garlic, minced
½ cup reduced-sodium chicken broth, defatted
3 tablespoons fresh lemon juice
3 tablespoons chopped fresh parsley
3 tablespoons snipped fresh chives
1 teaspoon grated lemon zest
¾ teaspoon salt
¼ teaspoon freshly ground black pepper
2 tablespoons grated Parmesan cheese
1 tablespoon plain dried bread crumbs

1. Heat a large pot of water to boiling, and cook the spaghettini until just tender. Drain well.

2. Meanwhile, in a large nonstick skillet, heat the oil until hot but not smoking over low heat. Add the garlic and cook, stirring frequently, until tender, about 5 minutes. Stir in the broth, lemon juice, parsley, chives, lemon zest, salt, and pepper and cook until the mixture is heated through, about 1 minute.

3. Transfer the spaghettini to a large bowl, add the garlic sauce, and toss to combine. Sprinkle with the Parmesan and bread crumbs and toss again. Spoon the spaghettini mixture into 4 shallow bowls and serve.

Suggested accompaniments: Sliced fresh tomatoes drizzled with a balsamic vinaigrette, and orange wedges for dessert.

FAT: 12G/25%
CALORIES: 438
SATURATED FAT: 2G
CARBOHYDRATE: 68G
PROTEIN: 13G
CHOLESTEROL: 2MG
SODIUM: 561MG

Cajun cooks know how to show off the superb texture and flavor of just-caught seafood. Frequently the most effective treatment for fresh fish and shellfish is the simplest. Here, a light, slightly peppery, lemon sauce coats the pasta, snapper, shrimp, and bell pepper. Serve the dish with crusty garlic bread dusted with chopped parsley.

CAJUN-STYLE SEAFOOD SAUCE

SERVES: 4
WORKING TIME: 30 MINUTES
TOTAL TIME: 30 MINUTES

10 ounces shaped pasta, such as medium shells or ruote (wagon wheels)

1 tablespoon olive oil

6 scallions, thinly sliced

4 cloves garlic, minced

2 ribs celery, thinly sliced

1 green bell pepper, cut into ½-inch squares

2 tablespoons flour

1 teaspoon paprika

¼ teaspoon cayenne pepper

¼ teaspoon freshly ground black pepper

1 cup bottled clam juice or reduced-sodium chicken broth, defatted

¾ pound medium shrimp, shelled, deveined (see tip), and halved lengthwise

½ pound skinless red snapper fillets, any visible bones removed, cut into large chunks

2 tablespoons fresh lemon juice

1. In a large pot of boiling water, cook the pasta until just tender. Drain well.

2. Meanwhile, in a large nonstick skillet, heat the oil until hot but not smoking over medium heat. Add the scallions, garlic, and celery and cook, stirring frequently, until the celery is tender, about 3 minutes. Add the bell pepper and cook, stirring frequently, until the bell pepper is crisp-tender, about 3 minutes.

3. Stir the flour, paprika, cayenne, and black pepper into the pan and cook until the vegetables are well coated, about 3 minutes. Gradually stir in the clam juice and ¼ cup of water and cook, stirring frequently, until the sauce is slightly thickened and no floury taste remains, about 4 minutes. Add the shrimp, snapper, and lemon juice. Cover and cook until the fish is just opaque, about 4 minutes. Toss the sauce with the hot pasta, divide among 4 bowls, and serve.

Helpful hint: Possible substitutes for red snapper—which can be quite expensive—include flounder, cod, haddock, and rockfish.

FAT: 7G/14%
CALORIES: 462
SATURATED FAT: 1G
CARBOHYDRATE: 62G
PROTEIN: 36G
CHOLESTEROL: 126MG
SODIUM: 295MG

TIP

To shell fresh shrimp, pull apart the shell at the belly of the shrimp with your fingers, splitting the shell, and remove. To devein, with the point of a sharp knife, score the shrimp along the back, and remove the dark vein.

FETTUCCINE WITH SPINACH AND FETA CHEESE

SERVES: 4
WORKING TIME: 20 MINUTES
TOTAL TIME: 30 MINUTES

If you've ever eaten spanakopita (Greek spinach pie), you know that spinach and tangy feta cheese taste great together. Here, the feta is "stretched" with part-skim ricotta, making this a cheese-rich—but low-fat—Mediterranean-style dish. Sun-dried tomatoes add a splash of color and bright tomato taste; to save time, they're heated in the broth rather than presoaked.

8 ounces fettuccine

1 cup reduced-sodium chicken broth, defatted

10-ounce package frozen chopped spinach, thawed and squeezed dry

⅓ cup sun-dried (not oil-packed) tomato halves

1 clove garlic, minced

1 cup part-skim ricotta cheese

¼ teaspoon freshly ground black pepper

¼ cup crumbled feta cheese

1. In a large pot of boiling water, cook the fettuccine until just tender. Drain well.

2. Meanwhile, in a medium saucepan, bring the broth, spinach, sun-dried tomatoes, and garlic to boil over high heat. Reduce the heat to a simmer, cover, and cook until the spinach is warmed through, about 5 minutes.

3. Stir the ricotta and pepper into the saucepan and cook until just warmed through, about 1 minute. Transfer the mixture to a large bowl, add the pasta and feta, and toss to combine. Divide the pasta mixture among 4 bowls and serve.

Helpful hint: To thaw the spinach in the microwave, remove all of the packaging, place the frozen spinach in a microwave-safe container, and microwave on high power for 2 to 3 minutes.

FAT: 9G/22%
CALORIES: 362
SATURATED FAT: 4.8G
CARBOHYDRATE: 51G
PROTEIN: 20G
CHOLESTEROL: 80MG
SODIUM: 402MG

ASIAN-STYLE CHICKEN AND VEGETABLE PASTA

SERVES: 4
WORKING TIME: 30 MINUTES
TOTAL TIME: 30 MINUTES

There's never a boring bite with this dish: Tender chicken contrasts with crisp vegetables, while ginger and garlic play against sesame and soy.

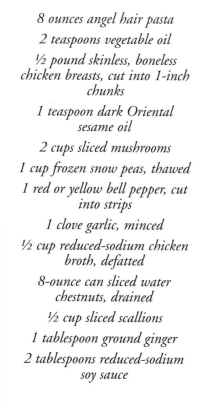

8 ounces angel hair pasta

2 teaspoons vegetable oil

½ pound skinless, boneless chicken breasts, cut into 1-inch chunks

1 teaspoon dark Oriental sesame oil

2 cups sliced mushrooms

1 cup frozen snow peas, thawed

1 red or yellow bell pepper, cut into strips

1 clove garlic, minced

½ cup reduced-sodium chicken broth, defatted

8-ounce can sliced water chestnuts, drained

½ cup sliced scallions

1 tablespoon ground ginger

2 tablespoons reduced-sodium soy sauce

1. In a large pot of boiling water, cook the pasta until just tender. Drain well.

2. Meanwhile, in a large nonstick skillet, heat the vegetable oil until hot but not smoking over medium-high heat. Add the chicken and cook, stirring, until browned, about 4 minutes. With a slotted spoon, transfer the chicken to a plate.

3. Add the sesame oil, mushrooms, snow peas, bell pepper, and garlic to the skillet. Cook, stirring, until the snow peas and bell pepper are crisp-tender, about 4 minutes. Add the broth, water chestnuts, scallions, ginger, and soy sauce. Return the chicken to the skillet. Cook until the vegetables are tender and the chicken is cooked through, about 3 minutes. Transfer the mixture to a large bowl, add the pasta, and toss to combine. Divide the pasta mixture among 4 plates and serve.

Helpful hint: Fans of spicy Szechuan dishes might like to add ¼ teaspoon of Chinese chili oil to this dish. Chinese chili oil is a fiery condiment made by steeping chilies in oil. It can be found in Asian grocery stores. Reduce the sesame oil by ¼ teaspoon and add the chili oil to the skillet at the same time.

FAT: 5G/12%
CALORIES: 366
SATURATED FAT: 0.8G
CARBOHYDRATE: 55G
PROTEIN: 24G
CHOLESTEROL: 33MG
SODIUM: 431MG

Egg Noodles with Ham, Cabbage, and Apples

Serves: 4
Working time: 30 minutes
Total time: 30 minutes

8 ounces "yolkless" egg noodles

1 tablespoon vegetable oil

1 onion, coarsely chopped

6 ounces reduced-fat ham, diced

1 teaspoon cumin seeds, or ½ teaspoon ground cumin

2 cups shredded cabbage

1 Red Delicious apple, cored and diced

1 cup reduced-sodium chicken broth, defatted

1 tablespoon cider vinegar

2 teaspoons Dijon mustard

1 tablespoon cornstarch

1. In a large pot of boiling water, cook the noodles until just tender. Drain well.

2. Meanwhile, in a large nonstick skillet, heat the oil until hot but not smoking over medium heat. Add the onion and ham and cook until the ham is lightly browned, about 4 minutes. Add the cumin seeds and cook until fragrant, about 1 minute. Add the cabbage, apple, and broth and bring to a boil. Reduce the heat to a simmer and cook until the cabbage is just tender, about 4 minutes.

3. In a small bowl, combine the vinegar, mustard, and cornstarch. Add the cornstarch mixture to the skillet and cook until the liquid is slightly thickened, about 1 minute.

4. Transfer the ham and cabbage mixture to a large bowl, add the noodles, and toss to combine. Divide the noodle mixture among 4 bowls and serve.

Helpful hint: Smoked turkey or chicken can be substituted for the ham.

Fat: 7g/18%
Calories: 345
Saturated Fat: 1.4g
Carbohydrate: 53g
Protein: 18g
Cholesterol: 20mg
Sodium: 850mg

Here's the German way to warm a cold winter day. Mustard, vinegar, and cumin seeds flavor the sauce.

HERBED TOMATO SAUCE

SERVES: 4
WORKING TIME: 15 MINUTES
TOTAL TIME: 20 MINUTES

The flavor of fresh herbs dissipates if they're cooked for more than a few minutes, so the tastiest sauce may well be one where they're not cooked at all. Here, basil, rosemary, and chives are stirred together with tomatoes and sautéed shallots and garlic. The herbs' flavors are released in a delicious waft of steam when you pour the sauce over the hot pasta.

2 tablespoons olive oil, preferably extra-virgin

3 shallots or 1 small onion, finely chopped

3 cloves garlic, minced

1½ pounds tomatoes, finely chopped

2 tablespoons no-salt-added tomato paste

½ cup chopped fresh basil

2 teaspoons chopped fresh rosemary, or ¾ teaspoon dried, crumbled

2 tablespoons snipped fresh chives or minced scallion greens

1¼ teaspoons salt

¼ teaspoon cayenne pepper

10 ounces medium tube pasta, such as ziti or penne

1. In a large nonstick skillet, heat 2 teaspoons of the oil until hot but not smoking over medium heat. Add the shallots and garlic and cook, stirring frequently, until the shallots are tender, about 5 minutes. Transfer to a large bowl.

2. Add the tomatoes, tomato paste, basil, rosemary, chives, salt, and cayenne to the bowl, stirring well to combine.

3. Meanwhile, in a large pot of boiling water, cook the pasta until just tender and drain well. Toss the hot pasta with the sauce and the remaining 4 teaspoons oil. Divide among 4 bowls and serve.

Helpful hint: Shallots are a member of the onion family with a mild, slightly garlicky flavor. Like garlic, shallots separate into cloves. Store shallots as you would onions, in a cool, dry place.

FAT: 9G/21%
CALORIES: 381
SATURATED FAT: 1.3G
CARBOHYDRATE: 66G
PROTEIN: 12G
CHOLESTEROL: 0MG
SODIUM: 713MG

FRESH FETTUCCINE WITH TOMATO CREAM SAUCE

SERVES: 4
WORKING TIME: 20 MINUTES
TOTAL TIME: 30 MINUTES

1 red bell pepper, halved lengthwise and seeded

1 cup evaporated low-fat milk

¼ cup grated Parmesan cheese

½ teaspoon salt

½ teaspoon freshly ground black pepper

1 teaspoon olive oil

3 tablespoons finely chopped prosciutto or Canadian bacon (1 ounce)

2 cups canned no-salt-added tomatoes, coarsely chopped with their juices

1 cup frozen peas, thawed

1 pound fresh fettuccine

1. Preheat the broiler. Place the bell pepper halves, cut-sides down, on the broiler rack. Broil the pepper 4 inches from the heat for 10 minutes, or until the skin is blackened. When the peppers are cool enough to handle, peel them and cut into thin strips. Start heating a large pot of water to boiling for the pasta.

2. Meanwhile, in a large bowl, combine the evaporated milk, Parmesan, salt, and pepper. Set aside.

3. In a large nonstick skillet, heat the oil until hot but not smoking over medium heat. Add the prosciutto and cook until lightly crisped, about 2 minutes. Add the tomatoes and red pepper strips and cook, stirring occasionally, until flavorful and lightly thickened, about 5 minutes. Add the peas and cook until heated through, about 2 minutes.

4. Cook the fettuccine in the boiling water until just tender. Drain and add to the milk and Parmesan mixture, tossing well to coat and to melt the cheese. Transfer the pasta to the tomato sauce in the skillet, toss to coat, and serve.

Helpful hint: You can substitute 12 ounces of dried fettuccine for the fresh pasta.

FAT: 10G/15%
CALORIES: 593
SATURATED FAT: 2.4G
CARBOHYDRATE: 98G
PROTEIN: 28G
CHOLESTEROL: 128MG
SODIUM: 823MG

340

The "cream" in this recipe is really evaporated low-fat milk. Here are the impressive figures on this "miracle" ingredient: Evaporated low-fat milk has a mere 3 grams of fat per cup, while the same amount of heavy cream has a whopping 90 grams! It's one of the more dramatic ways to cut fat in a sauce without sacrificing luxurious richness.

This will remind you of good old-fashioned spaghetti and meatballs, but without all the fat. For our meatballs, we've used lean ground meats, low-fat milk, a sprinkle of sharp Parmesan, and an egg white rather than a whole egg. If lean ground pork is not available, substitute an extra quarter pound of lean ground round.

SPAGHETTI AND LITTLE MEATBALLS

SERVES: 4
WORKING TIME: 20 MINUTES
TOTAL TIME: 25 MINUTES

1 tablespoon olive oil

1 medium onion, minced

2 cloves garlic, minced

¼ pound lean ground beef round

¼ pound lean ground pork

3 tablespoons chopped fresh parsley

½ teaspoon dried oregano

½ teaspoon salt

¼ teaspoon dried sage

¼ teaspoon freshly ground black pepper

2 slices (1 ounce each) white bread, crumbled

3 tablespoons low-fat (1%) milk

⅓ cup grated Parmesan cheese

1 egg white

14½-ounce can no-salt-added stewed tomatoes

8-ounce can no-salt-added tomato sauce

10 ounces spaghetti

1. Start heating a large pot of water to boiling for the pasta. In a large nonstick skillet, heat the oil until hot but not smoking over medium heat. Add the onion and garlic and cook, stirring frequently, until the onion begins to soften, about 5 minutes. Transfer the onion to a large bowl. Reserve the skillet.

2. Add the ground beef and pork, the parsley, oregano, salt, sage, and pepper to the onion and mix well. Stir in the bread, milk, 3 tablespoons of the Parmesan, and egg white until well combined. Shape into 32 small meatballs (see tip).

3. In the reserved skillet, combine the tomatoes and the tomato sauce, breaking the tomatoes up with the back of a spoon. Bring to a boil over medium-high heat, reduce to a simmer, and add the meatballs. Cover and cook until the meatballs are cooked through, about 7 minutes.

4. Meanwhile, cook the spaghetti in the boiling water until just tender. Drain well. Transfer the meatballs and sauce to a large bowl, add the spaghetti and the remaining Parmesan, and toss to combine. Spoon the spaghetti and meatballs onto 4 plates and serve.

Suggested accompaniments: Romaine and cherry tomato salad with an herbed buttermilk dressing, and pears poached in apricot nectar with grated lemon zest for dessert.

FAT: 15G/25%
CALORIES: 547
SATURATED FAT: 4.8G
CARBOHYDRATE: 76G
PROTEIN: 27G
CHOLESTEROL: 44MG
SODIUM: 570MG

TIP

Keeping the meatballs small distributes the meat more evenly throughout each serving, creating the sensation of richness in every bite. Lightly dampen your hands, pull off a piece of meat mixture about the size of a walnut, and gently roll into balls with your fingertips or the palms of your hands. Place on a clean plate.

Fresh asparagus, the harbinger of spring, is played to full advantage against a background of pasta and tender chunks of chicken, all tossed in a creamy sauce made with reduced-fat sour cream. When shopping for asparagus, select medium-green, firm, straight spears with smooth, unwrinkled stems and compact tips.

STIR-FRIED CHICKEN AND ASPARAGUS WITH LINGUINE

SERVES: 4
WORKING TIME: 20 MINUTES
TOTAL TIME: 20 MINUTES

6 ounces linguine

2 teaspoons olive oil

1 ounce smoked turkey, finely chopped

1 pound skinless, boneless chicken breasts, cut into 1-inch pieces

½ teaspoon salt

¾ pound asparagus, trimmed, peeled (see tip), and cut diagonally into 1-inch pieces

¾ cup reduced-sodium chicken broth, defatted

3 tablespoons light sour cream

2 tablespoons snipped fresh chives or finely chopped scallion

4 teaspoons coarsely chopped pecans

1. In a large pot of boiling water, cook the pasta until just tender. Drain, return the pasta to the cooking pot, and cover to keep warm.

2. Meanwhile, in a large nonstick skillet, heat the oil until hot but not smoking over medium heat. Add the turkey and cook, stirring frequently, until the turkey begins to brown, about 1 minute. Add the chicken and salt and cook, stirring frequently, until the chicken is lightly browned, about 3 minutes.

3. Stir in the asparagus and cook for 1 minute. Add the broth. Bring to a boil over medium-high heat, reduce to a simmer, and cook until the chicken is cooked through and the asparagus is tender, about 3 minutes longer. Remove from the heat. With a slotted spoon, transfer the chicken mixture to the pasta pot.

4. Stir the sour cream and chives into the sauce, pour over the chicken and pasta mixture, and toss to combine. Spoon the chicken-pasta mixture onto 4 plates, sprinkle with the pecans, and serve.

Suggested accompaniments: Shredded carrot salad with a reduced-fat poppy seed dressing, and small scoops of raspberry and orange sherbet for dessert.

TIP

To prepare for cooking, rinse asparagus well, paying particular attention to the tips. Trim off the woody ends. Unless the asparagus is pencil-thin, the outer layers can be tough, so peeling is recommended. Using a swivel-bladed vegetable peeler, remove the outside layers of the stems until you reach the tender centers.

FAT: 8G/20%
CALORIES: 359
SATURATED FAT: 1.7G
CARBOHYDRATE: 35G
PROTEIN: 36G
CHOLESTEROL: 73MG
SODIUM: 543MG

CURRIED VEGETABLE COUSCOUS

SERVES: 4
WORKING TIME: 25 MINUTES
TOTAL TIME: 25 MINUTES

Though it looks like no other pasta, North Africa's couscous is made of the same semolina flour and water that go into spaghetti and macaroni. This innovative dish crosses borders, combining the grainlike pasta with India's curry seasonings and chutney. Unlike other pastas, couscous is cooked very quickly in a small amount of liquid, so this entire meal can be cooked in one skillet.

2 teaspoons olive oil
1 red onion, diced
2 carrots, thinly sliced
2 cloves garlic, minced
2 teaspoons curry powder
2 teaspoons ground cumin
13¾-ounce can reduced-sodium chicken broth, defatted
15-ounce can chick-peas, rinsed and drained
¼ cup dried currants or raisins
2 tablespoons mango chutney
1 tablespoon white wine vinegar
2 teaspoons grated fresh ginger
½ teaspoon salt
¾ cup couscous
3 tablespoons chopped fresh cilantro or parsley

1. In a large nonstick skillet, heat the oil until hot but not smoking over medium heat. Add the onion and carrots and cook until the onion is softened, about 5 minutes. Stir in the garlic, curry powder, and cumin and cook for 1 minute to blend the flavors.

2. Add the broth, chick-peas, currants, chutney, vinegar, ginger, and salt to the skillet and bring to a boil. Remove the skillet from the heat, stir in the couscous, cover, and let stand until the couscous is tender, about 5 minutes. Stir in the cilantro and serve.

Helpful hints: If the fresh ginger you are using has thin skin, you don't need to peel it before grating. If the skin is thick and leathery, however, it's best to remove it with a vegetable peeler. Mango chutney often contains large chunks of mango; for even flavoring, you may need to chop the chutney before using it in this dish.

FAT: 5G/14%
CALORIES: 323
SATURATED FAT: 0.4G
CARBOHYDRATE: 60G
PROTEIN: 12G
CHOLESTEROL: 0MG
SODIUM: 780MG

MEXICAN CHICKEN AND SALSA PASTA

SERVES: 4
WORKING TIME: 20 MINUTES
TOTAL TIME: 20 MINUTES

There's a jar in your kitchen that will make quick and tasty pasta sauce, but it's not what you might expect—it's lively tomato salsa. Salsa, enhanced with additional cumin and cilantro, turns spaghettini, chicken, and corn into a meal worthy of a fiesta. Toss an accompanying salad with a cooling yogurt dressing.

8 ounces spaghettini
2 teaspoons vegetable oil
1 pound skinless, boneless chicken breasts, cut crosswise into 1-inch-wide strips
1 teaspoon ground cumin
1½ cups mild or medium-hot prepared salsa
10-ounce package frozen corn kernels
2 tablespoons chopped fresh cilantro or parsley

1. In a large pot of boiling water, cook the spaghettini until just tender. Drain well.

2. Meanwhile, in a large nonstick skillet, heat the oil until hot but not smoking over medium heat. Add the chicken and cook, turning once, until the chicken is golden brown, about 5 minutes. Add the cumin and cook until fragrant, about 30 seconds. Stir in the salsa and corn and bring to a boil. Reduce the heat to a simmer, cover, and cook until the chicken is cooked through, about 5 minutes.

3. Divide the pasta among 4 plates, spoon the sauce over, sprinkle with the cilantro, and serve.

Helpful hint: Heating the cumin brings out its toasty flavor and fragrance. Other spices, such as coriander and curry powder, benefit from this treatment, too.

FAT: 5G/10%
CALORIES: 447
SATURATED FAT: 0.9G
CARBOHYDRATE: 63G
PROTEIN: 36G
CHOLESTEROL: 66MG
SODIUM: 959MG

Vegetable Chow Mein

SERVES: 4
WORKING TIME: 30 MINUTES
TOTAL TIME: 30 MINUTES

Although "chow mein" is an authentic Cantonese dish, it has been in this country for so long (probably since the early 1850s) that it has nearly achieved traditional American cuisine status. Basically a noodle stir-fry, it can include all manner of ingredients; here we present a light, meatless version made with fettuccine in place of the usual fresh Chinese egg noodles.

8 ounces fettuccine

1 tablespoon dark Oriental sesame oil

6 scallions, thinly sliced

4 cloves garlic, finely chopped

2 tablespoons finely chopped fresh ginger

1 red bell pepper, cut into thin strips

1 green bell pepper, cut into thin strips

2 ribs celery, cut into ¼-inch slices

½ pound button mushrooms, halved

¼ teaspoon salt

2 teaspoons cornstarch

¾ cup reduced-sodium chicken broth, defatted

3 tablespoons reduced-sodium soy sauce

2 tablespoons dry sherry

1 tablespoon fresh lemon juice

1. In a large pot of boiling water, cook the fettuccine until just tender. Drain well.

2. Meanwhile, in a large nonstick skillet or wok, heat 2 teaspoons of the sesame oil until hot but not smoking over medium heat. Add the scallions, garlic, and ginger and stir-fry until the scallions are crisp-tender, about 1 minute. Add the bell peppers, celery, and mushrooms and stir-fry until the bell peppers and celery are crisp-tender, about 4 minutes. Add the pasta to the skillet and stir-fry until lightly crisped, about 1 minute.

3. In a small bowl, combine the salt, cornstarch, broth, soy sauce, sherry, lemon juice, and the remaining 1 teaspoon oil. Pour the mixture into the skillet and cook, stirring, until slightly thickened, about 1 minute.

Helpful hint: You can cut up the bell peppers and celery a few hours ahead of time; combine them in a sealable bag or a covered bowl and refrigerate until needed.

FAT: 6G/17%
CALORIES: 313
SATURATED FAT: 1G
CARBOHYDRATE: 52G
PROTEIN: 12G
CHOLESTEROL: 54MG
SODIUM: 744MG

CHICKEN WITH SPAGHETTI AND SUMMER SQUASH

SERVES: 4
WORKING TIME: 20 MINUTES
TOTAL TIME: 20 MINUTES

6 ounces spaghetti

2 teaspoons olive oil

3 cloves garlic, minced

1 pound skinless, boneless chicken thighs, cut into 1-inch chunks

10 ounces yellow summer squash, halved lengthwise and cut into ½-inch-thick pieces

1 red bell pepper, cut into ½-inch chunks

¾ teaspoon dried sage

1½ cups diced plum tomatoes

1 tablespoon red wine vinegar

½ teaspoon salt

2 tablespoons grated Parmesan cheese

1. In a large pot of boiling water, cook the pasta until just tender. Drain.

2. Meanwhile, in a large nonstick skillet, heat the oil until hot but not smoking over low heat. Add the garlic and cook, stirring frequently, until fragrant, about 30 seconds. Increase the heat to medium, add the chicken, and cook, stirring occasionally, until the chicken is lightly browned, about 3 minutes.

3. Add the squash, bell pepper, and sage and cook, stirring frequently, until the vegetables begin to soften, about 3 minutes. Add the tomatoes, vinegar, and salt and cook until the chicken is cooked through and the vegetables are tender, about 4 minutes longer.

4. Place the pasta on 4 plates and spoon the chicken and vegetables on top. Sprinkle with the Parmesan and serve.

Suggested accompaniment: Belgian endive and sliced tomato salad sprinkled with lemon juice and chopped fresh parsley.

This simple chicken sauce is ready in the amount of time it takes to cook the pasta. And you may substitute freely; zucchini for the yellow squash, balsamic vinegar for the red wine vinegar, and dried oregano or rosemary for the sage. Bow-ties or wagon wheels would be fun alternate pasta shapes to use in this dish.

FAT: 8G/21%
CALORIES: 348
SATURATED FAT: 1.6G
CARBOHYDRATE: 40G
PROTEIN: 29G
CHOLESTEROL: 94MG
SODIUM: 380MG

ROTINI WITH PORK, CHICK-PEAS, AND SPINACH

SERVES: 4
WORKING TIME: 20 MINUTES
TOTAL TIME: 25 MINUTES

The combination of meaty textures and warm, saucy flavors in this delightful sauce is sure to quell the hungriest diners.

1 tablespoon flour

6 ounces pork loin, trimmed and cut into 1½-by-¼-inch strips

1 tablespoon olive oil

1 red bell pepper, cut into thin strips

4 cloves garlic, minced

6 cups rinsed, dried, and coarsely chopped spinach leaves

3 tablespoons chopped fresh basil

¾ teaspoon salt

¼ teaspoon freshly ground black pepper

⅛ teaspoon ground nutmeg

½ cup reduced-sodium chicken broth, defatted

4 teaspoons Dijon mustard

1 cup canned chick-peas, rinsed and drained

12 ounces rotini pasta

1. Start heating a large pot of water to boiling for the pasta. On a plate, spread the flour. Dredge the pork in the flour, shaking off the excess. In a large nonstick skillet, heat the oil until hot but not smoking over medium heat. Add the pork and cook, stirring frequently, until the pork is golden brown and cooked through, about 4 minutes. With a slotted spoon, transfer the pork to a plate.

2. Add the bell pepper to the pan and cook, stirring frequently, until tender, about 5 minutes. Add the garlic and cook, stirring frequently, until fragrant, about 1 minute. Stir in the spinach, basil, salt, black pepper, and nutmeg and cook, stirring frequently, until the spinach has wilted, about 3 minutes. Add the broth and mustard and cook until the flavors are blended, about 1 minute. Add the chick-peas and pork and cook until heated through, about 2 minutes longer.

3. Meanwhile, cook the rotini in the boiling water until just tender. Transfer the pork mixture to a large bowl, add the rotini, and toss to combine. Spoon the rotini mixture onto 4 plates and serve.

Suggested accompaniments: Crusty rolls. For dessert, fresh mango slices drizzled with a purée of raspberries.

FAT: 9G/16%
CALORIES: 503
SATURATED FAT: 1.5G
CARBOHYDRATE: 79G
PROTEIN: 26G
CHOLESTEROL: 27MG
SODIUM: 824MG

FETTUCCINE WITH CHICKEN AND TANGY ONION SAUCE

SERVES: 4
WORKING TIME: 20 MINUTES
TOTAL TIME: 30 MINUTES

6 ounces fettuccine

1 teaspoon vegetable oil

1 pound skinless, boneless chicken thighs, cut into 2-inch chunks

1 large onion, halved and thinly sliced

3 cloves garlic, minced

2 carrots, cut into julienne strips

½ pound mushrooms, cut into quarters

½ teaspoon sugar

½ teaspoon salt

2 tablespoons red wine vinegar

1 scallion, cut into julienne strips

1. In a large pot of boiling water, cook the pasta until just tender. Drain.

2. Meanwhile, in a large nonstick skillet, heat the oil until hot but not smoking over medium heat. Add the chicken and cook, stirring frequently, until lightly browned, about 3 minutes. With a slotted spoon, transfer the chicken to a plate.

3. Add the onion and garlic to the pan and cook, stirring frequently, until the onion begins to soften, about 3 minutes. Add the carrots, mushrooms, sugar, and salt and cook until the vegetables begin to soften, about 4 minutes. Return the chicken to the pan and cook until the chicken is cooked through, about 4 minutes longer.

4. Stir in the vinegar and scallion. Place the pasta on 4 plates, spoon the chicken and vegetables on top, and serve.

Suggested accompaniments: Mixed greens with a mustard vinaigrette. For dessert, fresh fruit salad topped with raspberries puréed with a little red currant jelly.

FAT: 8G/20%
CALORIES: 360
SATURATED FAT: 1.7G
CARBOHYDRATE: 42G
PROTEIN: 31G
CHOLESTEROL: 135MG
SODIUM: 397MG

In this distinctive dish, a bit of wine vinegar complements the richness of the chicken and mushrooms.

Penne Caprese

SERVES: 4
WORKING TIME: 10 MINUTES
TOTAL TIME: 20 MINUTES

12 ounces penne pasta

2 teaspoons olive oil

3 cloves garlic, minced

1 pound plum tomatoes (about 4), coarsely chopped

½ cup diced cucumber

⅓ cup diced red onion

3 tablespoons chopped fresh basil

3 tablespoons chopped fresh parsley

½ teaspoon dried tarragon

½ teaspoon salt

6 ounces part-skim mozzarella cheese, diced (about 1½ cups)

¼ cup coarsely chopped, pitted brine-cured black olives (such as Calamata)

1. Heat a large pot of water to boiling, and cook the penne until just tender. Drain well.

2. Meanwhile, in a small nonstick skillet, heat the oil until hot but not smoking over low heat. Add the garlic and cook, stirring frequently, until tender, about 4 minutes. Transfer the garlic and oil to a large bowl. Add the tomatoes, cucumber, onion, basil, parsley, tarragon, and salt and toss to coat. Stir in the mozzarella and olives.

3. Add the penne and toss to combine. Serve immediately, or cover and refrigerate for up to 4 hours. May be served chilled or at room temperature. Spoon the penne salad into 4 bowls and serve.

U*sing just a few plump Calamata olives lends a mellow richness to this fresh-tasting combination of ripe tomatoes, pasta, mild cheese, and herbs—without adding excessive fat. French Niçoise olives would be another good choice. For a stronger flavored cheese, try Greek feta. And for an alternate pasta shape, use ziti or medium shells instead of the penne.*

FAT: 12G/22%
CALORIES: 491
SATURATED FAT: 4.9G
CARBOHYDRATE: 74G
PROTEIN: 23G
CHOLESTEROL: 25MG
SODIUM: 565MG

Fusilli alla Puttanesca

Serves: 4
Working time: 20 minutes
Total time: 25 minutes

1 tablespoon olive oil

1 large red onion, diced

4 cloves garlic, minced

1 rib celery, thinly sliced

14½-ounce can no-salt-added stewed tomatoes

2 tablespoons no-salt-added tomato paste

½ teaspoon red pepper flakes

½ teaspoon salt

¼ teaspoon dried oregano

¼ teaspoon dried rosemary

⅓ cup pitted green olives, halved

6⅛-ounce can water-packed tuna, drained and flaked

3 tablespoons chopped fresh parsley

8 ounces long fusilli pasta

1. Start heating a large pot of water to boiling for the pasta. In a large nonstick skillet, heat the oil until hot but not smoking over medium heat. Add the onion and garlic and cook, stirring frequently, until the onion has softened, about 7 minutes. Stir in the celery and cook until the celery is crisp-tender, about 3 minutes.

2. Add the tomatoes, breaking them up with the back of a spoon. Stir in the tomato paste, pepper flakes, salt, oregano, and rosemary until well combined. Add the olives and bring to a boil over high heat. Reduce to a simmer, cover partially, and cook until the flavors are blended and the sauce is slightly thickened, about 5 minutes. Stir in the tuna and cook until the tuna is heated through, about 2 minutes longer. Stir in the parsley.

3. Meanwhile, cook the fusilli in the boiling water until just tender. Drain well. Transfer the tuna mixture to a large bowl, add the fusilli, toss to combine, and serve.

Suggested accompaniments: Red wine, a salad of Boston lettuce and radicchio with sliced red onion in a citrus vinaigrette, and a finale of angel food cake.

Italy's well-loved puttanesca sauce is quickly prepared from ingredients usually on hand, and has become a standard favorite in this country as well. Our version replaces the traditional anchovies with fat-slashing water-packed tuna. Canned salmon would also be at home in this dish.

Fat: 6g/15%
Calories: 366
Saturated Fat: .8g
Carbohydrate: 56g
Protein: 22g
Cholesterol: 17mg
Sodium: 731mg

FETTUCCINE WITH CHICKEN, ASPARAGUS, AND PEAS

SERVES: 4
WORKING TIME: 15 MINUTES
TOTAL TIME: 25 MINUTES

To create this rich (yet low-fat) sauce, we've thickened it with a little cornstarch and stirred in light sour cream—off the heat to avoid separation. Although you may use frozen asparagus, tender fresh spears from early spring are best. Select bright green, firm stalks with tight tips. If stalks still seem tough after trimming the ends, peel them with a vegetable peeler.

1 tablespoon Oriental sesame oil

1 red bell pepper, cut into thin strips

6 ounces skinless, boneless chicken breasts, cut into ¼-inch-wide strips

6 scallions, cut diagonally into ½-inch pieces

½ pound asparagus, trimmed and cut into 1-inch pieces

¾ cup reduced-sodium chicken broth, defatted

2 teaspoons fresh lemon juice

1 teaspoon grated lemon zest

½ teaspoon salt

½ teaspoon dried thyme

⅔ cup frozen peas

2 teaspoons cornstarch

2 tablespoons light sour cream

10 ounces fettuccine

¼ cup grated Parmesan cheese

1. Start heating a large pot of water to boiling for the pasta. In a large nonstick skillet, heat the oil until hot but not smoking over medium heat. Add the bell pepper and cook, stirring frequently, until crisp-tender, about 3 minutes. Add the chicken and scallions, stirring to coat. Add the asparagus, broth, lemon juice, lemon zest, salt, and thyme and cook until the asparagus is crisp-tender, about 1 minute. Stir in the peas and cook until the peas are heated through, about 1 minute.

2. In a cup, combine the cornstarch and 1 tablespoon of water and stir to blend. Bring the chicken mixture to a boil over medium-high heat, stir in the cornstarch mixture, and cook, stirring constantly, until the mixture is slightly thickened and the chicken is cooked through, about 1 minute longer. Remove from the heat and stir in the sour cream.

3. Meanwhile, cook the fettuccine in the boiling water until just tender. Drain well. Transfer the chicken mixture to a large bowl, add the fettuccine and Parmesan, and toss to combine. Spoon the fettuccine mixture into 4 shallow bowls and serve.

Suggested accompaniments: Garlic toast, and orange sorbet sprinkled with melon liqueur for dessert.

FAT: 8G/17%
CALORIES: 423
SATURATED FAT: 2.3G
CARBOHYDRATE: 63G
PROTEIN: 25G
CHOLESTEROL: 31MG
SODIUM: 550MG

If you're looking for a quick meal with flair, search no further. Sweet, delicate scallops are always a treat; dusted with cumin, sautéed with vegetables, and served over freshly cooked linguine, they make a fine dinner for family or friends. Partner the main dish with a salad of dark leafy greens and cherry tomatoes.

SPICY SCALLOPS WITH LINGUINE

SERVES: 4
WORKING TIME: 30 MINUTES
TOTAL TIME: 30 MINUTES

8 ounces linguine

1 tablespoon flour

1 teaspoon ground cumin

¼ teaspoon salt

¼ teaspoon freshly ground black pepper

1 pound bay scallops or quartered sea scallops (see tip)

1 tablespoon olive oil

1 cup sliced scallions

1 clove garlic, minced

1 zucchini, cut into ¼-inch dice

1 yellow summer squash, cut into ¼-inch dice

2 tomatoes, diced

1 small fresh or pickled jalapeño pepper, seeded and minced

½ cup reduced-sodium chicken broth, defatted

1. In a large pot of boiling water, cook the linguine until just tender. Drain well.

2. Meanwhile, in a sturdy plastic bag, combine the flour, cumin, salt, and pepper. Add the scallops to the bag, tossing to coat. In a large nonstick skillet or wok, heat 2 teaspoons of the oil until hot but not smoking over medium-high heat. Add the scallops and stir-fry until the scallops are just opaque, 2 to 3 minutes. With a slotted spoon, transfer the scallops to a plate.

3. Add the remaining 1 teaspoon oil to the skillet. Add the scallions and garlic and stir-fry until the scallions are softened, about 1 minute. Add the zucchini, summer squash, tomatoes, jalapeño, and broth and bring to a boil. Cook, stirring, until the squash is crisp-tender, about 3 minutes. Return the scallops to the pan and cook until heated through, about 1 minute.

4. Divide the pasta among 4 plates, spoon the scallops and sauce over, and serve.

Helpful hints: It's best to buy scallops no longer than one day before you plan to use them. Before dredging them in the flour mixture, use paper towels to pat the scallops dry.

TIP

If the smaller and sweeter bay scallops are not available, use the larger sea scallops. Cut each one into quarters so they are about the same size as the bay variety.

FAT: 6G/14%
CALORIES: 389
SATURATED FAT: 0.7G
CARBOHYDRATE: 55G
PROTEIN: 29G
CHOLESTEROL: 38MG
SODIUM: 415MG

SPAGHETTI WITH CHILI SAUCE

SERVES: 4
WORKING TIME: 25 MINUTES
TOTAL TIME: 25 MINUTES

Making chili can be an all-day project; the Tex-Mex favorite is usually slow-simmered to blend the flavors of beans, meat, and complex spices. But this praiseworthy chili dinner is ready in less than half an hour. Just toss the chili with the spaghetti, crown it with a dollop of creamy yogurt sauce, and bring it to the table with a basket of seeded semolina bread.

8 ounces spaghetti
2 teaspoons vegetable oil
½ pound lean ground beef
1 onion, coarsely chopped
3 cloves garlic, minced
1 tablespoon chili powder
Two 14½-ounce cans no-salt-added stewed tomatoes
15-ounce can red kidney beans, rinsed and drained
4½-ounce can chopped mild green chilies, drained
¼ teaspoon salt
¼ cup plain nonfat yogurt
2 tablespoons reduced-fat sour cream
¼ cup sliced scallions

1. In a large pot of boiling water, cook the spaghetti until just tender. Drain well.

2. Meanwhile, in a large nonstick skillet, heat the oil until hot but not smoking over medium heat. Add the beef, onion, and garlic and cook, stirring to break up the meat, until the meat is browned, about 5 minutes.

3. Add the chili powder to the skillet and cook until fragrant, about 1 minute. Stir in the tomatoes, kidney beans, green chilies, and salt and bring to a boil. Reduce the heat to a simmer and cook until the chili sauce is slightly thickened, about 10 minutes.

4. Meanwhile, in a small bowl, combine the yogurt, sour cream, and scallions. Transfer the chili sauce to a large bowl, add the pasta, and toss to combine. Divide the pasta mixture among 4 plates, top with a dollop of the yogurt-scallion mixture, and serve.

Helpful hint: If you like your chili hot, you can increase the amount of chili powder and substitute chopped jalapeños for the mild green chilies.

FAT: 17G/27%
CALORIES: 565
SATURATED FAT: 5.7G
CARBOHYDRATE: 77G
PROTEIN: 27G
CHOLESTEROL: 45MG
SODIUM: 577MG

DESSERTS

Left, Hot Strawberry Sundaes
Above, Triple Chocolate Pudding

Chocolate-Dipped Fruits

SERVES: 4
WORKING TIME: 30 MINUTES
TOTAL TIME: 30 MINUTES PLUS SETTING TIME

4 ounces semisweet chocolate, coarsely chopped

1 teaspoon vegetable oil

1 green apple, cored, cut into 8 wedges, and patted dry

1 red apple, cored, cut into 8 wedges, and patted dry

1 cup whole strawberries, patted dry

¾ cup dried apricot halves

½ cup dried pear halves

1. In a small bowl set over, not in, a pan of simmering water, melt the chocolate, stirring frequently. Remove the bowl from over the pan, stir in the oil, and let cool slightly.

2. With a fork, spear each apple wedge and dip halfway into the melted chocolate. Place on a wire rack set over a sheet of wax paper. One at a time, by hand, dip the strawberries, apricots, and pears halfway into the melted chocolate and place on the rack. Let the fruits stand until the chocolate is firm. (If necessary, refrigerate for up to 30 minutes to help set the chocolate.) Divide the fruits among 4 dessert plates and serve.

Helpful hints: These are best served soon after the fruits have been dipped, since the chocolate will readily soften at room temperature. If serving on a buffet, arrange the fruits on a tray placed over a pan of ice water.

FAT: 10G/29%
CALORIES: 314
SATURATED FAT: 5.1G
CARBOHYDRATE: 62G
PROTEIN: 3G
CHOLESTEROL: 0MG
SODIUM: 7MG

What could be more tantalizing during the holidays than these delectable treats? Chocolate and fruit are one of those time- and taste-honored favorites, always popular, regardless of the season. Put a plate of these on a buffet table, and guests will make a beeline for them. Or serve with after-dinner cordials and coffee in front of the fire.

CARAMELIZED ORANGES WITH TOASTED ALMONDS

SERVES: 4
WORKING TIME: 10 MINUTES
TOTAL TIME: 15 MINUTES

Bring a touch of sun-washed southern Italy to your table with these glowing, sweetly glazed orange slices. Be sure to buy eating oranges (rather than juice oranges) for this recipe. Navel oranges are reliably sweet (and they're conveniently seedless), but juicier Valencias would work well in this recipe, too. A cup of cappuccino and a crisp cookie would go well with the oranges.

1 tablespoon slivered orange zest
½ cup sugar
2 tablespoons fresh lemon juice
4 large navel oranges
2 tablespoons sliced almonds, toasted

1. In a medium saucepan, combine the orange zest, sugar, and lemon juice, stirring well to combine. Cook over medium heat, without stirring, until the syrup is pale amber in color, about 5 minutes.

2. Meanwhile, with a paring knife, peel the skin and outer membranes from the oranges. Cut each orange crosswise into five ½-inch-thick rounds. Add the oranges to the hot syrup in the saucepan and gently spoon the sauce over the oranges. Divide the oranges among 4 plates and spoon the sauce and zest over. Serve at room temperature or chilled; sprinkle with the almonds just before serving.

Helpful hint: Be careful when adding the oranges to the pan of hot syrup: Lay the slices gently in the syrup so that it does not splatter.

FAT: 2G/9%
CALORIES: 196
SATURATED FAT: .2G
CARBOHYDRATE: 47G
PROTEIN: 2G
CHOLESTEROL: 0MG
SODIUM: 2MG

*I*f
fall weather brings the
grilling season to a
close in your part of
the country, be sure to
try this recipe before
you put your
equipment away for
the winter. Pears are
plentiful in the
autumn, and the
toasty taste of
butterscotch is just the
thing for a chilly-day
dessert.

GRILLED PEARS WITH BUTTERSCOTCH SAUCE

SERVES: 4
WORKING TIME: 25 MINUTES
TOTAL TIME: 25 MINUTES

4 large firm-ripe Anjou or Bartlett pears

3 tablespoons fresh lime juice

2 tablespoons granulated sugar

⅓ cup evaporated skimmed milk

2 tablespoons firmly packed light brown sugar

2 teaspoons unsalted butter

½ teaspoon vanilla extract

1. Preheat the grill and the grill topper to a medium heat. (When ready to cook, spray the rack—off the grill—with nonstick cooking spray; see page 6.)

2. Peel the pears, halve them lengthwise, and core (see tip). With a sharp knife, cut a very thin slice from the rounded side of each pear half so it will lie flat on the grill topper. In a medium bowl, toss the pear halves with the lime juice and granulated sugar.

3. Grill the pear halves on the grill topper for 4 minutes. Turn the pears over, drizzle with any remaining lime juice mixture, and grill for 5 minutes or until tender.

4. Meanwhile, in a small saucepan, combine the evaporated milk, brown sugar, butter, and vanilla. Cook directly on the grill or on the stovetop over medium heat, stirring constantly, until the mixture comes to a gentle boil. Cook until the sauce is smooth and slightly thickened, about 2 minutes. Divide the pears among 4 plates, drizzle with the butterscotch sauce, and serve hot or warm.

Helpful hint: The grilled pear halves—without the butterscotch sauce— would be a wonderful accompaniment to grilled poultry.

FAT: 3G/13%
CALORIES: 211
SATURATED FAT: 1.3G
CARBOHYDRATE: 48G
PROTEIN: 3G
CHOLESTEROL: 6MG
SODIUM: 27MG

With a paring knife, peel the pear. Halve the pear lengthwise and use a knife (or a grapefruit spoon) to cut out the core.

FRUIT WITH CANNOLI CREAM

SERVES: 4
WORKING TIME: 10 MINUTES
TOTAL TIME: 10 MINUTES

1 cup part-skim ricotta cheese

⅓ cup sugar

¾ teaspoon grated orange zest

3 tablespoons orange juice

2 tablespoons mini chocolate chips

1 apple, cored and cut into 8 wedges

1 pear, cored and cut into 8 wedges

1 plum, pitted and cut into 8 wedges

1 pint strawberries, hulled

1. In a food processor, combine the ricotta, sugar, orange zest, and orange juice and process until smooth. Transfer the mixture to a medium bowl and fold in 1 tablespoon of the chocolate chips.

2. Place the fruit on a platter, spoon the ricotta mixture on the side, sprinkle with the remaining 1 tablespoon chocolate chips, and serve.

Helpful hint: You can also arrange the fruit in four large goblets and top each portion with some of the cream and chocolate chips.

FAT: 7G/25%
CALORIES: 257
SATURATED FAT: 3.9G
CARBOHYDRATE: 44G
PROTEIN: 8G
CHOLESTEROL: 19MG
SODIUM: 78MG

Cannoli are crisp tube-shaped pastries filled with a chocolate-dotted ricotta cream; the cannoli shells are deep-fried before they're filled, making this a dessert to avoid if you're watching your fat intake. But you can still enjoy the flavor of the ricotta cream as a topping for fresh fruit. We've used part-skim ricotta for this slim but luscious treat.

LATTE COTTA

SERVES: 6
WORKING TIME: 10 MINUTES
TOTAL TIME: 15 MINUTES PLUS CHILLING TIME

You won't find a recipe for this velvety chocolate pudding in a standard Italian cookbook; it's our lightened version of a classic called "panne cotta" (cooked cream), made with "latte" (milk) instead. We don't stop with the cream though—we cut more fat by using cocoa powder rather than chocolate. Crumbled amaretti cookies make a crunchy topping.

1 envelope unflavored gelatin
2¼ cups low-fat (1%) milk
¼ cup unsweetened cocoa powder
¾ teaspoon cinnamon
¼ cup boiling water
½ cup firmly packed dark brown sugar
⅛ teaspoon salt
¾ teaspoon vanilla extract
6 amaretti cookies, crumbled

1. In a small bowl, sprinkle the gelatin over ¼ cup of the milk and let stand until softened, about 3 minutes. In another small bowl, combine the cocoa powder and cinnamon. Gradually add the boiling water to the cocoa mixture, whisking until smooth and no lumps remain. Set aside.

2. In a medium saucepan, combine the remaining 2 cups milk, the brown sugar, and salt. Whisk in the cocoa mixture until well combined. Bring to a boil over medium heat. Reduce the heat to a simmer, whisk in the gelatin mixture, and remove from the heat. Stir in the vanilla.

3. Divide the mixture among four 6-ounce dessert dishes and chill until set, about 2 hours. Sprinkle the amaretti cookies on top and serve.

Helpful hint: For a lump-free pudding, you will need lump-free brown sugar. If your sugar has hardened into rock-like pellets, place it in a microwavable dish and sprinkle it lightly with water; cover and cook on high power for 30 seconds.

FAT: 2G/12%
CALORIES: 145
SATURATED FAT: .9G
CARBOHYDRATE: 29G
PROTEIN: 5G
CHOLESTEROL: 4MG
SODIUM: 105MG

BANANA GRATIN WITH MARSALA CREAM

SERVES: 4
WORKING TIME: 10 MINUTES
TOTAL TIME: 10 MINUTES

In this delicious dessert, broiled bananas glazed with brown sugar are served over a creamy sauce flavored with Marsala.

⅓ cup reduced-fat sour cream

¼ cup plain nonfat yogurt

¼ cup firmly packed light brown sugar

2 tablespoons Marsala wine

¾ teaspoon grated lemon zest

⅛ teaspoon nutmeg

4 large bananas, peeled and sliced on the diagonal into ¾-inch long pieces

2 tablespoons fresh lemon juice

1. In a small bowl, combine the sour cream, yogurt, 2 tablespoons of the brown sugar, the Marsala, lemon zest, and nutmeg. Refrigerate until serving time.

2. Preheat the broiler. Arrange the banana pieces in a single layer on a broilerproof pan. Sprinkle the lemon juice over the bananas, then sprinkle with the remaining 2 tablespoons brown sugar. Broil 6 inches from the heat for 4 minutes, or until the sugar has melted and the bananas are heated through. Divide the Marsala cream among 4 plates, top with the bananas, and serve.

Helpful hint: To speed the ripening of bananas, place them in a plastic bag with a slice of apple and store at room temperature or in a slightly warm place.

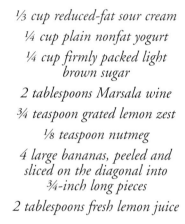

FAT: 3G/12%
CALORIES: 226
SATURATED FAT: 1.6G
CARBOHYDRATE: 48G
PROTEIN: 4G
CHOLESTEROL: 7MG
SODIUM: 29MG

Winter Fruit Salad with Honey-Yogurt Dressing

SERVES: 8
WORKING TIME: 30 MINUTES
TOTAL TIME: 30 MINUTES PLUS CHILLING TIME

½ cup plain nonfat yogurt

⅓ cup reduced-fat sour cream

½ cup honey

1 teaspoon grated lime zest

¼ cup fresh lime juice

3 cups cut fresh pineapple (½-inch chunks)

2 Granny Smith apples, cored and cut into ½-inch chunks

2 bananas, sliced

¾ cup halved seedless green grapes

¾ cup halved seedless red grapes

⅓ cup dried cherries or dried cranberries

½ cup coarsely chopped pecans

1. In a small bowl, whisk together the yogurt and sour cream. Whisk in 2 tablespoons of the honey and the lime zest and refrigerate until well chilled, about 1 hour.

2. In a large bowl, whisk together the lime juice and remaining 6 tablespoons honey until well combined. Add the pineapple, apples, bananas, grapes, cherries, and pecans, tossing gently to combine. Refrigerate until well chilled, about 1 hour.

3. Divide the fruit salad among 8 bowls, spoon the honey-yogurt dressing on top, and serve.

Helpful hints: For the best flavor and appearance, serve this salad soon after it's thoroughly chilled. Well-drained canned pineapple chunks can be substituted for the fresh and, if you prefer, orange will provide a softer tartness than lime.

FAT: 7G/24%
CALORIES: 241
SATURATED FAT: 1.1G
CARBOHYDRATE: 48G
PROTEIN: 3G
CHOLESTEROL: 4MG
SODIUM: 13MG

The tangy pineapple and lime-accented dressing of this fruit medley will awaken even the most party-tired palate.

PEACHES AND CREAM WITH RASPBERRY SAUCE

SERVES: 4
WORKING TIME: 10 MINUTES
TOTAL TIME: 10 MINUTES

Richly colored like a Renaissance tapestry, this dish poses sweet summer fruits on a "painted" backdrop. Be sure the peaches are at peak flavor and texture as well as picture perfect: The best time to try this dessert would be when locally grown peaches are plentiful.

12-ounce package frozen (not in syrup) raspberries, thawed
¼ cup honey
¼ cup plain nonfat yogurt
2 tablespoons reduced-fat sour cream
½ teaspoon vanilla extract
4 large peaches, halved and pitted
½ cup fresh raspberries

1. In a food processor, combine the frozen raspberries and honey and process to a purée. Strain the mixture through a fine-mesh sieve into a bowl; discard the seeds.

2. In a medium bowl, combine the yogurt, sour cream, and vanilla. Reserving ¼ cup of the raspberry purée, divide the remainder among 4 dessert bowls. Dividing evenly, place 2 or 3 dollops of the sour cream mixture on top of the raspberry purée and with a sharp knife, briefly swirl the sour cream mixture into a decorative pattern.

3. Place the peaches in the bowls. Top with the fresh raspberries and spoon the reserved raspberry purée on top. Serve immediately or chill for later.

Helpful hints: Choose peaches with a creamy-yellow background color: Whether or not there's a red blush depends on the variety, not the stage of ripeness. Don't buy rock-hard fruit—check for a slight softness at the peach's "seam." Store firm peaches in a paper bag at room temperature for a few days; they will soften and become more fragrant, but not sweeter.

FAT: 2G/9%
CALORIES: 211
SATURATED FAT: .5G
CARBOHYDRATE: 51G
PROTEIN: 4G
CHOLESTEROL: 3MG
SODIUM: 16MG

Tropical Tapioca Pudding

Serves: 6
Working time: 15 minutes
Total time: 20 minutes

3 tablespoons fresh lime juice

3 tablespoons honey

1 mango, peeled and cut into ½-inch chunks (see tip)

1 banana, quartered lengthwise and cut into ½-inch-thick slices

1 cup raspberries

¼ cup quick-cooking tapioca

¼ cup granulated sugar

¼ teaspoon salt

2 cups low-fat (1%) milk

1 large egg

1½ teaspoons vanilla extract

½ teaspoon coconut extract

1. In a medium bowl, combine the lime juice and honey. Add the mango, banana, and raspberries, tossing to coat. Cover and refrigerate until serving time.

2. In a medium heavy-bottomed saucepan, combine the tapioca, sugar, and salt. Gradually stir in the milk. Bring to a boil, stirring constantly, and remove from the heat.

3. In a small bowl, lightly beat the egg. Gradually whisk some of the hot milk mixture into the egg, then whisk the warmed egg mixture back into the saucepan. Return to the heat and cook, stirring constantly, for 1 minute. Remove from the heat and stir in the vanilla and coconut extracts. Spoon into 6 dessert bowls and serve warm, at room temperature, or chilled, topped with the reserved fruit mixture.

Helpful hint: Tapioca thickens as it cools, so the pudding will be slightly stiffer if you serve it chilled.

Fat: 2g/9%
Calories: 191
Saturated Fat: 0.9g
Carbohydrate: 41g
Protein: 4g
Cholesterol: 39mg
Sodium: 173mg

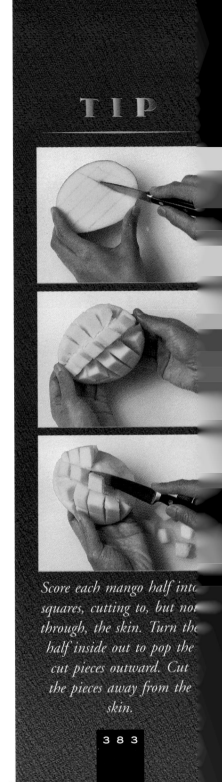

TIP

Score each mango half into squares, cutting to, but not through, the skin. Turn the half inside out to pop the cut pieces outward. Cut the pieces away from the skin.

*W*hen Italians dine at home they are more likely to close a meal with fruit and cheese than with cake and pastries. This sophisticated finale draws on the time-honored combination of pears and blue cheese; here, it's Italy's fine Gorgonzola that fills the spiced pears. If you're not a fan of blue cheese, try this recipe using a mild goat cheese, such as Montrachet.

POACHED PEARS STUFFED WITH GORGONZOLA

SERVES: 4
WORKING TIME: 20 MINUTES
TOTAL TIME: 30 MINUTES

1½ cups dry white wine

⅓ cup sugar

1 cinnamon stick

¼ teaspoon allspice berries

¼ teaspoon whole black peppercorns

4 firm-ripe pears, such as Bosc or Bartlett, peeled, halved, and cored

¾ cup crumbled Gorgonzola or goat cheese (3 ounces)

1 tablespoon reduced-fat cream cheese (Neufchâtel)

1. In a large saucepan big enough to fit 8 pear halves in a single layer, combine the wine, sugar, cinnamon, allspice, and peppercorns. Bring to a boil over medium heat, add the pears, and reduce the heat to a simmer. Place a piece of waxed paper directly over the pears (to keep them from becoming discolored) and simmer gently until the pears are just tender when pierced with a fork, about 7 minutes. Remove the waxed paper and with a slotted spoon, transfer the pears to a plate.

2. Bring the wine mixture to a boil over high heat. Cook until the liquid is reduced to a syrup thick enough to coat the back of a spoon, about 5 minutes. Strain through a fine-mesh sieve and cool to room temperature.

3. In a small bowl, mash the Gorgonzola and cream cheeses until well blended. Spoon the cheese mixture into a pastry bag with no tip attached (or use a sturdy plastic bag; see tip). Pipe the cheese mixture into the hollow of the pears. Divide the pears among 4 plates, spoon the reduced wine syrup over, and serve.

Helpful Hint: Ground spices will make the poaching liquid murky in appearance, but if you don't have allspice berries, peppercorns, or cinnamon sticks on hand, you can use ⅛ teaspoon ground allspice, ¼ teaspoon ground cinnamon, and ¼ teaspoon freshly ground black pepper.

FAT: 8G/26%
CALORIES: 279
SATURATED FAT: 5G
CARBOHYDRATE: 43G
PROTEIN: 6G
CHOLESTEROL: 21MG
SODIUM: 316MG

TIP

If you don't own a pastry bag, spoon the cheese mixture into a large, sturdy plastic bag. Twist the top of the bag closed, and snip off one bottom corner with scissors. Squeezing the bag gently, pipe the filling evenly into the pear halves.

ESPRESSO SEMIFREDDO

SERVES: 4
WORKING TIME: 10 MINUTES
TOTAL TIME: 20 MINUTES PLUS FREEZING TIME

As the name suggests, a semifreddo—a sort of frozen mousse—is only "half frozen." Heavy cream and eggs are the basis for a traditional semifreddo, but we've taken a lighter route with this coffee-flavored dessert, using low-fat milk, part-skim ricotta, and just one egg yolk (egg whites contain no fat). A banana adds creamy richness, as well.

2 cups low-fat (1%) milk
⅓ cup firmly packed light brown sugar
1 whole egg
2 egg whites
2 tablespoons instant espresso powder
¾ cup part-skim ricotta cheese
1 banana, cut into 3 or 4 pieces
2 tablespoons Frangelico or Amaretto
2 tablespoons plus 2 teaspoons chocolate syrup

1. In a medium saucepan, combine the milk and sugar and bring to a simmer over medium heat. Remove from the heat.

2. In a medium bowl, combine the whole egg and egg whites, whisking well. Gradually whisk a little of the hot milk mixture into the egg mixture. Stir the warmed eggs into the saucepan, return it to medium heat, and cook, stirring constantly, until the custard thickens enough to coat the back of a spoon, about 10 minutes. Add the espresso powder, stirring to combine.

3. Transfer the custard to a food processor. Add the ricotta, banana, and Frangelico and purée until smooth. Line an 8½ x 4½-inch loaf pan with plastic wrap, leaving a 4-inch overhang. Transfer the mixture to the prepared loaf pan and freeze until mostly frozen, but still easy to slice, about 4 hours. To unmold, run a small metal spatula between the plastic wrap and the sides of the pan to loosen the loaf. Invert the pan onto a platter or cutting board and remove the pan and the plastic wrap. Dip a long knife into hot water and slice the loaf into 8 even slices. Divide among 4 plates, drizzle with the chocolate syrup, and serve.

Helpful hint: Instant espresso is sold in many supermarkets (it comes in jars). If you substitute regular instant coffee, be sure to use powdered, not granular or freeze-dried, which will not dissolve as well.

FAT: 6G/19%
CALORIES: 288
SATURATED FAT: 3.6G
CARBOHYDRATE: 43G
PROTEIN: 13G
CHOLESTEROL: 72MG
SODIUM: 182MG

Hot Strawberry Sundaes

SERVES: 4
WORKING TIME: 20 MINUTES
TOTAL TIME: 30 MINUTES

What a spectacular combination: Jewel-like grilled strawberries in a warm orange sauce, spooned over vanilla frozen yogurt (peach yogurt would also be delicious). For an added note of sophistication, stir a teaspoon of orange liqueur, such as Cointreau, into the sauce along with the strawberries.

¼ cup orange juice
¼ cup strawberry spreadable fruit
1 teaspoon cornstarch
2 pints strawberries, hulled
2 cups low-fat vanilla frozen yogurt

1. Preheat the grill to a medium heat. (When ready to cook, spray the rack—off the grill—with nonstick cooking spray; see page 6.)

2. In a medium saucepan, combine the orange juice, strawberry spreadable fruit, and cornstarch. Set aside. Thread the strawberries onto 4 skewers.

3. Grill the kebabs, turning once, for 4 to 5 minutes. Meanwhile, place the medium saucepan directly on the grill or on the stovetop over medium heat and bring to a boil, stirring constantly. Cook, stirring, until the sauce is slightly thickened, about 1 minute.

4. Remove the strawberries from the skewers and stir into the sauce mixture in the saucepan. Cook until the mixture returns to a boil, 1 to 2 minutes. Divide the yogurt among 4 bowls, spoon the strawberry sauce over, and serve.

Helpful hints: This sauce is most impressive when served hot, but it's also good at room temperature or chilled. It could also be spooned over angel food cake that has been topped with nonfat vanilla yogurt for an extra-special "shortcake."

FAT: 2G/9%
CALORIES: 190
SATURATED FAT: 1G
CARBOHYDRATE: 41G
PROTEIN: 4G
CHOLESTEROL: 5MG
SODIUM: 62MG

TRIPLE CHOCOLATE PUDDING

SERVES: 4
WORKING TIME: 15 MINUTES
TOTAL TIME: 15 MINUTES PLUS CHILLING TIME

You can dive right into this intensely chocolaty pudding without a moment's hesitation: Even with its alluring topknot of whipped cream and chocolate shavings, it's still a low-fat treat. Like packaged pudding mixes, this recipe is based on cornstarch, but the resemblance ends there. No store-bought mix could ever be this deeply flavorful.

3 tablespoons unsweetened cocoa powder

3 tablespoons cornstarch

⅔ cup firmly packed dark brown sugar

3 cups low-fat (1%) milk

¼ teaspoon salt

1 vanilla bean, split lengthwise, or 1 teaspoon vanilla extract

2 ounces German sweet chocolate

1 ounce chocolate chips (about 2 tablespoons)

3 tablespoons whipped cream

2 teaspoons shaved chocolate (optional)

1. In a small bowl, combine the cocoa powder, cornstarch, ⅓ cup of the brown sugar, and ½ cup of the milk.

2. In a medium saucepan, combine the remaining 2½ cups milk, the remaining ⅓ cup brown sugar, the salt, and vanilla bean (if using). Bring to a boil over medium heat. Whisk the cocoa mixture into the boiling milk mixture and cook, whisking, just until thickened, about 4 minutes.

3. Stir in the sweet chocolate and chocolate chips, remove from the heat, and stir just until the chocolate is melted. Stir in the vanilla extract (if using). Spoon into 4 bowls and chill. Top with a dollop of whipped cream, sprinkle the shaved chocolate over, and serve.

Helpful hint: To make the chocolate shavings, have a bar of chocolate at room temperature and use a vegetable peeler to pare off thin shavings, letting them fall onto a plate. Pick up the shavings on the blade of a knife or with a metal spatula; they'll begin to melt if you handle them.

FAT: 12G/28%
CALORIES: 382
SATURATED FAT: 6.9G
CARBOHYDRATE: 67G
PROTEIN: 8G
CHOLESTEROL: 14MG
SODIUM: 248MG

PLUMS POACHED IN RED WINE

SERVES: 4
WORKING TIME: 10 MINUTES
TOTAL TIME: 30 MINUTES PLUS CHILLING TIME

Summer fruits poached in spiced wine are a favorite Italian dessert. Instead of a dollop of whipped cream or the super-rich cheese called mascarpone, the fruit here is topped with a creamy mixture of reduced-fat sour cream and nonfat yogurt. This topping would be lovely with other desserts—warm gingerbread, dried-fruit compote, or homemade applesauce, for instance.

⅔ cup plain nonfat yogurt

2 tablespoons reduced-fat sour cream

1 cup dry red wine

⅓ cup sugar

1 vanilla bean, split, or ½ teaspoon vanilla extract

Two 3 x ½-inch strips of orange zest

¼ teaspoon ground ginger

6 red or purple plums, halved and pitted

1. In a small bowl, combine the yogurt and sour cream. Cover and refrigerate until serving time.

2. In a medium saucepan, combine the wine, sugar, vanilla bean (if using the vanilla extract, do not add it now), orange zest, and ginger. Bring to a boil over medium heat, reduce the heat to a simmer, and add the plums, cut-sides down. Cook, turning once, until the plums are tender, about 12 minutes. With a slotted spoon, transfer the plums to a shallow bowl and set aside. Return the syrup to the heat and cook, stirring occasionally, until reduced to ½ cup, about 8 minutes. If using the vanilla extract, stir it into the mixture now.

3. Pour the reduced syrup over the plums and cool to room temperature. Chill the plums in the syrup for at least 1 hour and up to 3 days. To serve, remove the orange zest and vanilla bean. Spoon the plums and syrup into 4 dessert bowls and spoon a dollop of the yogurt cream into the bowl.

Helpful Hint: The vanilla bean can be reused after the plums have cooled: Rinse and dry the bean and place it in the container where you store your sugar to infuse the sugar with a subtle vanilla flavor.

FAT: 2G/12%
CALORIES: 149
SATURATED FAT: .6G
CARBOHYDRATE: 33G
PROTEIN: 3G
CHOLESTEROL: 3MG
SODIUM: 21MG

BUTTERSCOTCH SAUCE

MAKES: 6 HALF-PINTS
WORKING TIME: 15 MINUTES
TOTAL TIME: 15 MINUTES

4 cups firmly packed dark
brown sugar
2 cups light corn syrup
2 tablespoons unsalted butter
2 cups evaporated low-fat milk
1 teaspoon vanilla
½ teaspoon salt

1. Wash 6 half-pint jars and lids in hot soapy water and rinse well. Keep the lids and bands in hot water. To sterilize, place the jars, right-side up, in a large saucepan, cover with hot water by 1 inch, and then boil for 10 minutes. Keep the jars in the hot water until ready to use.

2. In a large saucepan, combine the brown sugar and corn syrup. Cook over medium-low heat, stirring occasionally, until the sugar dissolves, about 6 minutes.

3. Remove the mixture from the heat and stir in the butter until melted. Stir in the evaporated milk, vanilla, and salt until combined. Drain the sterilized jars. Pour the butterscotch sauce into the jars, seal the jars, and refrigerate for up to 1 week. This sauce cannot be processed in a boiling water bath.

Helpful hint: Heat the brown sugar and corn syrup over medium-low heat to avoid scorching the sugar.

VALUES ARE PER 1 TABLESPOON
FAT: 0.3G/5%
CALORIES: 61
SATURATED FAT: 0.1G
CARBOHYDRATE: 15G
PROTEIN: 0G
CHOLESTEROL: 1MG
SODIUM: 29MG

Our rendition of this classic dessert sauce tastes just as rich as the ice cream parlor favorite—but we've cut way back on the fat by using evaporated low-fat milk. Present it in heavy, glass-topped mason jars, wrapped in decorative foil paper. Spoon chilled or warm over frozen yogurt, toasted slices of fat-free pound cake, or even a bowl of mixed fresh berries.

Butterscotch Sauce
4 cups brown sugar
2 cups corn syrup
2 T unsalted butter
2 cups low-fat evap milk
1 t vanilla
1/2 t salt

2 syrup.

Open-Face Plum Tarts

SERVES: 4
WORKING TIME: 25 MINUTES
TOTAL TIME: 25 MINUTES

If you've never tried backyard baking, this is a good recipe to start with. These charming tartlets couldn't be easier to prepare, but they look quite special —like something you'd be served at a French country inn. Using flour tortillas instead of pastry crust is the secret to their simplicity.

Four 6-inch flour tortillas
⅓ cup apple jelly
4 large red and/or green plums, thinly sliced
1 tablespoon sugar
½ teaspoon cinnamon

1. Preheat the grill with the grill topper to a medium heat. (When ready to cook, spray the grill topper—off the grill—with nonstick cooking spray; see page 6.)

2. Brush each tortilla with 2 teaspoons of the apple jelly. Arrange the sliced plums in concentric circles on each of the tortillas. (If using 2 different colors of plum, alternate the colors.) In a small bowl, combine the sugar and cinnamon and sprinkle over the plums.

3. Grill the tortillas on the grill topper, covered, for 6 to 7 minutes or until the plums are tender. Divide the tortillas among 4 plates, brush the remaining apple jelly over the hot plums and serve.

Helpful hint: This is a perfect recipe for children to help with. Place each tortilla on a plate and let the kids add the plum topping. The plates will also make it easier for you to slip the tarts onto the grill topper with little risk of a mishap.

FAT: 2G/9%
CALORIES: 193
SATURATED FAT: .3G
CARBOHYDRATE: 43G
PROTEIN: 3G
CHOLESTEROL: 0MG
SODIUM: 105MG

STRAWBERRIES WITH BALSAMIC VINEGAR

SERVES: 4
WORKING TIME: 10 MINUTES
TOTAL TIME: 20 MINUTES

*J*ust as a squeeze of lime brings out the full flavor of melon, a bit of mild balsamic vinegar does wonderful things for strawberries. The syrup can be cooked the day before serving, but it's best to hull and slice the berries no more than an hour ahead of time. Pour the syrup over the strawberries just 20 to 30 minutes before serving, or the fruit will become mushy.

⅓ cup sugar
Three 3 x ½-inch strips of orange zest
Three 3 x ½-inch strips of lemon zest
3 tablespoons balsamic vinegar
2 pints strawberries, hulled and halved

1. In a small skillet or saucepan, combine the sugar and ¼ cup of water, stirring to blend. Add the orange zest and lemon zest and bring to a boil over medium heat. Boil for 2 minutes, remove from the heat, cover, and let cool to room temperature, about 20 minutes. Remove the orange zest and lemon zest and discard.

2. Transfer the syrup to a medium bowl and stir in the vinegar. Add the strawberries, tossing to coat. Spoon the berries and syrup into 4 bowls and serve.

Helpful hint: Any time you're about to eat an orange or juice a lemon, peel off the zest in wide strips, wrap it, and freeze it. This way, you'll always have citrus zest on hand when you need it.

FAT: 1G/8%
CALORIES: 116
SATURATED FAT: 0G
CARBOHYDRATE: 29G
PROTEIN: 1G
CHOLESTEROL: 0MG
SODIUM: 3MG

Each grilled peach half is like an individual fruit crisp: The hollows in the peaches overflow with a buttery, cinnamon-laced mixture of oats, almonds, and brown sugar. Almonds and peaches are related botanically, so perhaps that's why their flavors complement each other particularly well.

Grilled Stuffed Peaches

SERVES: 4
WORKING TIME: 10 MINUTES
TOTAL TIME: 25 MINUTES

4 large peaches

2 tablespoons fresh lemon juice

⅓ cup quick-cooking oats

2 tablespoons firmly packed light brown sugar

1 tablespoon finely chopped almonds

1 tablespoon unsalted butter, melted

½ teaspoon cinnamon

1. In a large pot of boiling water, cook the peaches for 30 seconds to blanch (see tip; top photo). Rinse them under cold water and carefully remove their skins (bottom photo). With a sharp knife, halve and pit the peaches and cut a very thin slice from the back of each peach half so it will lie flat on the grill topper. In a medium bowl, toss the peach halves with the lemon juice.

2. Preheat the grill and the grill topper to a medium heat. (When ready to cook, spray the grill topper—off the grill—with nonstick cooking spray; see page 6.)

3. Meanwhile, in a small bowl, combine the oats, brown sugar, almonds, melted butter, and cinnamon. Dividing evenly, fill the centers of each peach half with the topping. Place the filled peach halves on the grill topper and cook, covered, for 5 to 6 minutes or until the peaches are tender. Place the peach halves on 4 plates and serve hot or warm.

Helpful hint: Almost all the peaches on the market today are freestones— that is, peaches whose pits can be easily removed. Some older peach varieties, which you may find at orchards and farm stands, are clingstones; though delicious for eating whole, they are difficult to use in a recipe calling for halved, pitted fruit.

FAT: 5G/28%
CALORIES: 161
SATURATED FAT: 2G
CARBOHYDRATE: 31G
PROTEIN: 3G
CHOLESTEROL: 8MG
SODIUM: 4MG

TIP

Place the peaches in a medium saucepan of boiling water and cook for 30 seconds to blanch. This will help loosen the skins without cooking the fruit. With a sharp paring knife, carefully pull away the skin and discard.

DOUBLE CHOCOLATE FUDGE SAUCE

MAKES: 4 HALF-PINTS
WORKING TIME: 15 MINUTES
TOTAL TIME: 15 MINUTES

Semisweet chocolate and cocoa powder are the double flavor hits in this smooth, rich sauce. It's essential for spooning over holiday desserts— slices of angel food cake, poached pears or other fruit, a warm bread pudding, or anything else that begs for a delicious blanket of chocolate. Use the fudge sauce at room temperature or gently reheat.

8 ounces semisweet chocolate,
  coarsely chopped
1⅓ cups boiling water
½ cup light corn syrup
3 cups granulated sugar
1 cup firmly packed dark brown
  sugar
½ cup unsweetened cocoa
  powder, preferably Dutch process
¼ teaspoon salt
1 tablespoon vanilla

1. Wash 4 half-pint jars and lids in hot soapy water and rinse well. Keep the lids and bands in hot water. To sterilize, place the jars, right-side up, in a large saucepan, cover with hot water by 1 inch, and then boil for 10 minutes. Keep the jars in the hot water until ready to use.

2. In a medium saucepan, melt the chocolate over very low heat, stirring constantly. Stir in the boiling water and corn syrup. Add the granulated sugar, brown sugar, cocoa, and salt and stir well to combine. Cover, bring to a boil over medium heat, and cook without stirring for 3 minutes. Uncover and cook without stirring for 3 minutes longer.

3. Remove the mixture from the heat and stir in the vanilla. Drain the sterilized jars. Pour the fudge sauce into the jars, seal the jars, and refrigerate for up to 1 week. This sauce cannot be processed in a boiling water bath.

Helpful hint: For a mocha-flavored sauce, stir in a teaspoon of instant espresso powder with the vanilla.

VALUES ARE PER 1 TABLESPOON
FAT: 1G/14%
CALORIES: 76
SATURATED FAT: 0.7G
CARBOHYDRATE: 17G
PROTEIN: 0G
CHOLESTEROL: 0MG
SODIUM: 13MG

GLOSSARY

Allspice—A dark, round, dried berry about the size of a peppercorn, called allspice because it tastes like a combination of cloves, cinnamon, and nutmeg. Usually sold in ground form, allspice is often mistakenly thought to be a blend of spices.

Arugula—A peppery Italian salad green; also called rocket or roquette. Arugula's elongated dark-green leaves look something like dandelion leaves, but they're rounded rather than sharply toothed. This assertive green has a slightly hot, slightly bitter flavor that adds punch to salads; it can also be sautéed and served as a vegetable. Choose a crisp bunch of arugula that isn't yellowed; store it in the refrigerator for no longer than a day or two. After untying the bunch, trim the stems and wash the leaves carefully, as you would spinach.

Avocado—A fruit with a nutty flavor and a smooth, buttery consistency; used most often as a vegetable than a fruit. The flesh of the pebbly textured, black Hass variety is richer and meatier than that of the larger, smooth-skinned, green Fuerte. Select firm avocados that yield slightly to pressure without being mushy; avoid rock-hard fruit. To ripen, store in a loosely closed brown paper bag at room temperature. Because avocados are high in fat, they should be used in sparingly.

Balsamic vinegar—A dark red vinegar made from the unfermented juice of pressed grapes, most commonly the white Trebbiano, and aged in wooden casks. The authentic version is produced in a small region in Northern Italy, around Modena, and tastes richly sweet with a slight sour edge. Balsamic vinegar adds a pleasant tang to pasta sauces.

Broccoli—A versatile vegetable that takes the form of stout branches topped with bunches of tiny buds. Broccoli is one of the most nutritious vegetables and retains much of its nutrient value when frozen. When buying fresh broccoli, choose crisp stalks with tightly closed buds; they may have a purplish hue but should not be yellow. Store broccoli in a loosely closed bag in the crisper drawer.

Canadian bacon—A lean smoked meat, similar to ham. This bacon is precooked, so it can be used directly as is. For extra flavor, cook it in a skillet until the edges are slightly crisp. Just a small amount adds big flavor to sautés, baked dishes, and salads, but without all the fat of regular bacon.

Capers—The flower buds of a small bush found in Mediterranean countries. To make capers, the buds are dried and then pickled in vinegar with some salt: To reduce saltiness, rinse capers before using them. The piquant taste of capers permeates any sauce quickly, and just a few supply a big flavor boost.

Cayenne pepper—A hot spice ground from dried red chili peppers. Add cayenne to taste when preparing Mexican, Tex-Mex, Indian, Chinese, and Caribbean dishes; start with just a small amount, as cayenne is fiery-hot.

Chili powder—A commercially prepared seasoning mixture made from ground dried chilies, oregano, cumin, coriander, salt, and dehydrated garlic, and sometimes cloves and allspice; used in pasta salads, sauces, and baked pasta dishes for a Southwestern punch. Pure ground chili powder, without any added spices, is also available as cayenne. Chili powders can range in strength from mild to very hot. However, the heat in chili powder will fade with time, so for proper potency, use within 6 months of purchase.

Chutney—A sweet, spicy condiment ranging from smooth to chunky, generally made of fruit and spices. Chutney is most often used in Indian cooking, especially as an accompaniment to curries.

Cilantro/Coriander—A lacy-leaved green herb (called by both names). The plant's seeds are dried and used as a spice (known as coriander). The fresh herb, much used in Mexican and Asian cooking, looks like pale flat-leaf parsley and is strongly aromatic. Store fresh cilantro by placing the stems in a container of water and covering the leaves loosely with a plastic bag. Coriander seeds have a somewhat citrusy flavor that complements both sweet and savory dishes.

Citrus juice—The flavorful liquid component of oranges, lemon, limes, tangerines, and the like. Freshly squeezed citrus juice has an inimitable freshness that livens up low-fat foods. Frozen juice concentrates make a tangy base for sweet or savory sauces. An inexpensive hand reamer makes quick work of juicing citrus fruits.

Cornstarch—A fine flour made from the germ of corn. Cornstarch, like flour, is used as a fat-free sauce thickener; cornstarch-thickened sauces are lighter, glossier, and more translucent than those made with flour. To prevent lumps, combine the cornstarch with a cold liquid before adding it to a hot sauce; bring it gently to a boil and don't stir too vigorously, or the sauce may thin.

Cream cheese, reduced-fat—A light cream cheese, commonly called Neufchâtel, with about one-third less fat than regular cream cheese. It can be used as a substitute for regular cream cheese. A small amount used in sauces duplicates the richness of full-fat cheese or heavy cream.

Cumin—A pungent, peppery-tasting spice essential to many Middle Eastern, Asian, Mexican, and Mediterranean dishes. Available ground or as whole seeds; the seeds can be toasted in a dry skillet to bring out their flavor.

Curry powder—Not one spice but a mix of spices, commonly used in Indian cooking to flavor a dish with sweet heat and add a characteristic yellow-orange color. While curry blends vary (consisting of as many as 20 herbs and spices), they typically include turmeric for its vivid yellow color, ginger, cloves, cumin, coriander, and cayenne pepper. Commercially available Madras curry powder is hotter than other store-bought types.

Dill—A name given to both the fresh herb and the small, hard seeds that are used as a spice. Add the light, lemony, fresh dill leaves (also called dillweed) toward the end of cooking. Dill seeds provide a pleasantly distinctive bitter taste and marry beautifully with sour cream- or yogurt-based sauces.

Endive, Belgian—A bullet-shaped member of the chicory family with a pleasing bitter taste; its individual spears, or leaves, make wonderful "boats" for appetizer dips. Select small, firm heads that are creamy white with yellowish tips. Refrigerate in damp paper towels in a perforated plastic bag for no more than 2 days.

Evaporated milk, skimmed and low-fat—Canned, unsweetened, homogenized milk that has had more than half of its fat removed: In the skimmed version, 100 percent of the fat has been removed; the low-fat version contains 1 percent fat. Used in baking or cooking, it adds a creamy richness with almost no fat. Store at room temperature for up to 6 months until opened, then refrigerate for up to 1 week.

Flour, all-purpose—A refined wheat flour, made from a blend of hard and soft wheats, that is suitable for most cooking purposes. Also called plain flour, all-purpose flour comes bleached or unbleached; use whichever you prefer (the bleaching has no effect on the finished product).

Garlic—The edible bulb of a plant closely related to onions, leeks, and chives. Garlic can be pungently assertive or sweetly mild, depending on how it is prepared: Minced or crushed garlic yields a more powerful flavor than whole or halved cloves. Whereas sautéing turns garlic rich and savory, slow simmering or roasting produces a mild, mellow flavor. Select firm, plump heads with dry skins; avoid heads that have begun to sprout. Store garlic in an open or loosely covered container in a cool, dark place for up to 2 months.

Ginger—A thin-skinned root used as a seasoning. Fresh ginger adds a sweet pungency to Asian and Indian dishes. Tightly wrapped, unpeeled fresh ginger can be refrigerated for 1 week or frozen for up to 6 months. Ground ginger is not a true substitute for fresh, but it will lend a warming flavor to soups, stews, and sauces.

Honey—A liquid sweetener made by honeybees from flower nectar. It ranges in flavor from mild (orange blossom) to very strong (buckwheat). Deliciously versatile, honey can sweeten savory sauces or fruit desserts. Store honey at room temperature. If it crystallizes, place the open jar in a pan of warm water for a few minutes; or microwave it for 15 seconds, or until the honey liquifies.

Hot pepper sauce—A highly incendiary sauce made from a variety of hot peppers flavored with vinegar and salt. Use hot pepper sauce sparingly, drop by drop, to introduce a hot edge to any dish, especially barbecue sauces, rice dishes, and gumbos.

Jalapeño peppers—Hot green chili peppers about two inches long and an inch in diameter, with rounded tips. Most of the heat resides in the membranes (ribs) of the pepper, so remove them for a milder effect—wear gloves to protect your hands from the volatile oils. Jalapeños are also sold whole or chopped in small cans, although the canned version is not nearly as arresting as the fresh. Toss a little jalapeño into soups, sautés, baked dishes, or anywhere you want to create some fire.

Kidney beans—Deep red, pink, or white kidney-shaped beans with a meaty flavor. White kidney beans, popular in Italy, are also called cannellini. Canned kidney beans make a hearty foundation for low-fat meals such as vegetarian chili.

Lettuce, Bibb—A butterhead lettuce that forms a small, cup-shaped head of grass-green leaves. As the term "butterhead" suggests, Bibb lettuce leaves are soft and delicate, with a sweet, mild flavor. Use this lettuce when other salad ingredients and the dressing are not too strong-flavored or acidic.

Lettuce, red or green leaf—Two types of lettuces that grow in loose, open bunches, rather than forming tight heads. Leaf lettuces, fresh-tasting but not assertive in flavor, are versatile salad ingredients. The dark bronze color of the red-leaf type makes a handsome addition to an otherwise all-green salad bowl.

Lettuce, romaine—A sturdy lettuce whose leaves form an oblong, fairly loose head. Romaine (also called cos) has a distinctively sweet taste; its leaves are pale at the base, shading to a deep green at the tips. Romaine is the lettuce traditionally used for Caesar salad; it resists wilting and holds up well under acidic or warm dressings.

Mango—A yellow-skinned fruit with vivid orange flesh and an unmistakable sweet-tart flavor. Although they originated in India, mangoes are now cultivated in other parts of the world. Mangoes can range from about 10 ounces to about four pounds in weight; all have a large, flat seed from which the flesh must be cut away. An unripe mango can be placed in a brown paper bag at room temperature to ripen. When ripe, the fruit will give to slight pressure and will have a rich, flowery fragrance.

Mesclun—A mixture of baby lettuce leaves and other greens, fresh herbs, and, sometimes, edible flowers. Mesclun (pronounced MES-klen) is a Provençal word that means "mixture." When buying mesclun, which is sold both loose and packaged, check to be sure you're getting tiny, tender leaves, and not mature lettuce torn into small pieces; there should be a number of different greens for a pleasing variety of taste and texture. The mixture should smell fresh; a sickly-sweet aroma signals decay.

Marjoram—A member of the mint family that tastes like mildly sweet oregano. Fresh marjoram should be added at the end of the cooking so the flavor doesn't vanish. Dried marjoram, sold in leaf and ground form (the more intense leaf being preferable), stands up to longer cooking.

Marsala—A sweet, nutty, fortified wine made in Sicily. To make Marsala, sweet concentrated grape juice is added to strong white wine; the wine is then aged for several years and, in some cases, blended. Marsala is much used in cooking: Sweet Marsala is good for dessert-making, but a dry version should be used in savory sauces.

Mayonnaise, reduced-fat—A form of mayonnaise in which other thickeners, such as food starch, take the place of some of the oil. Reduced-fat mayonnaise is not quite as rich-tasting as regular, but it has a light, tangy flavor. Don't substitute

fat-free mayonnaise, which usually contains mostly water and is quite tasteless.

Mint—A large family of herbs used to impart a refreshingly heady fragrance and cool aftertaste to foods; the most common types are spearmint and peppermint. As with other fresh herbs, mint is best added toward the end of the cooking time. Dried mint is fairly intense, so a pinch goes a long way. Store fresh mint the same way as fresh cilantro.

Mozzarella cheese—A very mild-flavored Italian cheese with exceptional melting properties. Mozzarella was originally made from water-buffalo milk, but is now more commonly made from cow's milk; it is available in whole milk, part-skim, and fat-free varieties. The part-skim variety is the best option for cooking, as it is relatively low in fat but still has a nice texture and good melting properties. The rubbery texture of nonfat mozzarella makes it unsuitable for most recipes.

Olive oil—A fragrant oil pressed from olives. This oil is rich in monounsaturated fats, which make it more healthful than butter and solid shortenings. Olive oil comes in different grades, reflecting the method used to refine the oil and the resulting level of acidity. The finest, most expensive oil is cold-pressed extra-virgin, which should be reserved for flavoring salad dressings and other uncooked or lightly cooked foods. Virgin and pure olive oils are slightly more acidic with less olive flavor, and are fine for most types of cooking.

Olives—Small, oval fruits native to the Mediterranean region with an intense, earthy taste. Olives are picked green (unripe) or black (ripe) and then must be cured—in oil or brine—to mellow their natural bitterness and develop their flavor; herbs and other seasonings are added to create a wide variety of olives.

Spanish olives—green olives sold whole, pitted, or pimiento-stuffed—add jazzy color as well as piquant flavor. The Calamata, a purple-black, brine-cured olive, is a full-flavored Greek-style olive that works well in pasta sauces. Use all olives sparingly since they are high in fat (olive oil).

Oregano—A member of the mint family characterized by small, green leaves. Prized for its pleasantly bitter taste, oregano is essential to many Mediterranean-style dishes and is used in Mexican cooking as well.

Paprika—A spice ground from a variety of red peppers and used in many traditional Hungarian and Spanish dishes. Paprika colors foods a characteristic brick-red and flavors dishes from sweet to spicy-hot, depending on the pepper potency.

Parmesan cheese—An intensely flavored, hard grating cheese. Genuine Italian Parmesan, stamped "Parmigiano-Reggiano" on the rind, is produced in the Emilia-Romagna region, and tastes richly nutty with a slight sweetness. For a fine, fluffy texture that melts into hot foods, grate  the cheese in a hand-cranked grater. Buy Parmesan in blocks and grate it as needed for best flavor and freshness.

Parsley—A popular herb available in two varieties. Curly parsley, with lacy, frilly leaves, is quite mild and is preferred for garnishing, while flat-leaf Italian parsley has a stronger flavor and is better for cooking. Store parsley as you would basil. Since fresh parsley is so widely available, there is really no reason to use dried, which has very little flavor.

Peppercorns, black—The whole dried berries of a tropical vine, *piper nigrum*. A touch of this hot, pungent seasoning enlivens just about any savory dish, and the flavor of freshly ground pepper is so superior to pre-ground that no cook should be without a pepper grinder filled with peppercorns.

Pepper, Italian frying—A long, tapered pepper, also called *cubanelle*, that is sweeter than a regular bell pepper, and ranges in color from green to yellow to red. Sautéing enhances the sweet flavor.

Potatoes, small red—Round red boiling potatoes, usually harvested when they are no larger than 1½ inches in diameter. If sold soon after harvest, they're called "new potatoes;" these are very thin-skinned and have a high moisture content and a slightly sweet flavor. Potatoes that have been kept in cold storage have thicker skins and are starchier. You can use either type in our recipes; small white potatoes can be substituted for red.

Red pepper flakes—A spice made from a variety of dried red chili peppers. Pepper flakes will permeate a stew or casserole with a burst of heat and flavor during the cooking and eating. Begin with a pinch—you can always add more.

Rice, long-grain—A type of rice with grains much longer than they are wide. Available in white and brown forms, long-grain rice remains fluffy and separate when cooked and works well in dishes with gravy or an abundance of other liquid, such as stews or braised dishes. Converted rice, which has been processed to preserve nutrients, takes slightly longer to cook than regular white rice. Rice is ideal for low-fat cooking because it absorbs other flavors and is quite filling, yet it contributes almost no fat.

Rosemary—An aromatic herb with needle-like leaves and a sharp pine-citrus flavor. Rosemary's robust flavor complements lamb particularly well, and it stands up to long cooking better than most herbs. If you can't get fresh rosemary, use whole dried leaves, which retain the flavor of the fresh herb quite well. Crush or chop rosemary leaves with a mortar and pestle or a chef's knife.

Sage—An intensely fragrant herb with grayish-green leaves. Sage will infuse a dish with a pleasant, musty mint taste. In its dried form, sage is sold as whole leaves, ground, and in a fluffy "rubbed" version.

Sauerkraut—A fermented mixture of shredded cabbage, salt, and spices that adds texture and a distinctive "sour" flavor to a dish. It is available fresh in some ethnic delicatessens, in plastic bags in the refrigerated section of the supermarket, and in jars and cans. To lessen its salty flavor and sodium content, rinse well and drain before using.

Scallions—Immature onions (also called green onions) with a mild and slightly sweet flavor. Both the white bulb and the green tops can be used in cooking; the green tops make an attractive garnish. To prepare, trim off the base of the bulb or root end and any withered ends of the green tops. Remove the outermost, thin skin from around the bulb. Cut the white portion from the green tops and use separately, or use together in the same dish.

Sesame oil, Oriental—A dark, polyunsaturated oil pressed from toasted sesame seeds, that is used as a flavor enhancer in many Asian and Indian dishes. Do not confuse the Oriental oil with its lighter colored counterpart, which is cold-pressed from untoasted sesame seeds and imparts a much milder flavor. Store either version in the refrigerator for up to 6 months.

Snow pea—A flat pea pod that is fully edible, even uncooked. Slightly sweet and very tender, snow peas need only quick cooking and add both crunch and color. Select crisp, bright green pods, and refrigerate in a plastic bag for up to 3 days. String the peas and remove the tips before using.

Sour cream—A soured dairy product, resulting from treating sweet cream with a lactic acid culture. Regular sour cream contains at least 18 percent milk fat by volume; reduced-fat sour cream contains 4 percent fat; nonfat sour cream is, of course, fat free. In cooking, the reduced-fat version can be substituted for regular sour cream; use the nonfat cautiously since it behaves differently, especially in baking. To avoid curdling, do not subject sour cream to high heat.

Soy sauce, reduced-sodium—A condiment made from fermented soybeans, wheat, and salt used to add a salty, slightly sweet flavor to food. Soy sauce is especially at home in stir-fries and Asian-style salads. Keep in mind that reduced-sodium sauces add the same flavor but much less sodium.

Spinach, fresh—A nutrient-rich, dark-green, leafy vegetable. Fresh spinach has crisp, emerald green leaves; it will keep its bright color if not overcooked. When buying fresh spinach, choose springy, green bunches; avoid withered or yellowing leaves. Wash spinach carefully, as it is often gritty: Submerge the leaves in a large bowl of lukewarm water, swirl them with your hands, then lift out the leaves. Even bagged spinach labeled "prewashed" should be rinsed.

Squash, yellow summer—A slender, thin-skinned squash with delicate white flesh. Summer squash has a mild flavor that adapts to a variety of seasonings and sauces. Straightneck and crookneck yellow squash are interchangeable in recipes; zucchini can usually be substituted for yellow summer squash.

Sugar snap peas—A type of sweet peas with edible pods. Developed in the 1970s, sugar snaps are a cross between regular peas and snow peas. Unlike snow peas, which are flat, sugar snaps are plump, with fully formed peas inside the pods. Before eating sugar snaps, pinch off the tips and remove the string that runs along both the front and back of the pod. Eat sugar snaps raw, or steam or blanch them very briefly.

Sun-dried tomatoes—Plum tomatoes that have been dried slowly to produce a chewy, intensely flavorful sauce ingredient. Although oil-packed tomatoes are widely available, the dry-packed type are preferred for their lower fat content. For many recipes, the dried tomatoes must be soaked in hot water to soften them before using.

Tarragon—A potent, sweet herb with a licorice- or anise-like taste; often used with chicken or fish. Dried tarragon loses its flavor quickly; check its potency by crushing a little between your fingers and sniffing for the strong aroma. As with most herbs, you may substitute 1 teaspoon dried for each tablespoon of fresh.

Tomato paste—A concentrated essence of cooked tomatoes, sold in cans and tubes. This Italian ingredient is commonly used to thicken and accent the flavor and color of sauces; however, it is slightly bitter and should not be used alone or in large quantities. If you're using only part of a can of tomato paste, save the remainder by freezing it in spoonfuls.

Tomato sauce—A cooked, seasoned purée of fresh tomatoes, sold in cans or jars. Tomato sauce is usually seasoned with salt, spices, and corn syrup; some brands come in Italian- or Mexican-style versions with more assertive flavorings. The recipes in this book call for "no-salt-added" tomato sauce, because the regular sauce is quite high in sodium.

Tomatoes, canned—Fresh tomatoes processed and packed for easy use. Canned tomatoes come in several forms: They may be whole or diced (labeled "crushed"), packed with no added liquid, or with added juice, purée, or paste. The recipes in this book call for "no-salt-added" tomatoes. Some no-salt-added imported brands are not labeled as such—read the ingredient and nutrition labels for information on salt and sodium content.

Tomatoes, cherry—Round tomatoes roughly the size of ping-pong balls; may be red or yellow. These bite-size tomatoes add a colorful touch to pasta dishes and are great for salads. Cherry tomatoes are usually sold in baskets. Choose well-colored specimens and store them at room temperature to preserve their flavor.

Tortillas, flour—Round, thin Mexican flat-breads made from wheat flour. Traditionally, flour tortillas are made with lard; however, those you'll find in the supermarket are usually made with vegetable shortening.

Vinegar, red and white wine—Vinegars made by fermenting red or white wine. Use these vinegars in vinaigrettes and other dressings, especially those that employ Italian or French flavors. (Use red wine vinegar with assertive ingredients, white wine vinegar in more delicate salads.) For a change, try champagne or sherry vinegar, or an herb-flavored vinegar.

Vinegar, rice—A pale vinegar made from fermented rice, it is milder than most other types of vinegar. Rice vinegar's light, clean flavor, much favored in Asian cooking, allows you to make dressing with less oil. Japanese rice vinegar is widely available; be sure to buy the unseasoned type.

Watercress—A slightly peppery-tasting aquatic herb that adds zip to salads and cooked dishes. The assertive flavor of watercress provides a peppery counterpoint to savory or sweet flavors. To prepare, rinse the bunch of watercress under cold water and blot dry with paper towels. Remove the tough stalks and use just the tender stems, or, for a more delicate flavor, use only the leaves.

Worcestershire sauce—A richly savory condiment based on vinegar, molasses, garlic, anchovies, tamarind, and onion. It takes its name from Worcester, England, where it was first bottled. Worcestershire is frequently used with meat—as a table condiment and in sauces or marinades. If the bottle is kept tightly capped, this potent condiment will keep almost indefinitely at room temperature.

Yogurt, nonfat and low-fat—Delicately tart cultured milk products made from low-fat or skim milk. Plain yogurt makes a healthful base for marinades, and its acidity tenderizes the meat a bit and helps seasonings to penetrate. (Tandoori-style chicken, for example, is marinated in a yogurt-based sauce before cooking.)

Zest, citrus—The thin, outermost colored part of the rind of citrus fruits that contains strongly flavored oils. Zest imparts

an intense flavor that makes a refreshing contrast to the richness of meat, poultry, or fish. Remove the zest with a grater, citrus zester, or vegetable peeler; be careful to remove only the colored layer, not the bitter white pith beneath it.

INDEX

TIME LIFE BOOKS

Time-Life Books is a division of Time Life Inc.

TIME LIFE INC.

PRESIDENT and CEO: George Artandi

TIME-LIFE CUSTOM PUBLISHING

VICE PRESIDENT and PUBLISHER: Neil Levin

Director of Acquisitions and Editorial Resources:
  Jennifer Pearce
Editor for Special Markets: Anna Burgard
Production Manager: Carolyn Bounds
Quality Assurance Manager: James D. King

Interior design by David Fridberg of Miles Fridberg
  Molinaroli, Inc.

TIME-LIFE BOOKS

PUBLISHER/MANAGING EDITOR: Neil Kagan

Director of Finance: Christopher Hearing
Directors of Book Production: Marjann Caldwell;
  Patricia Pascale
Director of Publishing Technology: Betsi McGrath
Director of Photography and Research: John Conrad Weiser
Director of Editorial Administration: Barbara Levitt
Chief Librarian: Louise D. Forstall

Books produced by Time-Life Custom Publishing are
available at special bulk discount for promotional and
premium use. Custom adaptations can also be created to
meet your specific marketing goals.
Call 1-800-323-5255

REBUS, INC.

PUBLISHER: Rodney M. Friedman

Editorial Staff for *Quick & Light*
Director, Recipe Development and Photography:
  Grace Young
Editorial Director: Kate Slate
Senior Recipe Developer: Sandra Rose Gluck
Recipe Developers: Helen Jones, Paul Piccuito,
  Marianne Zanzarella
Managing Editor: Julee Binder Shapiro
Writers: Bonnie J. Slotnick, David J. Ricketts
Editorial Assistant: James W. Brown, Jr.
Nutritionists: Hill Nutrition Associates

Art Director: Timothy Jeffs
Photographers: Lisa Koenig, Vincent Lee, Corinne Colen,
  René Velez, Edmund Goldspink
Photographers' Assistants: Alix Berenberg, Bill Bies, Bain
  Coffman, Eugene DeLucie, Russell Dian, Katie Bleacher
  Everard, Petra Liebetanz, Rainer Fehringer, Robert
  Presciutti, Val Steiner
Food Stylists: A.J. Battifarano, Helen Jones, Catherine
  Paukner, Karen Pickus, Roberta Rall, Andrea B.
  Swenson, Karen J.M. Tack
Assistant Food Stylists: Mako Antonishek, Catherine
  Chatham, Charles Davis, Tracy Donovan, Susan Kadel,
  Amy Lord, Ellie Ritt
Prop Stylists: Sara Abalan, Debra Donahue
Prop Coordinator: Karin Martin